Multiculturalism in Indian Tradition and Literature

Multiculturalism in Indian Tradition and Literature

Edited by

M. Rajagopalachary
K. Damodar Rao

ATLANTIC
PUBLISHERS & DISTRIBUTORS (P) LTD

Published by
ATLANTIC
PUBLISHERS & DISTRIBUTORS (P) LTD
7/22, Ansari Road, Darya Ganj, New Delhi-110002
Phones : +91-11-40775252, 23273880, 23275880, 23280451
Fax : +91-11-23285873
Web : www.atlanticbooks.com
E-mail : orders@atlanticbooks.com

Branch Office
5, Nallathambi Street, Wallajah Road, Chennai-600002
Phones : +91-44-64611085, 32413319
E-mail : chennai@atlanticbooks.com

Reprint 2018

Printed in India at Nice Printing Press, A-33/3A, Site-IV, Industrial Area, Sahibabad, Ghaziabad, U.P.

Preface

Any country that aims at moving on a path of social and economic development faces the challenge of grappling with co-existence of contraries. As such, imbibing the principles of tolerance, cultural pluralism and democracy becomes more of a necessity. Much before Western nations declared multiculturalism as their state policy, India had followed, as a way of life, the twin principles of tolerance and pluralism over many centuries without stating it overtly. Democracy as a political tool became part of its ethos in the previous century. The country offers a model of postmodern mosaic of contradictions co-existing in its social-cultural-political matrix, often considered a puzzling marvel. Despite aberrations like occasional incidents of intolerance, its multicultural roots are strong and the fabric of its middle path that shuns extremes is sound, based on millennia-old experience of accommodation, syncretism and plurality as it is reflected in the chapters included in the book.

The Department of English, Kakatiya University, Warangal, organized a UGC-sponsored national seminar, "Multiculturalism in Indian Literatures" during March 19-20, 2012 under SAP-DRS-I. Some of the papers presented at the seminar, and invited articles constitute the content of this anthology. The twenty-three articles in the volume deal with manifestations of Indian multiculturalism as evidenced in its tradition and literature. We thank all the contributors for their valuable observations. We also thank Bhai Harjeet Singh of Atlantic Publishers & Distributors (P) Ltd. and his team for taking care of every aspect in publishing this volume.

The book will be useful for the students and teachers of Indian English Literature and Sociology, and researchers in these fields.

M. Rajagopalachary
K. Damodar Rao

Contents

List of Contributors

M. Rajagopalachary, (Retd) Professor of English and Emeritus Fellow, Department of English, Kakatiya University, Warangal, Telangana.

K. Damodar Rao, Associate Professor and Head, Department of English, Kakatiya University, Warangal, Telangana.

S. Ramaswamy, Formerly a Fulbrighter at the University of California, Los Angeles (1964-66), a Senior Fulbright Fellow in California (1988) and a third Fulbright at the Universities of Yale and Texas (1991), and a Fellow of Silliman College, Yale University. A renowned scholar in English and Sanskrit.

P. Mallikarjuna Rao is Retired Professor of English, Kakatiya University, Warangal, Telangana.

Sumita Roy, Professor of English, Osmania University, Hyderabad.

A.V. Suresh Kumar, Professor of English, Osmania University, Hyderabad.

B. Yadava Raju, Professor and Head, Department of English, Osmania University, Hyderabad.

B. Krishnaiah, Assistant Professor of English, Osmania University, Hyderabad.

T.N. Gurudutt, Associate Professor in Visveswarapura College of Arts and Commerce, Bangalore.

Rajeshwar Mittapalli, Professor of English, Kakatiya University, Warangal, Telangana.

Anita Ahmadi, Research Scholar, Kakatiya University, Warangal, Telangana.

M. Suresh Kumar, Associate Professor and Head, Department of English, Acharya Nagarjuna University, Nagarjunanagar, Guntur.

Simran Luthra, Academic Support Manager for Educational Initiatives in Hyderabad.

D. Vijaya Prakash, Academic Assistant, Satavahana University, Karimnagar, Telangana.

Shikha Bhatnagar, Associate Professor and Head, Humanities and Sciences Dept., Sindhura College of Engg & Tech, JNTUH, NTPC, Godavarikhani.

G. Damodar, Professor of English, Kakatiya University, Warangal, Telangana.

Alapati Rama Naga Hanuman, Assistant Professor of English, Department of Humanities and Social Sciences, Andhra University, Visakhapatnam.

N. Ramesh Chandra Srikanth, Assistant Professor of English, Govt. Degree College, Thorrur.

S. Devika, Associate Professor in English, VTMNSS College, Dhanuvachapuram, Trivandrum District, Kerala.

N. Anil Krishna, Assistant Professor of English & Public Relations Officer, Osmania University, Hyderabad.

Baishali Bhaumik Mitra, Senior Assistant Professor of English, VNR Vignan Jyothi Institute of Engineering and Technology, Hyderabad.

B. Gopal Rao, Retired Professor of English, Osmania University, Hyderabad.

Soumyajyoti Banerjee, Assistant Professor, Department of Applied Sciences, Haldia Institute of Technology, Haldia, West Bengal.

Amrita Basu, Assistant Professor, Department of Applied Sciences, Haldia Institute of Technology, Haldia, West Bengal.

Introduction

M. Rajagopalachary and *K. Damodar Rao*

> In order to save mankind we have to learn to live together in concord in spite of traditional differences of religion, civilization, nationality, class and race.
>
> —Arnold Toynbee

> Whence this vitality that overcomes destruction and death? Whence this wisdom that reconciles opposite truths? The story of India's culture unravels the secret of that vitality and that wisdom. It is a story of unity and synthesis, of reconciliation and development, of a perfect fusion of old traditions and new values.
>
> —Humayun Kabir

> The only thing that truly links every Indian today is a knowledge, first hand and constant, of diversity.
>
> —Pico Iyer

Indian democracy has survived for nearly seven decades despite ominous predictions to the contrary, and Indian tradition has survived over five millennia despite periodic setbacks and recent challenges. Its social diversity and cultural pluralism have proved to be its strengths, in fact, its structural principles. Added to these, its stability and continuity have made it truly 'functional' at every level—social, political and cultural. India's experience of living together with different religious faiths, of accommodating diverse ethnic groups and languages might not have the linguistic denomination of multiculturalism but the fact remains that

India happened to be one of the first few countries to have celebrated cultural pluralism as a way of living. The markers with which it came to be characterized are many, including 'unity in diversity,' 'cultural pluralism,' 'living together separately,' 'religious neutrality,' 'honeycomb,' 'syncretistic,' and the recent 'multiculturalism' and 'hybridity.'

The linguistic denominators vary from one country to the other. Besides, ancient civilisations like India may not carry the burden of modern markers like multiculturalism and secularism, but may still have lived the experience. It is well known that each language has its own history, geography and symbols, and a specific cultural context: "One language differs from another, not only in its sounds, intonations and the meaning its words convey, but also in its 'world view.' Each language looks at the universe in a particular manner, tests it and translates it into its own meanings in a special way" (Verma 265-6).

The subcontinent has become home to a staggering array of languages and spiritual creeds, and "myriad literary, intellectual, musical and artistic traditions as well as diverse political philosophies, economic systems and ways of living" (Priyamvada 66). It believed in the Rig Vedic dictum: *Aano bhadra kratavoyanti visvatah*, ("Let noble thoughts come to us from all sides"). As a social reality in India, inclusiveness and accommodation were celebrated as a way of life. If Hindu, Muslim, Christian, Sikh, Buddhist, Bahaai, Jain, and Parsi and various other ethnic communities have continued to co-exist for many centuries now, it only celebrates the multicultural nature of its ethos. Asim Roy says that the Indian ethos operated on a system of fission and fusion:

> India's social diversity and pluralism had always been her strength. A vast mosaic of cross-cutting divisions of class, caste, tribe, religion, sect, language and region, each social compartment was more or less insulated from the other and compartmentalized. In this sense, society functioned on the principle of fission. The principle of fusion was, on the other hand, equally operative in that there were competing and interacting groups and interests, which held the balance of order and stability. As Indian

> society had not been organized on the basis of a single mega-circuit system, but as a multiple-circuit system, a breakdown in one circuit kept the others going. (Roy 19)

As a linguistic construct and a political policy, 'multiculturalism' is a recent European phenomenon. 'Multiculturalism' was first officially introduced in Canada in 1971 under the leadership of Pierre Trudeau as an acknowledgment of their cultural and ethnic diversity. Canada was an amalgam of Anglophone and Francophone groups, European immigrants since the middle of the nineteenth century, its aboriginal peoples, and the more recent immigrants from Asian countries. It is followed by Australia, Argentina, USA, UK, Europe, Germany and several other countries. The experience of the ancient civilizations like India, and migration of populations, especially of European origin, to different parts of the globe led sociologists and political philosophers hold that cultural pluralism was crucial to social humanism, which in turn would help build an egalitarian society.

The anti-colonial leaders of Indian freedom struggle while devising strategies for its independence were also trying to come to terms with the idea of India. In fact, what constitutes Indianness and what unites India are issues that have been raised time and again. Equally, many answers have been attempted. The smorgasbord of diversity, it has been cited, instead of being a weak link, proved to be a pillar of strength in Indian ethos. Tolerance, the basic ethic of Indian society, provides an affirmative value to multicultural democracy. Citing the example of Asoka's ideas of secularism and tolerance nearly 2,300 years ago, Amartya Sen says, "The Indian emperor Asoka's dedicated championing of religious and other kinds of tolerance in the third century B.C... is certainly among the earliest political defenses of tolerance anywhere" (Sen 2006: 50). Another Indian emperor, Akbar followed a similar path of tolerance. Jawaharlal Nehru was an articulate spokesman who emphasized the unity in diversity in India: "The diversity of India is tremendous, it is obvious. It lies on the surface and anybody can see it. It concerns itself with physical appearances as well as with certain mental habits and traits.... Yet, with all these differences, there is no mistaking the impress of India" (61-2).

Nirmal Verma says that the desire to seek freedom in India was different from the aggressive, egoistic sentiments that lay behind the modern nation states, which came into existence only after the various races, nationalities and folk languages were annihilated as in the West. In India its roots could be traced to its cultural traditions:

> That the Indian national awareness was free of a self-involved rigidity right from its inception was because it had not been forcibly imposed from above, but its roots lay deep in the Indian cultural traditions. The various dialects and languages of India, despite their distinctiveness, shared an inherent unity, and this could never obstruct the growth of national unification. (Verma 273)

II

Even as they were preoccupied with the idea of India and what constitutes Indianness, the early nationalist leaders and intellectuals who ushered Indian Renaissance understood that homogenizing models of nationalism would not suit the purpose of India. Tagore, despite his modernity, was opposed to homogeneous nationalism. He considered it as an import from the west. Viewing it as 'a great menace', he termed it as *bhougolik apadevata*, a geographical demon (quoted in Nandy 7). Tagore rules out this kind of nationalism based on 'a conspiracy of fear.' In this narrow sense, he says, India "has never had a real sense of nationalism" (64). Instead, he looks back to India's past that sustained a tradition of co-existence of diverse faiths. He also viewed debate and dissent 'as essential to collective self-understanding' (Priyamvada 65). Gandhi's non-violent nationalism was in tune with the traditional Indian way of pursuing non-aggressive, non-imperialist policies. He also believed that India possessed a civilizational unity long before the British arrived, countering the view that India emerged as a single nation-state as a consequence of the interventionist policies of the British. He warned against 'simply mirroring the practices of European nation-states.' Priyamvada Gopal observes: “Though a devout Hindu, he insisted that religion and nationality were not synonymous. This is why those who would reduce the nation to some simplistic religious formula have never been comfortable with either great man” (65). According to Ashis Nandy, Gandhi’s unbridled antagonism to the concepts of nationalism and modernism and his defence of Indian traditions carried with it “intimations of a postmodern consciousness” (2).

The freedom struggle, satyagraha and non-violence as viable modes of struggle, subsequent independence of India from colonial rule and the making of the Constitution were all processes of and pointers to the continuing tradition of dialogue and debate, the bedrock of cultural pluralism. The role and participation of Dr. B.R. Ambedkar in the making of India during and after the freedom struggle is a case in point. He stood up to Gandhi and other leaders of the freedom movement insofar as social and religious matters are concerned and held his ground for most part. But for his interventions at crucial times, India would not have enjoyed the status of successful democracy that it is bestowed with now. A visionary who personified the spirit and essence of Indian thought, he looked beyond, and far ahead of, his times. N. Ram observes:

> He had a number of interesting things to say about complicated and different national problems—Kashmir, language, nationhood, citizenship, ethnicity, and so on. His analysis lit up the field for a proper democratic understanding of cooperative federalism and Centre-State relations in India. On international questions and foreign policy, his approach is that of a conservative dissenting from the non-alignment and from the Nehruvian, not to mention the Left’s world view. (7)

Faced with the daunting task of translating ‘history and its lessons’ into the Constitution, Ambedkar more than his peers, accomplished it with gusto. It was no small achievement in that his contemporaries were overawed by the ‘fear of freedom:’ “By foregrounding freedom from fear, Ambedkar fundamentally challenged the fear of freedom that characterized the majority’s anxiety at the time of making the Constitution” (Arvind Elangovan 12). An intellectual of a rare order, he was nonetheless confined to the margins as a subnational and sectional leader for long. History has a way of correcting itself and it is fascinating to see that Ambedkar is given his due place as one who played a key role in the making of India. In a poll conducted by the magazine, *Outlook* (August 20, 2012) on the issue who could be the greatest Indian after Gandhi, Ambedkar was way ahead of others including Jawaharlal Nehru—a clear testimony to a dialogic nation where pluralism is valued.

The Constitution of India is at once a fine reflection of the Indian cultural mosaic and a practical demonstration of the continuing dialogic tradition. While recognizing the rich diversity, it gave equal rights to all its citizens, irrespective of creed, colour, region or language. Hitherto a social reality, the inclusive pluralism has been institutionalised and given a codified constitutional sanction. It enshrined into rights and principles the way of life of a people. As a mark of tolerance and co-existence, minority communities were given the right to preserve their culture and follow religious practices; to ameliorate the plight of subalterns, constitutional guarantees were given to hitherto deprived communities and tribes in education and jobs; and dialogue was recognized as part of social-cultural discourse paving way to healthy social practices, religious amity, and cultural inclusiveness. Without terming it as multiculturalism, the Constitution has celebrated, enshrined its spirit in earnest. Sitakant Mahapatra says:

> Any culture like that of India, which has grown over the centuries on the bedrock of a great tradition and a host of little traditions surrounding it, generates a large number of contradictions, ambivalences, uncertainties, and dialectic oppositions within its fold. In the case of India, the latter are so many and so complex that, sometimes, it may even appear doubtful whether there is a unity which connects these apparently diverse streams—an integrity or a specific identity. Multiculturalism is the word often employed in this context. (293-94)

India was born a postmodern state when it attained freedom from British colonial rule.

There were many doomsday predictions that didn't give much of a chance to the newly born country to survive. They were eager to announce that India could not withstand the challenges of its diversity and was likely to collapse under its own burden sooner than later. But the reality in India is different. It is much too huge to apply any rules here. It is beyond a rigid framework of types and categories. It is multidimensional and variegated and that knowledge percolates deep down the social surface. Pico Iyer observes: "But if independence means anything, it is that India is, and ought to be, less uniform, more contradictory... than it ever was when Britain tried to push it into straight lines and parentheses" (Iyer 98). The question of identity, nationhood, Indianness, and other definitions may sometimes turn divisive but the debate goes on. As a multicultural democracy India has stood the test of time despite occasional pitfalls and 'its share of historical hurt' (Prasannarajan 25).

The problem arises when ideologies of different parties, including extreme right and left, consider themselves benign, the divine way, even while following or advocating a path of unrelenting violence. A closer scrutiny reveals that the two extreme versions, of the right and the left, do not represent the mainstream culture or practices in India. In fact, in the past, people have expressed their disenchantment with such extreme colourings in no uncertain terms. Their holding sway over popular imagination is but transitory. Their advocating violence needs to be seen in the specific context in which these posed a challenge to the mainstream, but may not be generalized as part of the mainstream culture of India, of following a middle path.

One finds, by the same token, a middle path in cultural and religious matters too. Commenting on the theme of violence in cultural and political narratives, Prof. Kancha Ilaiah, author of the hugely popular *Why I am Not a Hindu?* (1996), in a recent essay raises some important questions in respect of Indian culture and practices. He argues that Hindu gods carry different weapons and in people who worship such gods, violence is ingrained (4). If the gods are violent, and culture veered around violence, our freedom struggle would have followed a similar course; democracy would not have found a place here; co-existence of religions and cultures would not have become our way of life; and we would have flirted with dictatorships like our neighbouring countries and other postcolonial nations in Africa and Latin America; dialogue and debate would not have formed the basis of our society. The middle path or a balanced one has led us to a life full of contradictions, yet showing a way of living with them comfortably. Gods, in any religion, are benign. Hindu gods are no different. Since our way of life here gives scope to dialogue and dissent we must thank our gods. Our practice of secularism, too, is not anti-religion but advocates equal respect to all religions (*sama dharma sambhava*), a distinct socio-religious philosophy enshrined in the Constitution that allows religious neutrality (*dharma nirapekshta*). Ashis Nandy and T.N. Madan, two of the influential social philosophers of our times, believe that religion itself could be a resource to fight against religious bigotry. They didn't attest the hegemonic potentials of ideological secularism resorting to religious delimitation and devalutation. Madan, in his significant work, *Modern Myths, Locked Minds: Secularism and Fundamentalism in India*, says: "The construction of an Indian ideology of religious pluralism and tolerance... had been rendered problematic by the processes of secularization which tend to, if they do not actively seek to, delimit and devalue the role of religion in society" (Madan 276).

III

Asim Roy notes that the 'assimilative and inclusive traits of the Indic culture' have assumed 'almost the salience of an unquestionalble historical verity' until relatively recent times when its syncretistic tradition has been 'engaged, challenged, and undermined by various historical forces and contesting ideologies.' He identifies three major developments that undermined the fabric of pluralism. Firstly, it is the impact of British colonialism and its attendant ill-effects such as Orientalism that created exclusive and competing models of religious-cultural traditions in the region. Secondly, it is Muslim separatism, and thirdly there is the emergence of the radical political Hindutva. He says:

> Having virtually ignored the intricate and complex processes of interaction of living religions and cultures

> in India, especially at a popular level, Orientalism contributed a great deal to the construction of barriers among plural cultural traditions in the end. The second serious challenge came, at a somewhat later stage, from the Islamicists or the Islamic 'essentialists' and the champions of Muslim 'separatism'.... The third is the most recent and potentially the most threatening and subversive challenge. This is embodied by the proponents of Hindu nationalism with its ahistorical, monolithic, cultural, and political credo of *Hindutva* during the colonial and, more aggressively and significantly, post-colonial periods. (Roy 2)

Any discussion of Indian culture is incomplete without a mention of the caste system, its misery and curse for centuries: "Any attempt to redefine Indian culture has also to contend with the past and present of the caste system..." (Mahapatra 302). The stratified hierarchy has been, in more ways than one, proved to be detrimental to the continuing tradition. A constant stumbling block in the cherished tradition, it faced severe interrogation without the prospect of plausible answers. The fabric of the system was torn by the seemingly perennial problem. It cannot be denied that it has been a source of violence, physical and psychological, in an otherwise tolerant society. While mentioning the conflict between Indian culture's metaphysics and the social reality, a critic observes that one may preach that "all human beings are children of God and, hence, by implication, equal.... But then you may practise the caste system with all its stratifications" (Mahapatra 294). Such practices of inhumanity as well as the binary of 'majorityism vs minorityism' stress the need for a quick changeover from cultural pluralism to egalitarian pluralism in contemporary Indian situation.

One of the important features of postcolonial-postmodern nation is its identity-hybridity equation. In the realm of politics and culture it rejects a unified centre of authority. It implies multiple cultural centres in terms not merely of nation, but also in respect of class, caste, gender, profession and beliefs. The notion of 'belonging' lies at the heart of all communities. The word has two linguistic and social connotations. A sense of belonging marks a person's identity in the sense of attachment and affection, and at another level, it is "deemed to be the possession of a place, people, or institutions" (Joshi 8). The latter implies ownership, homogeneity. Belonging, in this sense, is a source of violence which India has experienced occasionally. It is its antithesis, the core of pluralism that veered it away from violence towards a path of tolerance. Hybridity recognizes many 'in-betweens' rather than 'us/them' binaries. Pramod K. Nayar says:

> "Hybridity" is the rejection of a single or unified identity, and preference for multiple cultural locations and identities. Hybridity might take the form of a nativist revival of a pre-colonial past—such as folk or tribal cultural forms—or the adaptation of artistic and social productions to present-day conditions of globalization, multiculturalism and transnationalism. Hybridity is thus a postcolonial answer to the dangers of cultural binarism (us/them) and the fundamentalist urge to seek "pure" cultural forms. (6)

The people of the country have avoided extremes at crucial times. The fact remains that "Indian unity is a repudiation of their extremities.... It is never monotonous. It defies the tyranny of homogeneity. When arguments divide nations, India is united by their variety" (Prasannarajan 25). The common man has shown his discretion and wisdom a number of times. This, despite aberrations like the role of money and other inducements during election time; and despite upheavals like demolition of Babri Masjid, violence in Bombay, Godhra carnage in Gujarat, and communal disturbances elsewhere. But the middle path is not shaken, even if tested, by these. While stressing the nature and strength of the dialogic tradition that flourished in India, Amartya Sen observes:

> The contemporary relevance of the dialogic tradition and of the acceptance of heterodoxy is hard to exaggerate. Discussions and arguments are critically important for democracy and public reasoning. They are central to the practice of secularism and for even-handed treatment of adherents of different religious faiths.... Going beyond these basic structural priorities, the argumentative

> tradition, if used with deliberation and commitment, can also be extremely important in resisting social inequalities and in removing poverty and deprivation. Voice is a crucial component of the pursuit of social justice. (Sen xiii)

This dialogic tradition and the spirit of Indian tradition are best exemplified in the interaction between the larger and smaller traditions over centuries. Sometimes within the larger tradition there is questioning of the accepted modes. The Bhakti movement and literature is an illustration of this dialogic tradition. Movements like Virashaiva, Haridasa, Srivaishnava revolted against orthodoxy and banal ritualism of the larger Hindu tradition. The humanism and reformist zeal of the Bhakti Literature and movements represented by the Alwars, Nayanars, Karaikkal Ammaiyar, Bahinabai, Ganga Sati, Janabai, Tulsidas, Chaitanya, Kabir, Mira Bai, Tukaram, Adi Shankara, Madhavacharya, Srimadramanuja, Annamayya, Kshetrayya, Rudrakavi, Basavanna, Akka Mahadevi, Allama Prabhu, Sri Aurobindo, and Tagore added to the value of democratic social system, cultural values and peaceful co-existence.

The focus on the underprivileged sections in the pre- and post-Independence Indian literatures has been a significant phenomenon. Prem Chand, Tagore, Mulk Raj Anand, Ismat Chughtai, and Mahasveta Devi have offered sympathetic portrayals of dalits, tribals, the rural poor, and other suppressed sections of the society in their fiction. Since Independence the new voices and standpoints not only demanded attention but also became assertive, making the concept of nationhood fragmented into several versions. In the last quarter of the twentieth century, different minorities, and ethnic and religious sub-cultures began to assert their identity moving away from the margins. Nationhood assumes new colouring because "many new voices, perceptions and locations begin to contest a mono-ethnic, monolithic concept of elitist, upper class, patriarchal hegemony" (Santosh Gupta 10). Parsee, Muslim and women writers and many submerged voices have asked for greater acceptance intervening in the consolidation of a simple dominant state ideology. The increasing space that these forces created for themselves within the existing power structure, in the process, questioned the validity of political meta-narratives and the assertion of Third World fiction as national allegories.

The papers presented by teacher-scholars across the country at the Department of English, Kakatiya University, Warangal in the UGC sponsored National Seminar on "Multiculturalism in Indian Literatures" during March 19-20, 2012 under SAP-DRS-I form part of this anthology. Besides, we have invited other scholars to contribute articles with a view to enriching the content of the book. The twenty-three articles included in the volume deal with the manifestations of Indian multiculturalism as reflected in its tradition of accommodation, and literature of syncretism. We thank all the contributors for partaking of this enterprise.

Works Cited

Elangovan, Arvind. "Freedom from fear and the fear of freedom." *Frontline* (May 15, 2015). 9-12. Print.

Gopal, Priyamvada. "The Freedom Song." *India Today* (August 20, 2007). 64-68. Print.

Gupta, Santosh. "Introduction." *Contemporary Indian Literature: Positions and Expositions.* Jaipur: Rawat Publications, 2000. 9-21. Print.

Ilaiah, Kancha. *Adhyatmika Himsa, Rajya Himsa.* (Spiritual Violence, State Violence) *Andhra Jyothi* (26 May 2015). 4. Print.

Iyer, Pico. "Divided we Stand." *India Today* (August 20, 2007). 96-97. Print.

Joshi, Sanjay. "What does it mean to belong?" *The Hindu.* Monday (June 8, 2015). 8. Print.

Madan, T.N. *Modern Myths, Locked Minds: Secularism and Fundamentalism in India.* New Delhi: Oxford UP, 1997. Print.

Mahapatra, Sitakant. "Indian Culture: Quest for Perspective—Dualities, Resolutions and Transcendence." *The Writer as Critic: Essays in Literature, History and Culture.* Ed. Jasbir Jain. Jaipur: Rawat, 2011. 291-306. Print.

Nandy, Ashis. *The Illegitimacy of Nationalism.* Delhi: Oxford UP, 1994. Print.

Nayar, Pramod K. "Postcolonialism Now." *Littcrit* 35. 1 & 2 (June—Dec., 2009). 3-15. Print.

Nehru, Jawaharlal. *The Discovery of India.* Calcutta: Signet Press, 1946. Print.

Prasannarajan. "What Unites India." *India Today* (August 20, 2007). 24-25. Print.

Ram, N. "The Relevance of Ambedkar." *Frontline* (May 15, 2015). 4-8. Print.

Roy, Asim. "Introduction." *Living Together Separately: Cultural India in History and Politics*. Eds. Mushirul Hasan and Asim Roy. New Delhi: Oxford UP, 2005. 1-25. Print.

Sen, Amartya. *The Argumentative Indian*. London: Penguin, 2005. Print.

———. *Identity and Violence: The Illusion of Destiny*. London: Allan Lane, 2006. Print.

Tagore, Rabindranath. *Nationalism*. Madras: Macmillan, 1985. Print.

Verma, Nirmal. "Language and National Identity." *The Writer as Critic: Essays in Literature, History and Culture*. Ed. Jasbir Jain. Jaipur: Rawat, 2011. 259-76. Print.

1

Shaiva Canon in Indian Literatures

S. Ramaswamy

Multiculturalism is inextricably connected with multi-lingualism and I am particularly drawn to the Bhakti Movement as represented in the various languages of India. Bhakti literature comprises the Alwars, Nayanmars, Kabir, Tagore, Annamayya, Kshetrayya, Rudrakavi, Basavanna, Akka Mahadevi, Allama Prabhu, etc. For the sake of focus, I have chosen Shaivism as represented throughout India from Kashmir Shaivism to Tamil Shaiva tradition through the Virashaiva Movement of Karnataka, cutting across regions of multi-lingualism.

But before analyzing Shaivism, it is necessary to have a bit of a background about the Bhakti Movement in India. From Acharya Adi Shankara, the Bhakti Movement started gaining momentum all over India. Shankara in *Viveka Chudamani* declared that Bhakti is the best means of obtaining *Moksha* or Liberation—"*Mokshasadhana saamagriyam Bhaktireva gariyasi.*" The later Acharyas Ramanuja, Madhva and Vallabha propagated Vaishnavism or Faith in Vishnu, whereas Appaiah Dikshitar, Neelakanta Dikshitar and Srikantacharya preached Shaivism or devotion to Lord Shiva. The emergence of Tulsidas, Surdas, Kabir, Madhusudana Sarasvati and Mira Bai of Chittor from the North, Purandara Dasa and Kanaka Dasa from Karnataka, Thyagaraja, Muthuswamy Dikshitar and Shama Shastry from Tamil Nadu, Bhadrachalam Ramadas from Telangana, Eknath, Sant Jnana Dev and Tukaram from Maharashtra, Chaitanya Mahaprabhu from Bengal, Narsi Mehta from Gujarat, Swati

Tirunal from Kerala are only a few names in the tradition of Bhakti Movement.

Bhagavata Mahapuranam mentions nine kinds of devotion called "*Nava Vidha Bhakthi.*" The first is "*Sravanam*"—listening to the names of the Lord, the second is "*Keertanam*"—composing and singing songs in praise of God, the third is "*Smaranam*" or Meditation, the fourth is "*Pada Sevanam*"—worshipping his feet, the fifth is "*Archanam*"—doing puja with flowers, the sixth is "*Vandanam*"—prostrating before God, the seventh is "*Dasyam*"—serving as a faithful servant of the Lord, the eighth is "*Sakhyam*"—serving as a friend and the ninth is "*Atma Nivedanam.*" In our Bhakti tradition we find examples for all these varieties—Parikshit Maharaja for *Shravanam*, Lakshmi took pleasure in *Padasevanam*, Hanuman for *Dasyam*, Arjuna for *Sakhyam*, Bali Chakravarti for *Atmanivedanam*, Akroora for *Vandanam*, and Dhruva for *Smaranam*. In traditional Indian philosophy, there are four ways of attaining the knowledge of God—Bhaktiyoga, Karmayoga, Jnanayoga and Rajayoga. Of these Bhaktiyoga is the Path of Devotion. Sage Narada said that the path of devotion is the easiest path. This is the path of love. For example, the love of the Gopies to Krishna is such and is called *Madhurabhakti*. In Vishistadvaita of Bhagavad Ramanuja, Bhakti takes the form of total surrender—*Prapatti* or *Sharanagati*. As the Bhagavadgita says, *Sarvadharman parithyajya mamekam sharanam vraja*" (Chapter 18. Verse 65). Another belief is that there is no difference between Jnana and Bhakti and says—"*Shemushi Bhaktiroopa.*" A classic about Bhaktimarga is Narada's *Bhaktisutras*. There are eighty-four aphorisms here. The Advaitic stand is that in the supreme state of Bhakti, worshipper and worshipped will be realised as One. In addition to all this, there is *Gurubhakti*. With this background, now we can turn to Indian literatures in various regions and languages and focus on Shaivism.

II

Shaivism is naturally related to Shiva worship and Shiva is known by various synonyms. At the Vedic level, the '*Rudradhyaya*', in the fifth '*Prashna*', fourth Canto of *Taittiriya Samhita* mentions the following—Visveswara, Kalagni, Rudra, Neelakanta, Mrithrunjaya, Mahadeva, Sarveswara and Sadashiva.

As Karan Singh, the well-known Kashmiri scholar and statesman puts it:

> Kashmir is not only one of the most beautiful places in the World; it has also in our history been one of the most creative in the fields of Philosophy and intellectual activity. There is reason to believe that some of the earliest Vedic writings took place in Kashmir and certainly two thousand years ago it was a flourishing centre.... (3)

This is a revealing statement to contemplate two thousand years later in 2002 A.D. Kashmir has produced not only poets and philosophers but it has been the home of literary theory and Shaivism. Kashmir Shaivism consists of Shiva and Shakthi. Recognizing this aspect Adi Shankaracharya composed his *Soundaryalahari* in Kashmir as different from his *Shivanandalahari* which he is said to have composed in Srishailam in Andhra Pradesh (It may be mentioned in passing that the same tradition is continued in contemporary Sanskrit poetry and a work called "Shivadvaita Lahari" has been written by Shatavadhani R. Ganesh, who I am proud to say, is a friend and former student of mine). The '*Shiva Sutras*' which form the basis of Kashmir Shaivism are stated to have been revealed in a dream to Vasugupta (8th Century A.D.) by Lord Shiva Himself. Kashmir Shaivism is different from Shaivism, as we generally understand it. Shaivism existed from great antiquity as '*Shaivagama*' the beginnings of which can be traced even to the Vedas, as has been pointed out already. Kashmir Shaivism may be called a type of Advaita. The followers of Kashmir Shaivism recognize a three-fold classification namely 'Para' which is 'Jnanapradhana', 'Apara' which is 'Kriyapradhana' and 'Parapara' which is a combination of 'Jnana' and 'Kriya'. The essence of this form of Shaivism is based on the concept 'Trika' which consists of three elements—(1) 'Pati', (2) 'Pashu' and (3) 'Pasha'. 'Pati' is Paramashiva, 'Pashu' is the imprisoned 'Jiva'. 'Pasha' constitutes the shackles that separate the 'Jiva' from the 'Paramashiva' placing it in the midst of worldly existence. When the 'Jiva' realizes that he is not different from Shiva, the shackles disappear. This is the Ultimate Realization in the Advaita system of Philosophy. The pithy statement '*Shivayityahamitubhau na bhinnau Shivayevaham aham Shivassayaiva*' which means 'I am Shiva. I am Shiva myself. There is no difference'. The 'shackles' mentioned in Kashmir Shaivism are the same as '*Granthi*' (the knot) mentioned in the *Mundakopanishad*, the severance of which results in Self Realization:

> *Bhidyate hridaya granthihi Chidhyante sarvasamshayaha* I
> *Ksheeyantechasya karmani tasmin drashte paravare* II
> (II, 2.6).

which means that in the case of the person who is a Self-Realized Soul, all his 'shackles' or *Granthis* or knots get broken, all his doubts are severed, and all works (Karma) get dissolved (free translation by me).

This is the reason why Dr. S. Radhakrishnan says that the later works of Kashmir Shaivism show a distinct leaning towards Advaitism. The Realization 'I am Shiva' has come down the centuries to our own times. For example, Shankaracharya's *Nirvanashatkam*,

> *Aham nirvikalpo nirakara rupo* I
> *Chidananda Rupah Shivoham Shivoham* II
> (*Collected Works of Shankaracharya* 394-95).

> I am beyond imagination, form of the formless,
> Form of Consciousness and Bliss:
> Shiva I am, I am Shiva. (Raja Rao 116)

This is rendered most accurately even in the French translation. (Raja Rao's *The Serpent and the Rope* has been translated into French by George Fradier. In fact, the translation is so good that Raja Rao told me that had he written the novel in French himself, it couldn't be better).

> *Je suis immuable, sans forme*
> *Je suis ce qui est present en toute choses,*
> *Je suis Savoir et Bonheur, je suis*
> *Shiva, je suis Shiva.* (Fradier 90-91)

III

Various appellations of Shiva in the *Rudradhyaya*, *Taittiriya Samhita* have been mentioned in the previous section. The various roles that Shiva has played in Indian literary sensibility are associated with these appellations. It is good to begin with the anthropomorphic idea of Lord Shiva in the pan-Indian literature of classical Sanskrit. Kalidasa's epic, *Kumarasambavam* describes the event leading upto the events of Kumara (also called Lord Subrahmanya), the son of Shiva born to bring about the defeat of the demon Taraka. For the present purpose, only two stanzas, verses 40 and 42 from the Third Canto are quoted:

Srutapsarogitirapi ksane'smin
harah prasamkhyanaparo babhuva |
atmeswavaranam na hi jatu vighnah
samadhibedaprabhavo bhavanti ||

...

Drstiprapatam parihrtya tasya
kamah purah sukramiva prayane |
prantesu samsaktanamerusakham
dhyanaspadam bhutapatervivesa || (Kalidasa 32)

Here, the situation is that the gods have realized that the only hope against Taraka is a General who shall be born as the son of Shiva and Parvati. But Shiva has no thoughts of marriage and is engaged in profound meditation in the remote mountain-forest of Himalaya. The Third Canto narrates how Indra, who has come from the Council of the Gods, seeks the help of Kama, the god of love whose task it is now to cause Shiva to fall in love with Parvati. The translation of the two stanzas is:

Yet Shiva still remained in meditation
Absorbed, although he heard the singing elves.
Can anything have power of perturbation
Of souls completely masters of themselves?

...

As on a journey under baleful omen,
Trying in fear from Shiva's eyes to hide,
To the Lord's sacred ground came Love the bowman

Emerging through creeper-thickets from the side. (Brough 110)

Now let us turn to Hindi. Who has not heard the name of the mystical poet of the 15th century—Kabir? Born to Muslim parents in Benares, he became a disciple of Ramananda who had brought to North India the religious revival of Ramanujacharya of the South. Kabir was a weaver, a simple man who earned his living at the loom. Kabir's songs are written in popular Hindi, not in the literary tongue and were addressed to the ordinary people in imagery drawn from universal experience.

Now we move from Hindi to Kannada Literature of the 12th century to "Vachana Sahitya." Akka Mahadevi in one of her Vachanas talks of Shiva as a husband.

Manavemba sakhiya prasadadinda
Anubaavava kalitenu Shivanodane
Karachelva Srishaila Channamallikarjuna
Sajjana gandana madikombe.
(*Sati-Pati Bhavada Vachanagalu* 12)

In this Vachana the idea of Shiva as husband continues. In the lines quoted Akka Mahadevi says that with the help of the mind as a friend she has chosen to take Lord Channamallikarjuna of Srishailam for her husband. To give an idea about how the Vachana reads in English, let us turn to the translation by a bilingual poet in Kannada and English—A.K. Ramanujan. In his *Speaking of Siva* we read—

I love the beautiful one
with no bond nor fear
no clan no land
no landmarks
for his beauty.

So my lord, white as jasmine, is my husband.
(Ramanujan 134)

Ramanujan himself points out that Akka Mahadevi 'left Kalyana and wandered off towards Srishaila, the holy mountain where she found Him (Shiva) and lost herself.... She enlists the traditional imagery of pan-Indian secular love poetry for personal expression. In her, the phases of human love are metaphors for the faces of mystic ascent' (Ramanujan 113). (I had occasion to discuss this translation with Dr. Ramanujan in Chicago in June 1987 along with his *Love Poems from a Classical Tamil Anthology* entitled *The Interior Landscape* published by Indiana University Press, Bloomington and London. It is good to remember that Ramanujan received the Mac Arthur "Genius Award").

The Tamil Shaiva canon comprises the twelve "*Thirumurai.*" The first seven (collectively called "*Thevaram*" are the outpourings of Thirujnana Sambandar, Appar and Sundarar). Thirumandiram is the mystic recording of Thirumalar. An important document in this context is "Periyapuranam." It weaves into a splendid epic narrative the lives of sixty-three Shaiva saints known as Nayanmars or "Servitors of the Lord." Lord Shiva whom these Shaiva siddantins worshipped is not a sectarian Deity but the Supreme Creator, Preserver and Destroyer of the Universe. Just a few lines from Sambandar in an English translation by G.V. Pillai—

> Behold Him
> With an ear having a plug of rolled palmyra leaf
> Stuck in his pierced lobe,
> The Rider of the bull,
> The wearer of pure white moon on his locks,
> The one smeared
> With the hot ashes of cremation general
> All over his body
> The stealer of my heart. (Qtd in Sekkizhaar xiv)
>
> (*Periya Puranam* is a Tamil Classic on the great Saiva Saints of South India by Sekkizhaar. Condensed English version is by G. Vanmikanthan).

Manikkavachakar's *Tiruvachagam* is a Tamil classic. *Tiruvachagam* is so voluminous and stupendous a work that one cannot even begin to talk about it in a short essay like this. The excellent English translation of this work by Rev. G.U. Pope is an achievement in translation. In his monumental edition Rev. Pope says, 'The sacred mystic poetry of people reveals their character and aspirations.... The fifty-one poems which are here edited, translated and annotated are on every one's lips and are dear to the hearts of vast multitudes of people' (Pope ix). In *Tiruvachagam* there are many ten stanza units—decads. The author Manikkavachakar was Chief Minister to a great Pandian King and when he went to Perun-turrai on a mission to buy royal steeds for his King, he sees Shiva who appears in the form of a human Guru and is immediately transformed. His ego is completely annihilated and he attains enlightenment. Just as Akka Mahadevi journeyed from Kalyana to Srishailam, Manikkavachakar's pilgrimage takes him from Perun-turrai to Tillai, his final place of arrival from where there are no more departures. Tillai is Chidambaram, the Sanskrit word, the derivation of which is 'Chideva Ambaram' (Chit or Consciousness is the Ambaram or Akasham). Just a few lines are quoted here to connect *Tiruvachagam* with Shaivism.

> The potsherd and the skull I deemed my kin;
> my soul dissolved;
> Wealth to be sought was Sivan's foot alone,
> I clearly saw;
> With soul and body to earth in worship bent, a slave,
> I'VE REACH'D HIM WHERE HE DANCES,
> LORD OF TILLAI'S HOME AND JOY.
>
> (Pope 304)

This leads to the idea of Shiva as a dancer, known as 'Nataraja' performing the 'Rudra Thandava' (cosmic dance). It is in this form that He is worshipped by the classical dancers. What is to be observed here is that this figure in metal has become an object d'art in the West but its symbolic significance is enormous and it holds a key to the highest level of Self-Realization.

> Nataraja or the Dancing Shiva is a symbol of Self-Realization personified. All the details are significant in achieving this final totality. The Ganga in the matted hair is the symbol of holiness and plenty, the half moon is a symbol of time and the mind, the circle of flames surrounding the murti of Nataraja is a symbol of perfection, the hair that is floating about is a symbol of space, the third eye is symbolic of *jnana*, the two right hands symbolize power of creation and sustenance, the

two left hands symbolize fire as the destructive power as well as a symbol of purification. The serpent round Shiva's neck symbolizes the power of the *kundalini* and the other serpents symbolize natural functions in everybody. The position of the left hand must be taken in conjunction with the position of the left foot. The left hand pointing downwards, known in dance as *dolahasta*, and the left foot pointing upwards symbolize the upward thrust of the *jiva*, the individual soul attracted by the union with the universal, Absolute. The demon on whom the right foot is firmly planted symbolizes Mortality, Ignorance and the dark forces. The skin cloth and anklets symbolize valour and inner strength and the expression on the face of Lord Nataraja shows the inner poise which is the result of abiding in the Self. (Put together by me from various sources, including a book on Dance)

It is not for nothing that perhaps the greatest cosmopolitan critic of our times who makes no distinction between East and West and who has taken all knowledge into his purview, Ananda Coomaraswamy calls one of his books *The Dance of Shiva*, where he is aware of the above explanation.

While the various aspects of Shiva are being discussed it must be remembered that he is also the originator or Grammar and Language in general. The famous Maheswara Sutras of Panini reveal the sound that was produced by the Damaruga (small hand-operated drum) accompanied by The Dance of Shiva. Shiva as The Supreme Teacher goes under the name of Dakshinamurthy. The famous *Dakshinamurthy Stotram* of Sri Shankaracharya defines this aspect. Only the first stanza is quoted here.

Viswam darpanadrsyamananagaritulyam nijantargatam ।
pasyannatmani mayaya bahirivodbhutam yatha nidraya ॥
Yah saksatkurute prabodhasamaye svatmanamevadvayam ।
tasmai srigurumurtaye nama idam sridaksinamurtaye ॥

(*Collected Works of Shankaracharya* 91)

Instead of giving my own translation of the above lines, I would rather quote Raja Rao's version in his novel *The Serpent and the Rope*. This, along with *Nirvanashatkam* is always humming in the consciousness of Ramaswamy, the protagonist of the novel—

Like a city seen in a mirror is the universe,
Seen within oneself but seemingly of Maya born,
As in sleep;
Yet is it really in the Inner Self
Of Him who sees at the point of Light
Within Himself, unique, immutable—
To Him incarnate as the holy Guru,
To Sri Dakshinamurti be my salutation. (Raja Rao 296)

Since translations have already been used in this essay it may not be inappropriate to give the French version of these lines from the French translation by George Fradier—

Telle une ville dans un miroir
L'univers est contenu en Lui
mais comme produit par mirage
comme en songe
et cependant existent en verite dans le Soi.
A lui qui dans l'eclat de la Pure Conscience
ne realise que son propre Soi,
a lui donc incarne dans le Maitre Bien—Aime,
a Dakshinamurti, notre salutation. (Fradier 237)

As this has been a brief survey of the Bhakti Movement in the literary sensibility in Indian National Consciousness in various languages and geographical regions, ranging from *Rudradhyaya*, through the classical Sanskrit of Kalidasa to Indian writing in English of Sri Aurobindo and Raja Rao, the poem entitled "Shiva" by Sri Aurobindo may be mentioned at this juncture. Sri Aurobindo has a Petrarchan Sonnet entitled "Shiva" where he talks about both Space and Time. Only the Octave is quoted here:

On the white summit of eternity
A single Soul of bare infinities,
Guarded he keeps by a fire-screen of peace
His mystic loneliness of nude ecstasy.

But, touched by an immense delight to be,
He looks across unending depths and sees
Musing amid the inconsistent silence
The Mighty Mother's dumb felicity. (Sri Aurobindo 36)

IV

It is clear that the journey motif has been used here and in our journey from the Himalayas to Chidambaram, from the anthropomorphic concept of Shiva from Kalidasa to Akka Mahadevi, from the context of myth and legend to the context of the Bhakti Movement of India of thinking of Shiva as the husband, the concept of Shiva as a Guru or the teacher, the concept of Shiva as the dancer, the concept of Shiva the originator of language. What really unifies the whole of Indian National consciousness is the classic stotram—*Dvadasha Jyotirlinga Stotram* which unifies the entire length and breadth of India—

Sourashtre Somanatha cha Srishaile Mallikarjunam I
Ujjainiyam Mahakalamonkaramamaleswaram II

Paralyam Vaidyanatham cha dakinyam bhimashankaram I
Sethubande tu ramesham nagesham darukavane II

Varanasyam tu visvesham triyambakam goutamitate I
Himalaye tu kedaram ghrusrusham cha shivalaye II
(*Brihat Stotra Ratnakaram* 211)

The meaning is self-evident. If one remembers the location of these various 'Shiva Kshetras' it becomes clear that the National integration was always a part of our culture—(1) Somanatha in Sourashtra, (2) Mallikarjuna in Srishailam, (3) Mahakala in Ujjaini, (4) Omkaram in Amaleswaram, (5) Vaidyanatha in Parali, (6) Bhimashankaram in Dhakini, (7) Rameswara in Rameswaram, (8) Nageswara in Daraka, (9) Visveswara in Varanasi (Kashi), (10) Triyambakeswara in Gouthami on the banks of Godavari, (11) Kedareswar in Kedar, and (12) Sruneswar in Shivalaya. This sense of unity prevailed of the whole of India.

What has been done is to steadily move from the concrete to the abstract, from the consciousness *of* Shiva to Shiva *as* consciousness, resulting in the Self-Realization of '*Abheda*

Bhavana,' 'Chidananda rupaha shivoham shivoham.' After all, the dance of Shiva is taking place not only in the temple of Chidambaram but in every Indian heart.

Works Cited

Bhagavadgita—Chapter 18. Verse 65. Print.

Brihat Stotra Ratnakaram, Part II. Hyderabad: Tagore Publishing House, 1995. Print.

Brough, John. Translated with an Introduction. *Poems from the Sanskrit.* New Delhi: Penguin Books 1988. Print.

Collected Works of Shankaracharya. Sri Shankara Granthavali. Vol. XI, Srirangam: Sri Vani Vilas Press, 1972. Print.

Fradier, Georges. Calmann-Levy, Editeurs. Le Serpent et la Corde *Traduit de l'anglais par.* Tr. Into French of Raja Rao's *The Serpent and the Rope.* Paris: 3, Rne Amber, 1959. Print.

Kalidasa. *The Kumara Sambhavam.* Ed. Suryakanta, Ggeneral Introduction by Dr. S. Radhakrishnan. New Delhi: Sahitya Academy, 1962. Print.

Karan Singh, "Foreword," K.S. Nagarajan. *Contribution of Kashmir to Sanskrit Literature.* Bangalore: V.B. Subbaiah and Sons, 1970. Print.

Mundakopanishat. II, 2.6. Print.

Pope, Rev. G.U. English Translation, Introduction and Notes. *The Tiruvachagam.* Oxford: Clarendon Press, 1990. Print.

Raja Rao. *The Serpent and the Rope,* London: John Murray, 1960. Print.

Ramanujan, A.K. Translated with an Introduction. *Speaking of Siva.* New Delhi: Penguin Books, 1973. Print.

"Sati-Pati Bhavada Vachanagalu," *Mahadevi Akkamma Vachanagalu.* Print.

Sekkizhaar. *Periya Puranam.* Tr. G. Vanmikanthan "FOREWORD," General Editor, Dr. N. Mahalingam, Madras: Sri Ramakrishna Math, 1925. Print.

Sri Aurobindo. "SHIVA," *Sonnets.* Pondicherry: Sri Aurobindo Ashram, 1980. Print.

2

Bhakti as Counter-Cultural Discourse

P. Mallikarjuna Rao

This paper discusses Bhakti literature as a discourse that offers an alternative system of the relationship between God and His devotee, devotee and his fellow beings. It can be considered as a redefinition of a devotee's relationship with God, Cosmos, liturgy, tradition—social, cultural and literary, the language in which he feels and emotes, and the social hierarchy he is entrenched in.

Bhakti literature, according to Andrew Schelling, represents a countercultural discourse as it acts subversively even while apparently operating within the traditional parameters. It is essentially a religious movement with socio-cultural and sometimes political ramifications and it is more reformist in its character. Besides challenging the traditional notions about God, it interrogates the caste, gender and such other inequalities fostered by the conventional and orthodox religious beliefs and practices. In the process it challenges the social stratifications, gender inequalities and also contests the Vedic concept of impersonal God, that is the notion of the Brahman.

For a Bhakti poet God is not just an abstraction beyond human reach, nor an elusive notion beyond human comprehension, but a concrete reality absolutely personal and within the easy reach of the devotees. Further, Bhakti poetry does not postulate God as an impersonal entity, who can be contemplated and meditated upon, but as one who is perceived as a father, mother, husband, child, friend, master and above all an elusive lover; thus it gives God a local colour and a habitat. Lord Siva is Cenna Mallikarjuna, a lover, for Mahadevi Akka and Lord of the meeting rivers for Basavanna, Ram for Kabir, Vitobha for Jana Bai, etc. As Ramanujan says the devotees have added families to their gods. We have the whole family of Siva comprising Parvati, Ganesha and Kumara (Ramanujan 1989).

The stress upon the local god not only added colour but also sometimes, as in the case of Veerasaivas and Vaishnavites, the language of worship too. While it is Kannada in the case of the former, it is Tamil (Manipravala) in the case of the latter. As Ramanujan says "To the 'culture language' of Sanskrit they oppose their own 'language of nature' and they insist upon their self-images as persons of wild, untutored, spontaneous passion" (Ramanujan 1993: 130). It is this feature of Bhakti literature which presses into service the vernacular as a medium for expressing intensely personal feelings and emotions and bestows upon it the respectability it did not enjoy before in matters of rituals and worship. Language for them is not a mere perfected piece of artefact, but a living and vibrant medium of expression of their spontaneous and overwhelming emotion of devotion. As Kabir says "Sanskrit is standing water, bhasha (vernacular) is flowing water." Consequently, these devotional compositions in vernacular came to be used, in temple rites and rituals as found in Tamil. The hymnal literature of 7th and 10th centuries has come to be described as "Tamil Veda."

The Bhakti poetry combined in it both the literary and oral traditions as these songs were rendered to the accompaniment of musical instruments and often performed. The best example that we can recall to our mind is that of the songs of Sri Chaitanya Mahaprabhu or abhangs of Vitobha, which are often performed in groups. As Ramanujan says, "A bhakti is not content to worship a god in word and ritual, nor is he content to grasp him in theology; he needs to possess him. He needs also to sing, to dance..." (Ramanujan 1993: 116). Thus the Bhakti poets produced what Dilip Chitre describes as Orature, a confluence of literary and oral (Schelling xix). This is what makes it stand out from the traditional scriptural literature.

Many Bhakti poets have challenged the gender inequalities and their relevance to a devotee's relation with God. These poets felt that one has to transcend the sex and gender differences to be one with God. In other words, they wanted to be 'human' and to be human is "to be qualified."

In this paper an attempt is made to focus on Bhakti poets and their unconventional ways so as to bring out the theme of protest in their poetry. Their relation with their god is intensely personal, emotional and often they express their love of God making use of the conventions of Sanskrit love poetry. Their imagery is sometimes raw and earthy and sometimes socially unacceptable. As Andrew Schelling Observes, "...the passions given speech in their poems were designed to shatter any fetters of belief that would limit the ferocity of experience" (Schelling 2011: xv). In their devotional fervour they never hesitated to violate social and cultural norms including their modesty as in the case of Akka Mahadevi and Lalla Ded. They abandoned their homes and families in quest of God and became spiritual vagabonds, if one may say so.

In its effort to develop counter-culture it has bestowed upon the sub-cultures the respectability they did not enjoy hitherto "...at a level deeper than what a poem or a song says, occurs disruptions or subversions that appear both spiritual and linguistic. These include forbidden emotions, raw vernacular vocabulary, riddles, secret codes, and non-rational images. There is also a question of context: the disruptive force of speech, prayer, liturgy, or song when used by people who have been forbidden" (Scheling 2011: xv). What is interesting is that these sub-cultures even while being subversive are not in clash with the mainstream culture; on the contrary they are absorbed into the latter contributing to the multicultural fabric of the Indian society. A.K. Ramanujan has rightly pointed out in his Introduction to *Speaking of Siva* that there has always existed a symbiotic relation between the "Great Tradition" and the "Little Traditions." There was a porous and permeable membrane dividing these two. He cites the example of the Mahabharata to establish his point (Ramanujan 1973: 4-11).

Significance of Bhakti

Bhakti stresses upon the direct, unmediated experience unrestrained by intellection and literary conventions. Its essence is Anubhava. The poet focuses less on the auspicious and divine qualities of the god he worships than on his fervour as a devotee. Unlike the traditional hymnal literatures their concern "...is with the subject rather than the object (of worship)" (Ramanujan 1973: 35).

As a Social Movement

Bhakti movements are also social movements which are reformist in character. In Bhakti a man and a woman enjoy equal status in spite of their caste and gender differences and they are equally qualified to realize their god. To be human is the qualification; to be able to feel and experience is the qualification. That is why, "*Feelings are more important than learning, status and privilege.* In fact, status, punditry, even maleness and pride that goes with such things are seen as obstacles to a true experience of god. Once such position is taken, anyone at all is qualified to experience god. To be human is to be qualified" (Ramanujan 1989: 9) (*Emphasis added*).

One of the charges made against Hinduism is that it is polytheistic and it has an overwhelming pantheon of gods. In spite of the Vedas postulating the all-pervasive Parabrahman, a single God without a name and a form, they are supposed to be three crores in number. The Vachanakaras who are the ardent devotees of Siva sneer at the number of gods we have. They proclaim Siva as the only god. Basavanna ridicules this proliferation of divinities in a couple of his vachanas:

> The pot is a god. The winnowing
> fan is a god. The stone in the
> street is a god. The comb is a
> god. The bowstring is also a
> god. The bushel is a god and the
> spouted cup is god.
>
> Gods, gods there are so many
> there's no place left
> for a foot.

There is only
one god. He is our Lord
of the meeting rivers.
Basavanna,

(Ramanujan 1973: 66)

He becomes more scathing and devastating in his criticism of these multiple gods and shows utter scorn for them in another vacana:

Certain gods
always stand watch
at the doors of people.
Some will not go if you ask them to go.
Worse than dogs, some others.
What can they give
These gods,
who live of the charity of people.
O lord of the meeting rivers?

("Basavanna," Ramanujan 65)

Two other poets Lalla Ded of Kashmir and Vemana, the Telugu poet, whose devotion to God is rooted in yogic practices scoff at idolatry. Their notion of god characterised by Vedantic thought and reformist zeal exhort people to seek god within oneself and other human beings rather than in lifeless stone idols. They are very unsparing in their attack:

The god is stone.
The temple is stone.
Top to bottom everything's stone.
What are you praying to, learned man?

("Lal Ded," Schelling 105)

Shaping god out of stone and installing it in a dark room
And worshipping it is not be done O fools
In beings He is found, not in stones.

(Verse 64)

Piling up a few stones humans make beautiful temples
And install in it a stone idol to gain fame

Even after the worship does it speak to bless?

("Vemana," Verse 65. Translation mine.)

Bhakti besides being a religious movement shared a few characteristics of a social reform movement. It is reformist in nature as it had the limited objective of bringing about equality among all the castes and clans which is more spiritual than social. Obviously its purpose was not to overhaul the existing order with all its stratifications, but to demand equality of all in terms of spirituality. As such they are not apologetic for being "lowly born."

The Bhakti poets challenge the existing caste hierarchy that has been plaguing the Indian society for millennia. They question how their caste can ever prevent them from experiencing the divine. Kabir, a fifteenth century saint poet, redefines caste in his own terms. He delinks it from birth, which no one has a choice about and insists that it is one's devotion to god that decides the 'lowliness' or 'exaltation' of one's birth. Ravidas insists that experiencing the divine has nothing to do with the externalities like caste, etc. as it is purely an inner transcendental experience.

No one is lowly born.
The only lowly are those
Who never talk of Ram.

(Hawley 2009: 54)

So, I'm born a weaver,
So what?
I've got the Lord in my heart.

("Kabir," Hawley 2009: 58)

Oh well-born of Benares, I too am born well known:
My labour is with leather. But my heart can boast the Lord.

("Ravidas," Hawley 9)

On the other hand Chokhamela, a varkari saint from Maharashtra, was denied schooling, access to scriptures, village well and temple being an outcaste. He prays to god to step into his shoes and experience what it means to be an outcaste. Puzzled by the prevailing iniquities and discrimination in the society he poignantly questions god:

> Doubts prey
> On my mind,
> What
> Can I do?
> ....
> A throne for one,
> A hovel for another, yet one other wanders bare.
> One half-fed, another feasting,
> for some not a scrap for the asking;
> high glory for one,
> good posts for a few,
> others beg from village to village.
> Such, it seems,
> is the law of your world?
>
> (Schelling 87-88)

> Why have you thrown
> this challenge god?
> Solve this riddle of mine;
> Enter my shoes, know
> in your own self:
> an outcaste,
> what rights do I enjoy?
> Says Chokha
> this low born
> human body every
> one drives away.
>
> (Schelling 87)

He feels enormously helpless and reconciles to his fate saying "...my fate lies in this." Albeit, he insists that it is the inner core that is more important than the outer shell as the core is same in everyone.

> The sugarcane is crooked,
> but not its juice.
> The bow is curved,

not the arrow.
The river is bent,
but not its water.
Chokha is twisted,
not his faith.
Why are you drawn
to the shape of a thing?

(Schelling 89)

He does not want to be looked at but looked into. The irony is while the world shoos him away his god embraces him.

Someone whose touch offends the world
You have enveloped with yourself.

(Hawley 24)

The practice of untouchability is related to our notions of 'purity' and 'pollution' which are as old as the human civilization. This discrimination is not peculiar to India; while it exists in India in the form of caste, elsewhere it is based on race, colour, creed, etc. In India these notions are related to the caste vocation. Those who deal with the skin of dead animals popularly known as chamars are considered untouchables along with those who are scavengers. These obnoxious and irrational practices come under the scythe of the bhakti poets who are made up of different caste groups.

Kalavve, the pious wife of Urlingapeddi, who challenges the very notions of 'purity' and 'pollution' scathingly indicts the hypocrisy of the Brahmins:

Bags are made of cow's hide
for ghee and for water.
Senseless Brahmins who drink
Ghee and water from such leather bags
thinking it sacred
They can't escape
utmost perdition.
The master of Urlingapeddi
doesn't approve of such men.

(Shivaprakash 81)

Palm wine (toddy), which is the staple drink of many working class men and women, is shunned as it is considered pollution to consume it. Ravidas ridicules this notion of impurity in the following verse. He says "liquor is liquor whatever its source", whether it is Ganges or a toddy tree. While the tree is considered impure its leaves are considered sacred enough to write the scriptures on them.

> See how you honour the purest of the pure,
> Water from the Ganges, which no saint will touch
> If it had been made into intoxicating drink—
> Liquor is liquor whatever is its source;
> and this toddy tree you consider impure
> Since the sacred writings have branded it that way,
> But see what writings are written on its leaves:
> The Bhagavta Purana you so greatly revere.
>
> (Hawley 25)

According to tradition the food defiled by the mouth is not worthy of offering to gods as libation. This notion of pollution is gently mocked at by Ravidas in one of his verses. Basavanna too plays upon with the same idea in one of his vachanas. These poets with a radical spiritual vision cannot discriminate between the pure and impure in God's creation and ridicule ritualism that has degenerated into obscurantism. They seem to point out that foolish people stick to form forgetting the spirit.

> Mother, she asks, with what can I worship?
> All the pure is impure. Can I offer milk?
> The calf has dirtied by it in sucking its mother's teat.
> Water, the fish have muddied; flowers the bees—
> No other flowers could be offered than these.
> The sandalwood tree, where the snake has coiled, is spoiled.
> The same act formed both nectar and poison.
> Everything's tainted—candles incense, rice—
> But still I can worship with my body and my mind
> And I have the Guru's grace to find the formless Lord.
> Rituals and offerings—I can't do any of these.

What, says Ravidas, will you do with me.
(Hawley 26)

Milk is leftover
From the calves,
Water is leftover
From the fishes,
Flowers, from the bees.

How can I worship,
O' Siva, with such offal?

But it's not for me
To despise leftovers,
So take what comes,
Lord of the meeting rivers.
("Basavanna," Ramanujan 1973: 72)

Bhakti poets have scant respect for learning and punditry as far as communion with god is concerned. In fact they consider it an inhibiting factor which stands in the way of one's experience of god. It is not mind but heart which should open their portals to god. God is not an "objective reality" to be contemplated upon, but a "subjective experience" to be enjoyed as Paramahamsa Yogananda avers.

Kabir considered knowledge of scriptures useless so long as it remains unhelpful to a devotee to realize god. Knowledge and punditry are no substitute to epiphany; on the contrary they may deny one from having the divine experience as they may erect the barriers of pride in one. Having been influenced by Sufism and Nath yoga tradition Kabir seems to believe that the experience of the divine must be spontaneous and natural unpropped by any practices. The word used in this context is "Sahaj." It embodies "spontaneous spirituality." The British Nath teacher Mahendranath writes:

> Man is born with an instinct for naturalness. He has never forgotten the days of his primordial perfection, except insomuch as the memory became buried under the artificial superstructure of civilization and its artificial concepts. Sahaja means natural.... The tree

> grows according to Sahaja, natural and spontaneous in complete conformity with the Natural Law of the Universe. Nobody tells it what to do or how to grow. It has no swadharma or rules, duties and obligations incurred by birth. It has only svabhava—its own inborn self or essence—to guide it. Sahaja is that nature which, when established in oneself, brings the state of absolute freedom and peace. (www.yogisahaj.com)

So Kabir says:

> Vedas, Puranas—why read them?
> It's like loading an ass with sandalwood!
> Unless you catch on and learn how Ram's name goes,
> how will you reach the end of the road?
>
> ("Kabir," Hawley 51)

He also ridicules those who observe strict Brahmacharya and practice Yogic exercises without a deep-seated longing for god.

> Brother, if holding back your seed
> Earned you a place in paradise,
> Eunuchs would be the first to arrive.
>
> (Hawley 35)

> What if one perfects yogasana
> Has not attained mind's desire
> Like the bullock of the oilman
> Though near home thinks it far.
>
> (G.N. Das 70)

His conviction is that god who is all pervasive and infinite cannot be experienced through any sectarian path. He advocates one to rise above caste, creed, religion and such other divisions, which are man-made. He exhorts a true seeker to move from fragmentation to integration, from multiplicity to unity.

> If God had wanted to make me a Muslim,
> Why didn't he make the incision?
>
> (Hawley 35)

Akka Mahadevi, a 12th century Veerasaiva poet, asserts that knowledge of scriptures will not lead one to god, but one's intense longing supported by mind control.

Look all of you
All the Vedas, Shastras, Agamas, Puranas
Are the grit and husk
From beaten paddy.
Why beat it? Why strike it?
Once you purge the mind
From flowing here and there,
Pure light dawns, Chennamallikarjuna.

(Shiva Prakash)

For Adaiah, another Veerasaiva poet, the scriptures cannot give one the experience of god as they are mere 'similes' with the limited function of describing god. Can such descriptions ever help one experience the experience they describe? he appears to ask. Language is a poor substitute to experience.

Four Vedas are similes;
So are sixteen Shastras
Eighteen Puranas
Twenty-eight sacred Agamas
Thirty-two Upanishads
Seven million great mantras.
Similes, all just similes
Countless words, scriptures,
Systems of logic and grammar—
Similes
Many many mantras, tantras
The mastery of yantras or black magic—
Similes.
Hearing the unheard
Attaining the unattainable
Penetrating the impenetrable—
Similes always.
Unable to stop similes
Unable to transcend the web of similes
Unable to free themselves
From the thick paste of similes and non-similes
Unable to prevent the contamination of feelings
Thought forming or not,
Unable to see the truth

Of Sowrashtra Someshwara
These similes-bound people
Make similes with smiles
Come into being with similes.

(Shiva Prakash 3)

Siddharama, another Veerasaiva poet, strikes the nail on the head when he says:

The vacana experience
Is not a construct of speech, O, my heart.
It is not a construct of speech
Vachanubhava vacho naiva
This is established in the revelations
O Kapilasiddhamallikarjuna.

He says that the experience of a vachanakara is too ineffable to be articulated, for in that mystical experience the 'seer' and the 'seen' and the 'object' and the 'subject' become one leaving nothing. A.K. Ramanujan sees in it a "fierce rebellion against petrification...a call to return to experience" (Ramanujan 1973: 14-15).

Bouddhika vs Kayaka

Traditionally the intellect is considered superior to body and this notion is evident in the social organisation of our society. The manual labour is depreciated as against the mental labour which is extolled. We can recall to our mind the *Purusha Sukhtam* in this context in which Brahmins are said to have emerged from the face of the Brahman, while the Sudras from His feet. This stratification may hold good in the social sphere where the pyramid is structured based on one's vocation. But in the spiritual realm this hierarchy simply crumbles as all are same without any inequities. The glorification of the intellectual labour and the depreciation of the manual labour is strongly resented and assailed by the bhakti poets. While some are reconciled to this idea, many others question it. The Veerasaiva poets vehemently assert that manual labour is equally important.

Maraiah the rice gleaner, a Veerasaiva poet uses the expression "*Kayakave kailasa.*" The culture of hand is represented by the

Kayaka philosophy, in other words labour is glorified, a typical characteristic of the productive classes. The Veerasaivas do not carry a disdainful attitude towards the body as being mortal and a hurdle to one's spiritual realization. On the contrary they consider it sacred as it is the abode of Siva, Kailasa. If *kaya* (body) is Kailasa and the soul is Siva, then whatever labour one performs with it will become a mode of worship of Siva. So, instead of making them feel mortified for being in a profession looked down upon by the society, this attitude bestows upon them certain pride in being engaged in their caste vocations.

As if to assert their caste identity in a mood of defiance, they draw their images from their caste vocations.

> The master weaver, whose skills
> Are beyond our knowing,
> Has stretched his warp
> Through the world.
> He has fastened his loom
> Between earth and sky,
> Where the shuttlecocks are the sun
> and moon.
> He fills the shuttle with the thread
> Of easy spontaneity,
> and weaves and weaves
> an endless pattern.
>
> But now, says Kabir, that weaver!
> He breaks apart his loom
> And tangles the thread
> in thread.

("Kabir," Hawley 55)

> After erecting three pillars
> The gross, the subtle and the causal bodies.
> After beating the buffaloes' rough hide
> After removing the flesh
> With the staff of the manifest and the hidden,
> After tanning the hide with the fibre of dualism
> After pouring the caustic juice of quintessence

Into the hide-pouch of awareness,
The blemishes of the soul thus destroyed
I have come
To take the sandals to his feet.
Take care,
Not of the ground below,
But of the path your feet and sandals take.
Do not be enslaved
By the hand-awl, blade or peg
But realize
Ramarama, your own true self, the joy of joys.
("Chennaiah, the Cobbler," Shiva Prakash 87)

The result is a refreshing poetry with rich imagery drawn from their day-to-day life, where the 'trivial' becomes the 'exalted' and the 'profane', the 'sacred'. Besides the conventional imagery of the Sanskrit literature they have also rejected the language itself by switching to vernacular languages namely, Hindi, Tamil, Kannada, Telugu, etc. to articulate their devotional ecstasy. As A.K. Ramanujan says, "In Bhakti all arts become "techniques of ecstasy," incitements to possession" (Ramanujan 1993: 116).

The bhakti movements gave rise to many social upheavals in the Indian society. The canonical figures of bhakti movements were not all Brahmans. They came from different castes. The rise of vernaculars and the rejection of Sanskrit by the bhakti poets appear to be the natural corollary of overthrowing the Brahman hegemony as Sanskrit was associated with the privileged classes of the society and symbolised social and cultural power. A.K. Ramanujan says, "Sanskrit had antiquity, hieratic pan-Indian prestige; it was the lingua franca of pundits, philosophers, epic poets, lawgivers, courts, and kings. It was unrivalled as model, metalanguage, as source of forms, a standard, an ancestor even to languages unrelated to it. *Sanskrit was culture*" (*Emphasis is mine*; Ramanujan 1993: 127). This aspect of culture was spurned by the bhakti poets and as such they rejected it. Kabir also says, "Sanskrit is standing water, bhasa is flowing water." If Sanskrit is 'Sthavara,' Vernacular languages are 'Jangama.' As Raja Rao says in his preface to *Kanthapura* Sanskrit is the language of intellectual make-up, the vernacular is the language of the emotional make-up of Indians.

The use of the Kannada language and the new literary form of Vachana by the Vachanakaras marks a watershed in the history of Kannada literary culture. As Nagaraj rightly points out, "One of the most important problematic of the history of Kannada literary culture is the emergence of radically new epistemes—core notions about the social and cultural order—and the reformulation of these epistemes overtime. A dramatic instance of such emergence occurred in the twelfth century, when an entirely new communicative form appeared, along with a new religious practice" (Nagaraj 346-47). So, "The Vacana should be seen not so much as an external form but rather as a convergence of a style of language and an attitude toward authority both religious and secular" (Nagaraj 352).

Manipravala was used by the Tamil bhakti poets, for these poets "insist on their self-images as persons of wild, untutored spontaneous passion" (Ramanujan 1993: 130). Manipravala is a mix of Sanskrit and Tamil. Here Sanskrit is the diamond, Mani, while Tamil is the Coral, Pravala. In other words, it is a highly Sanskritized form of Tamil.

Shortly under the influence of bhakti movement the use of vernacular became a pan-Indian phenomenon. Commenting on this phenomenon JTF Jordens observes, "The positive effects of bhakti were the liberation of language from the artificial conventions of the courtly writing that characterised the works of the ancient period; the creation of shorter genres of literature like the vachanas and the kirtans, which are more accessible to common man than long involved narratives of the previous age" (Jordens 266).

Further, the language the bhakti poets used often was full of riddles and it encrypted many esoteric philosophical concepts. Because of its abstruseness and ambiguity this language is known as "Sandhya Bhasa." Sandhya Bhasa is a pan-Indian phenomenon popular among the bhakti poets. Mercia Eliade observes in his book *Yoga: Immortality and Freedom* that there exists a long tradition of secret languages in India, which is known in Sanskrit as Sandhya Bhasa, "twilight speech or intentional speech;" it is a "process of destroying and reinventing language...a universe of analogies, homologies and double meanings" (Ramanvian 1973). The Virashaiva poets wrote what are known as Bedagina vachana drawing from the "common pool of symbols and concepts drawn from yogic psychology and Tantric philosophy" (Ramanujan 30). To cite an example from Allamaprabhu: "A necklace of nine jewels/ lies buried, intact, in the face of the night,/ in the face of day a tree/ with leaves of nine designs." Another vachana in Sandhya Bhasa by Dasari Dasimayya:

> Look here,
> The legs are two wheels;
> The body is wagon
> Full of things.
> Five men drive
> The wagon
> And one man is not
> Like another.
>
> Unless you ride it
> In full knowledge of its ways
> The axle
> will break,
> O Lord of caves.
>
> (Ramanujan 1993: 131)

In the medieval devotional poetry the dividing line between the profane and the Sacred gets erased and as consequence the erotic becomes the exalted. Many poets used sometimes very sensual imagery to articulate their devotional fervour. The common image of devotee as a harlot outrages our sense of propriety and prudence even today. It is 'Agape' expressed in terms of 'Eros.' Take for instance the devotional poetry of Vaishnava bhakti poet Andal. Her imagery is erotic and bizarre. She longs for a divine copulation with the Lord of Dwarka, Sri Krishna.

> From early childhood
> I yearned for

The lord of Dvarka,
Adored him alone,
Dedicated to him
My budding breasts.
Kamadeva, unite me to him soon.

I dedicated my swelling breasts
To the lord who holds
The conch and flaming discus.

(Schelling 11)

Suddenly the imagery propels into the celestial and sacred realms from the mundane. She thinks that it is sacrilegious to have a human lover or a husband.

O Manmatha,
Would you permit a roving jackal
To sniff and eat
The sacrificial food
The Brahmins offer
To celestial gods?

(Schelling 11)

An echo of similar sentiment can be found in Mira Bai in the north and Akka Mahadevi in the South. In one of her vachanas the latter utters her feelings thus:

"He bartered my heart,
Looted my flesh
claimed as tribute
my pleasure,
took over
all of me.

(Schelling 46)

It is common in Indian devotional poetry to perceive God as a lover, a husband and sometimes, as in the Padams of the Telugu bhakti poet Kshetrayya, as a customer. Interestingly it cuts across the sex and gender differences as God is looked upon as the only male, Purusha and the rest as female. In one of her vachanas Akka Mahadevi says "I saw the haughty Master/ for whom men, all men,/ are but women, wives" (Ramanujan 1973: 102). Basavanna a fellow vachanakara writes:

> Look here dear fellow;
> I wear these men's clothes
> only for you.
>
> Sometimes I am man,
> sometimes I am woman.
>
> O lord of the meeting rivers
> I'll make wars for you
> but I'll be your devotees' bride.
>
> (Ramanujan 1973: 69)

Akka Mahadevi treats the Lord of Srisaila Chenna Mallikarjuna as her lover and husband defying all the ethics of traditional marriage namely loyalty to husband. She shudders at the thought of sleeping with her husband whom she married under pressure:

> Other men are thorn
> Under the smooth leaf...
> Mother,
> Because they all have thorns
> In their chests,
> I cannot take
> Any man in my arms but my lord
> White as jasmine.
>
> (Schelling 46)

Unlike the lord who is formless and eternal the mortal husbands decay and die.

> So my lord, white as jasmine, is my husband.
> Take theses husbands who die,
> decay, feed them
> to your kitchen fires!
>
> (Ramanujan 1973: 116)

She finds it extremely difficult to live in this world and the world of her own, the spiritual world simultaneously, as they represent the two opposite poles. So she says:

Husband inside,
lover outside.
I can't manage them both.
This world
and that other,
cannot manage them both.

O lord white as jasmine

I can't hold in one hand
Both the round nut
And the long bow.

(Schelling 46)

Akka's devotional fervour was so strong that she hardly paid any attention to her bodily care. She even sheds her modesty and the clothes much against the social norms as these are man-made and wonders how she can be modest in the presence of her lord who is all pervasive.

People,
male and female,
blush when a cloth covering their shame
comes loose.

When the lord of lives
Lives drowned without a face
in the world, how can you be modest?

When all the world is the eye of the lord,
onlooking everywhere, what can you
cover and conceal.

(Schelling 47)

She is too radical to have any consideration for mundane matters as she has risen over the societal norms:

To the shameless girl
Wearing the White Jasmine Lord's
Light of morning,
You fool,
Where's the need for cover and jewel.

(Ramanujan 1973: 111)

As she had evolved spiritually and surrendered herself to her god Shiva, her body ceased to hold any importance to her:

> Who cares
> who strips a tree of leaf
> once the fruit is plucked?
>
> Who cares
> who lies with a woman
> You have left?
>
> Who cares
> who ploughs the land
> You have abandoned?
>
> After this body has known my lord
> who cares if it feeds
> A dog
> Or soaks up water?

(Schelling 47)

Sule Sankavva goes a step ahead and draws a parallel between the predicament of a devotee and a harlot in the following vachana:

> In my harlot's trade
> having taken one man's money
> I dare not accept a second man's sir.
> and if do,
> they'll strip me naked and
> Kill me.
>
> And if I lie down
> with someone polluted,
> they'll sever my hands
> ears and nose with a
> red-hot knife sir.
>
> Ah, no
> Knowing your reputation I will not.
> This is my word,
> O god without shame.

(Schelling 51)

Jana Bai, a great devotee of Vitobha who could make Him perform all her chores as a maid of Namadev and address the Lord as a woman "Vithala(bai)", likens herself to a "slut" to reach Him.

> Cast off all my shame,
> And sell yourself
> in the marketplace;
> then alone
> can you hope
> to reach the Lord...
> Jani says, My Lord
> I have become a slut
> to reach Your home.
>
> (Schelling 84)

Basavanna too makes use of the image of devotee as a harlot. He describes the miserable plight of the devotee who is torn between his/her god and the worldly temptations with that of a harlot who has to share the time between her customer and her suckling child.

> When a whore with a child
> Takes on a customer for money,
>
> Neither child nor lecher
> Will get enough of her.
>
> She'll go pat the child once
> Then go lie with the man once.
>
> Neither here nor there.
> Love of money is relentless,
> My lord of the meeting rivers.
>
> ("Basavanna," Ramanujan 1993: 55)

Kabir uses the image of a woman who is unfaithful to her husband yearning for her lover:

> My beloved is awakened, how can I sleep?
> Day and night he is calling me,
> And instead of responding to his call
> I am like an unchaste girl, living with another.

Saith Kabir: O clever confidant,
The meeting with the dearest is not possible without love.

("Kabir," Schelling 110)

If they see
breasts and long hair coming
they call it woman,

If beard and whiskers
they call it man:

But, look, the self that hovers
in between
is neither man
nor woman.

("Dasari Dasamayya," Ramanujan 1973: 92)

Conclusion

Thus the bhakti poetry does not merely have its spiritual significance but has wider and deeper implications for the Indian society. It can be read for its radicalism, protest elements, and reformist zeal. In spite of its defiance and subversive character, it operates within the boundaries of traditional Hindu religion. It offers a counter-cultural discourse:

Antarjyoti bahirjyoti pratyagjyoti paratparah
Jyotirjyoti swayamjyoti atmajyoti shivosmyaham

(Light is on the inside, light is on the outside,
Light is in myself, beyond the beyond.
The Light of lights, I myself am light,
the Self is light, I am Shiva.)

Works Cited

Das, G.N. (Trans. Ed. & Compiled). *Couplets from Kabir*. New Delhi: MBD, 2001. Print.

Nagaraj, D.R. "Critical Tensions in the History of Kannada Literary Culture." *Literary Cultures in History*. Ed. Sheldon Pollock. New Delhi. Oxford UP, 2004. Print.

Hawley, J.S. and M. Juergensmeyer (Trans. & ed). *Songs of the Saints of India*. New Delhi: Oxford UP, 2009. Print.

Jordens, J.T.F. "Medieval Hindu Devotionalism." *Cultural History of India*. Ed. A.L. Basham. New Delhi: Oxford UP, 2002. Print.

Prakash, Shiva. (Trans. & ed.) *I Keep Vigil of Rudra*. New Delhi: Penguin, 2011. Print.

Ramanujan, A.K. *Speaking of Siva*. New Delhi: Penguin, 1973. Print.

———. *Nammalvar: Hymns for the Drowning*. New Delhi: Penguin, 1993. Print.

———. "Talking to God in the Mother Tongue." New Delhi: Manushi, 1989. Print.

Schelling, Andrew (Ed.). *The Oxford Anthology of Bhakti Literature*. New Delhi: Oxford UP, 2011. Print.

3

Towards a Multicultural Celebration—Concept of *Bhakti* in Indian Philosophic Prose in English

Sumita Roy

The term multiculturalism is an experiential reality in today's global village. Juxtaposition and overlap of culture, cultural plurality and coexistence of diversity, spatial and temporal changes resulting in multiplicity of cultures—these and many other aspects merge into the term multiculturalism. Bhikhu Parekh in his essay "What is multiculturalism?" defines the concept thus: "Multiculturalism is best understood neither as a political doctrine with a programmatic content nor a philosophical school with a distinct theory of man's place in the world but as a perspective on or a way of viewing human life." Elaborating on the theme, he says:

> Its central insights are three.... First, human beings are culturally embedded in the sense that they grow up and live within a culturally structured world and organize their lives and social relations in terms of a culturally derived system of meaning and significance.... Second, different cultures represent different systems of meaning and visions of the good life.... Third, every culture is internally plural and reflects a continuing conversation between its different traditions and strands of thought. (Parekh)

It is this third point that is of great significance when we discuss a concept such as *bhakti* in Indian systems of thought—especially as it has evolved down the centuries and millenniums. Finally, Parekh also gives a significant conclusion: "This does not mean that it [multiculturalism] is devoid of coherence and identity, but that its identity is plural, fluid and open." Irene Bloemraad of the University of California, Berkeley suggests that "Multiculturalism as a philosophical orientation recognizes *de facto* pluralism in a society, and celebrates that diversity" (Web).

The celebration of diversity that spells multiculturalism can find no better context than Indian thought—especially philosophy and spirituality as is evident from its resilience of thousands of years, in spite of many cultural invasions and conflicts. As Harihar Bhattacharyya in his essay "Multiculturalism in Contemporary India" says: "Multicultural concerns have long informed India's history and traditions, constitution and political arrangements. Much of the writings on Indian history, culture and politics are marked by some kind of multicultural concern" (Web).

II

Indian philosophic prose in English—a fairly neglected area with immense research potential—shows an interesting aspect of multicultural celebration in the manner in which it handles the concept of *bhakti*—both traditional and innovative. For instance, in the doctrines of the Brahmo Samaj—especially in the writings of Rammohan Roy who can be considered the Father of Indian English prose—we find references to complete devotion to the Almighty with words like "You are my all in all." As is well-known, Brahmo Samaj was the fruit of Roy's efforts to find a Hindu-Christian meeting point and this has been recognized as one of the most creative multicultural responses to the colonizer's missionary endeavours.

The bhakti tradition itself, from its inception, symbolizes multiculturalism. In fact, it is this multicultural adaptability and assimilation that kept the traditional tenets of Hinduism active. Bhakti emerged as an approach to the divine which was not according to the dictates of the mainstream devotional practices prescribed by the so-called high priests of piety. It resulted from cultural invasions as well as subversions of the hegemonic discourses associated with love of God. As the Penguin Handbook suggests:

> During the Muslim period in India, and especially from the fifteenth century, Hinduism was vital and alive. *Bhakti* sects flourished, the vernacular languages were used, most of the population was involved at some level, and caste, however much loathed by certain groups, provided social stability and identity. In the face of this, Islam made surprisingly little headway, except perhaps to strengthen Hindu self-identity. (Hinnells 281)

A significant multicultural offshoot of this contact with Islam is the Sufi tradition which gives a novel dimension to devotion. And with the coming of the colonizer, the process of evolution of bhakti took on a new form as the Penguin Handbook notes:

> But it is in the modern period, in the nineteenth and twentieth centuries...that Hinduism faced its greatest self-examination as it confronted Western culture and Christianity. (Hinnells 281)

The Indian Renaissance is possibly one of the most tangible returns which have percolated from this 'greatest self-examination.'

With the passage of time, cultures pass through distinct changes even if the locale remains the same. This temporal dimension, which keeps alive some aspects of the past, contemporizes some and juxtaposes some new ones on the traditionally accepted models, creates a multicultural fabric into which are woven myriad definitions of a popular concept such as bhakti. The concept of bhakti has therefore been variously explicated by some significant prose writers such as Vivekananda, Sri Aurobindo, Tagore, Meher Baba, Rajneesh—to name just a few. Analyzing these different perspectives is the thrust of the present article.

III

Vivekananda's Western education, his affinity to the Brahmo Samaj with its Christian leanings and his inner quest for the meaning of existence make for a multicultural consciousness into which the impact of his guru Ramakrishna created a tremendous new perception. Communicating to the world in English what he heard from his largely unlettered Master in colloquial Bengali was another aspect of his multicultural contribution. His exposition of bhakti yoga in his essay "The Yoga of Love and Devotion" highlights the unification of diverse yogas ultimately leading to cosmic interconnectivity (Vivekananda Vol. III: 32).

Vivekananda also defines the term bhakti in this essay: "Bhakti is a series or succession of mental efforts at religious realization beginning with ordinary worship and ending in a supreme intensity of love for Ishvara" (Vivekananda Vol. III: 36). In the same essay, he talks extensively about all aspects of bhakti from the guru to the mantra to the concept of incarnation and the qualities of an aspirant or bhakta.

And in his essay on "Bhakti or Devotion" he seems to move away from specific Hindu to the universal applicability of the term bhakti. Also, in doing so, he seems to draw a word-picture of his guru's experiential lesson of devotion without disclosing the source of his description. Significantly, the language and vocabulary, the audience to whom he is describing this concept—all these make it a telling instance of communication across cultures. Vivekananda says:

> The true lovers of God want to become mad, inebriated with the love of God, to become "God-intoxicated men". They want to drink of the cup of love which has been prepared by the saints and sages of every religion, who have poured their heart's blood into it, and in which have been concentrated all the hopes of those who have loved God without seeking reward, who wanted love for itself only. The reward of love is love, and what a reward it is! (Vivekananda Vol. II: 53)

Vivekananda's words clearly point to the subtexts of bhakti bringing to mind the inebriation of Mira, the madness of the blind poet Surdas, the toil of Tulsidas who pours his 'heart's blood' into *Ramcharitmanas*—a compendium of devotion, the selfless surrender of Ramprasad or Tukaram, the stupendous reward which we glimpse in the song of Kamalakanta. There are also strains of Vaishnava bhakti here as it had gained ground in Bengal following the birth of Chaitanya Mahaprabhu. Another multicultural exposure which he had in the company of Ramakrishna was that of the devotional songs of Bauls—a conglomeration of cultures and melodies—which the Master was deeply fond of and Vivekananda also sang often.

Aurobindo, who acknowledges his debt to Vivekananda and the Ramakrishna tradition, began as an outsider to his own culture because his formative years were spent in England. By self-study he became familiar with Indian culture and then used it for political awakening. Subsequently, a mystical vision transformed him and invested his consciousness with a vision of Supramental transformation. He retired from active politics and administration to a life of contemplation—a huge cultural leap. Then he devoted his life to the experiment of executing the next step of human evolution which, according to him, would take place in the realms of consciousness.

This amalgam of cultures and experiences resulted in some of the most insightful pieces of Indian philosophic prose to flow from Aurobindo's pen. His essays on aesthetic truth and beauty and his conception of super-conscious evolution map the path of bhakti which begins with unswerving loyalty to the ineffable ideal. Among his significant contributions is his interpretation of foundational texts of Indian culture as supporting documents for his philosophy of Supramental transformation.

Commenting on the seminal text dealing with devotion among other things—that is the *Gita*—Aurobindo says: "It is bhakti with knowledge which the Gita demands from the disciple and it regards all other forms of devotion as good in themselves but still inferior" (284). He also speaks of the four categories of bhaktas thus:

> ...the Gita distinguishes between four kinds of *bhaktas*. There are those who turn to him as a refuge from sorrow and suffering in the world, *arta*. There are those who seek him as the giver of good in the world, *artharthi*. There are those who come to him in the desire for knowledge,

> *jijnasu*. And lastly there are those who adore him with knowledge, *jnani*. All are approved by the Gita, but only on the last does it lay the seal of its complete sanction.

Aurobindo's words have a completely different dimension where 'inebriating love' is tempered with 'knowledge' because this was most suited to his concept of mental and supramental evolution. Bhaktas of the highest order, according to him, therefore, need to be able to merge their 'adoration' with 'knowledge.'

Another noteworthy prose writer whose literary legacy makes significant contribution to the concept of bhakti or devotion is Rabindranath Tagore. Tagore's renowned Nobel Prize winning poem *Gitanjali* is a celebration of devotion. In his prose, Tagore has portrayed his philosophy which highlights his concept of bhakti as inextricably linked with worship of nature and its beauty. The eminent philosopher and another important name in the arena of Indian philosophic prose, Dr. S. Radhakrishnan writes extensively about Tagore's philosophy in a full-length volume. According to Radhakrishnan,

> Rabindranath has the eye which pierces into the secret of which the natural fact is the sign and prophecy. He is a poet of nature in whose hands the crudest stuff of existence acquires a poetic colouring. The spiritual phases of nature leap up to his God-filled eyes, kindle devotion in his heart, and set song on his lips. (Web)

Devotion was to Tagore the basis of his creativity and not only in his poetry but in most of his prose pieces there is some aspect of bhakti which is overtly or covertly explored. For instance, Tagore's *Creative Unity* shows his pantheistic preoccupation. It speaks at length about the creative process which for him was a path towards the divine: "To give perfect expression to the One, the Infinite, through the harmony of the many; to the One, the Love, through the sacrifice of self, is the object alike of our individual life and our society" (Web).

The merging of the individual and the cosmic—the One and the many—through the thread of Love is Tagore's perception of bhakti. Not only this, but he also considers this to be the aim and objective of everyone's life—individually and collectively. And for this he has prescribed the sacrifice of the self. Such a vision is not new but the manner in which it has been concretized in his writings is what makes Tagore's words add a significant dimension to the concept of bhakti.

An exceptional teacher and a realized soul Meher Baba, considered by his followers as an *avatara* or incarnation, has explored the concept of bhakti in his volume entitled *God Speaks,* among other works. This volume—entirely written by his disciples Ivy O. Duce and Don E. Stevens (San Francisco, California) on the basis of his hand gestures at a time when he was observing a vow of silence illustrates technicalities about the evolution of consciousness in which bhakti or self-surrender to the divine occupies a prominent place. From his descriptions we are told that *bhav* or bhava (ecstasy) is a form of devotion (in relation to the Deity) (284).

Bringing tenets of Sufi gnosis into his explanation of the Vedantic term *bhav* he says that it is the same as *hal.* Meher Baba explains:

> In the general sense of the word, *hal* is the inner experience (which includes ecstasy, both controlled and uncontrolled) of relative existence on the first through the sixth planes (stages) of the Path. In a particular sense, *hal* is the state of divine ecstasy and is always experienced in degrees of potency.... (248)

The depth and acuity of insight displayed in this description is one more dimension from which devotion can be approached. The inwardness which becomes evident in the above quoted words, their reference to the Sufi school and their juxtaposition with the Vedantic concept together signifies that the concept of devotion transcends cultural boundaries and makes multicultural explorations not only possible but also desirable.

A professor of philosophy and a name that spelled controversy for decades is Osho. Notwithstanding his outspokenness and permissive ways, his prose writings are as impressive as his ideas are worth exploring. Rajneesh's volume entitled *Krishna—The*

Man and his Philosophy highlights his views on bhakti; the volume deals with all the aspects of Krishna's message in which devotion is crucial. Here Rajneesh says:

> ...devotion means that the devotee becomes an emptiness, a nothingness, a non-being. To know the truth that "I am not" is to be a devotee, is to be with God. And conversely, to know that "I am" and to cling to this ego is to go far away from God. The declaration that "I am" makes for the separation and distance between the seeker and the sought. (Osho 353)

Illustrating this with a significant multicultural example, he continues:

> Rumi has written a beautiful song. It is the song of the Sufis, who know what devotion is. Sufis are among those few people on this earth who know what upasana is. If anyone can understand Krishna fully it is the Sufis. Although they are Mohammedans, yet it makes no difference.

IV

The above are just a sample of possibilities. Exponents such as Paramahamsa Yogananda who brought a scientific flavor to bhakti, Mata Amritanandamayi who propagates devotion as love and service, numerous other contemporary gurus like Sri Ravi Shankar and his Art of Living as a path of devotion, Sukhbodhananda (Spiritual and Management guru), and many others who can be seen propounding their own brand of bhakti through the electronic media are adding more colour to celebrate the plurality which makes concepts such as devotion or bhakti so vibrant and multifaceted. The discussion has endless potential.

Therefore, it is evident that the tradition of bhakti in its varied manifestations—including interreligious strains from Christianity, Islam and Sufi tradition, to name a few—find a distinct representation in Indian philosophic prose in English. A multicultural feast in fact!

Works Cited

Aurobindo, Sri. *Essays on the Gita*. Pondicherry: Sri Aurobindo Ashrama, 2006. Print.

Baba, Meher. *God Speaks: The Theme of Creation and Its Purpose*. Walnit Creek, CA: Sufism Reoriented, 1955, 1973. Print.

Bhattacharyya, Harihar. "Multiculturalism in Contemporary India" http://www.unesco.org/new/en/social-and-human-sciences/resources/periodicals/diversities/past-issues/vol-5-no-2-2003/multiculturalism-in-contemporary-india/ 30-10-2012. Web.

Bloemraad, Irene. "The Debate over Multiculturalism: Philosophy, Politics, and Policy" (http://www.migrationinformation.org/Feature/display.cfm?ID=854) 30-10-2012. Web.

Hinnells, John R. ed. *The Penguin Handbook of the World's Living Religions*. London: Penguin Books. 2010. Print.

Osho. *Krishna—The Man and his Philosophy*. Mumbai: Jaico Books. 2009. Print.

Parekh, Bhikhu. "What is Multiculturalism?" (http://www.india-seminar.com/1999/484/484%20parekh.htm) 30-10-2012. Web.

Radhakrishnan, S. *The Philosophy of Rabindranath Tagore,* 1918. (http://en.wikisource.org/wiki/The_Philosophy_of_Rabindranath_Tagore) 04-11-2012. Web.

Tagore, Rabindranath. *Creative Unity*. (http://www.gutenberg.org/catalog/world/readfile?fk_files=591146&pageno=2)04-11-2012. Web.

Vivekananda, Swami. *Complete Works of Swami Vivekananda*. (Volumes I to IX). Kolkata: Advaita Ashrama. 2009. Print.

Yogananda, Sri Sri Paramahamsa. *Man's Eternal Quest*. Kolkata: Yogada Satsang Society of India, 2008. Print.

4

Many Ways of Studying Literature

A.V. Suresh Kumar

There can be many ways of studying literature, one of which is comparative—an attempt to examine the otherness or explore the 'kindredness' in literatures growing within or beyond national boundaries. One thing needs to be stressed here that it is unwise to study literature solely as research in social psychology or as history of culture and not as a study of properties in literary texts which would explain their reception primarily as literature. But at the same time it is true that eliciting aesthetic experience in a text by any recipient depends upon the socio-cultural background of the recipient. Similarly, any study of the aesthetic function of a text will depend upon the socio-cultural context in which the text has grown. And this context varies from one language to another in the multilingual situation of India, and from one culture to another in the context of the other countries of the world. One can give examples to prove this; for instance, the division between art and religion in Indian culture seems to be less sharp than what it is in Europe and China. In the same way in Indian poetics under *Vritti* and *Riti* the cultural variability of texts in different Indian languages is discussed and analysed.

However, it is true that any intra-cultural and inter-cultural study can liberate us from cultural prison and, at the same time, help determine universally valid rules for artistic success. After all "there is a common feature in all art" or "literary invariables" occurring in all literature as explained by two famous comparative critics, Rene Wellek and Rene Etiemble. This does not mean that one would be happy and contented only with locating points of identities while studying comparative literature. In fact, in the Indian context it is not possible. We have both our identities and our diversities. We have, in fact, sustained ourselves through our diversities. So if it is said that Indian literature is one because it is written in many languages it cannot be far from truth. And at the same time, oneness or commonness of literary expression in the literature of twenty-two languages is also a reality. What people say so wonderfully holds good that for a north Indian there are a lot many differences to be seen and found in South India. But the element of commonness can also be felt which quickens our blood and assures us of our oneness.

Intra or inter-literary study focuses on literary invariables or on the expression of the human message implicit in all major literary works. Messages can have different shades of thought, but a message there will be. But, then, the big question is: can this kind of study help us know the position of Indian literature in the reading public of the world as a whole? Is the West interested in our literature? What is our present image *vis-a-vis* our literary creation?

The westerners do talk about our literature, but not so much about the living, contemporary Indian literature. Of course, they have a fascination for Tagore. But that is a different matter, which I shall take up later. When Schlegel said in 1800, "It is in the Orient that we must search for the highest Romanticism," he meant *Shakuntala* and the *Upanishads* (qtd in Said). So far as one can tell, most of the early English orientalists in India like William Jones were impelled by the dual purpose of investigating "the sciences and arts of Asia, with the hope of facilitating ameliorations there and of advancing knowledge and improving the arts at home" (Pargiter viii).

The study made by the Anglo-French or German scholars was an exercise in intellectual authority over India within Western culture. Scholars like Silvertre de Sacy made it clear that oriental literature could survive a European's taste, intelligence or patience, provided it was properly transformed by the orientalist before it could begin to be appreciated. Sacy further says that even if one does go through the rigours of specialised training, much of the description in poetry (Arabic) will not be accessible to Europeans "who have attained to a higher degree of civilization" (107, 110-12).

Lord Macaulay in his famous *Minute* of 1835 asserted that "our native subjects" have more to learn from us than we from them. Even if India was discussed during that time in an exotic manner for its pantheism, its spirituality, its stability, its enduringness, it was invariably followed by an underestimate of India as being underhumanized, antidemocratic, backward, barbaric and so forth. Theses of oriental backwardness, degeneracy and inequality were developed and the West most easily associated itself early in the nineteenth century with ideas about the biological bases of racial inequality (Said 206). Even if interest was shown about the people and languages of India, it was to consolidate the imperial designs. Lord Curzon told the House of Lords on 27 September 1909:

> Our familiarity, not merely with the languages of the people of the East but with their customs, their feelings, their traditions, their history and religion, our capacity to understand what may be called the genius of the East, is the sole basis upon which we are likely to be able to maintain in the future the position we have won, and no step that can be taken to strengthen the position can be considered undeserving of the attention of His Majesty's Government or of a debate in the House of Lords. (http://hansard.millbanksystems.com/lords)

In the early 20th century Western orientalists delivered India to the West by interpreting India for their compatriots. The relation between these orientalists and India was essentially hermeneutical: standing before a distant, barely intelligible civilisation or cultural monument, the Orientalist scholar reduced the obscurity by translating sympathetically portraying, inwardly grasping the hard-to-reach object. Yet for most of the westerners India remained beyond the kin of the west. This cultural, temporal and geographical distance was expressed in phrases like "the veils of an Eastern bride" or "the inscrutable orient" which eventually passed into the common language. This is the disappointing conclusion of E.M. Forster's *A Passage to India*, where Aziz and Fielding attempt and fail at reconciliation:

> Why can't we be friends now? Said the other, holding affectionately. It's what I want. It's what you want.
>
> But the horses didn't want it—they swerved apart; the earth didn't want it, sending up rocks through which riders must pass single file; the temples, the tank, the jail, the palace, the birds, the carrion, the Guest House, that came into view as they issued from the gap and saw Man beneath: they did not want it, they said in their hundred voices, No, not yet, and the sky said, 'No, not there'. (Chapter 37)

Despite this pessimism, Orientalists like Professor Sylvain Levi asserted in 1925, "Our duty is to understand Oriental civilization. These people are the inheritors of a long tradition of history, of art, and of religion, the sense of which they have not entirely lost and which they are probably anxious to prolong." We must not forget that long before what Levy said Tagore had got the Nobel Prize for literature in 1913 which created some kind of interest in the Western mind for Indian literature. Yeats found a 'fresh rediscovery of landscape' and 'joyous movement', and if not the 'voluptuous body', at least 'the tale of the nuptials of the soul with its ultimate destiny with voluptuous love details...' and 'Eastern contemplation...carrying that into the very depths of the soul, restoring to us the meaning of tonight's mystery.' This description caught the imagination of the foreign readers who found deep mystical and spiritual significance even in the love poems translated in *The Gardener*. This kind of emphasis did not help develop the right appreciation for Rabindranath Tagore. Many of his Western readers practically ceased reading him because of their apathy towards spiritualism or obscure mysticism. His reputation declined very fast among the Western readers also because of his lectures on nationalism and his return of the Knighthood after the massacre of Jalianwala Bagh in 1919 and, on top of it, because of the translations of his writings done by him, or later done by Thompson. Tagore was aware of 'cracks and gaps' in his translations and was sorry that he had ever attempted 'to cover them up with some pretty designs that may give them an appearance of wholeness.' But with new translations will he regain his true position in the Western mind?

William Radice recently translated selected poems of Tagore about which Khushwant Singh rapturously remarked, "At long last we have a translator who has succeeded better than anyone else and brought out one of the greatest of the great poets of all times." It is true that through this translation Western readers found in Tagore not only an eastern mystic but also a humanist social critic whose poetry matched well with the literary sensibility of the present era. Even then his position did not improve much in the eyes of the Western readers.

Ian Jack in *The Sunday Times* says that a prosaic Briton likes the concrete. High-flown Bengal has had a long affair with the abstract. Richard Caseby writes in *The Oxford Times* that realizing the limited appeal of poems dallying with transcendence one need not doubt that there will be no stampede at the bookstalls. The love affair with the East and all-embracing abstraction has long cooled. Does it mean that there is a cultural disparity based on different worldviews and ethos, which restrains a Western reader from accepting our literature? No doubt, there is a disparity, but the real cause is our own failure to present our best literature to the West in proper translation. Why blame a Western reader?

Gibb's article on 'Literature' published in 1931 says, "Oriental literature has begun to be studied again for its own sake, and a new understanding of the East is being gained. As this knowledge spreads and the East recovers its rightful place in the life of humanity, oriental literature may once again perform its historic function, and help us liberate ourselves from the narrow and oppressive conceptions which would limit all that is significant in literature, thought and history to our own segment of the globe" (Gilale 209). Gibb wanted to confront East as a sort of humanistic challenge to the local confines of Western ethnocentricity. 'The glory that was India' fascinated the lover in Andrew Marvell's 'Coy Mistress' who assures his beloved, "Thou by the Indian Ganges' side/should rubies find." Writers like Marvell have regarded India as an exotic land of sadhus, snakes and suttee; others like Kipling, Forster and Mark Twain, have found a varied spectacle of humanity in this vast land and interaction between an Indian character and the Western mind of absorbing interest; still others, like Whitman and Thoreau, Maugham and Eliot have felt the perennial appeal of Indian thought and philosophy. But we could not cash this interest in India and failed miserably in projecting our literature abroad. In 1951 the same Gibb contributed an essay to a book significantly entitled *The Near East and the Great Powers* in which he tried to explain the need for an expansion of Anglo-American programmes of Oriental studies:

> We can no longer rely on that factor of prestige which seemed to play a large part in pre-war thinking, neither can we any longer expect the peoples of Asia and Africa or of Eastern Europe to come to us and learn from us, while we sit back. We have to learn about them so that we can learn to work with them in relationship that is closer to terms of mutuality. (Qtd in Said)

The interest shown towards Oriental literature, now because of such considerations, has become political and has hardly remained simply scholarly. The overtly imperial concern has never ceased to play its role. The Soviet Russia and the East European countries have as a part of some policy objective before *perestroika,* translated Indian literature in abundance, and in the process this interest has caught up with the demand of the reading public. After all, great work of art, quite obviously, is an expression of a great personality; by whatever standard you may have it, eastern or western.

Russian and Eastern European universities are now producing fluent speakers of different Indian languages and they are translating Indian literature. One may agree that the study of Indian languages is becoming an instrument of propaganda, but then it is also helping in the propagation of Indian literature in those countries. Indian authors like Tagore, Premchand, R.K. Narayan, Mulk Raj Anand, Shivarama Karanth, Manik Bandyopadhyaya, S.K. Pottekkat, Akilon, U.R. Anantha Murthy, Bhisham Sahni, Amrita Pritam, and many others have written about their experiences, their values, their humanity and thereby effectively demolished the various images, clichés, and abstractions by which India was generally represented.

A literary text speaks more or less directly of living reality. Its power is felt not because it is in Hindi or French or English; its power lies in its encounter with life and in the dynamic vitality of words in which it is embedded. Besides this, one should not forget the enthusiasm of the Russian and the East European readers in accepting the humanistic tradition of involvement in a national culture or literature which is not their own. However, the situation is fast changing after the *perestroika* and *glasnost* in Soviet Russia, and the downfall of communism in many Eastern European countries. I cannot give the socio-political reason of upheaval, but one shudders to see the tremendous impact of the Western consumer culture which is fast eroding the very basis of the literary culture of these countries. Now there is a spurt in translation and sale of novels written by Hadley Chase, Sheldon, Ian Flemming and others. Even then at this point of time the interest in Indian writers has not completely fagged out.

Why is it not so in America and Western Europe and Britain? The study of cultural relativism has broadened the vision of scholars in these countries. Now one wishes to avoid the accusation of modernist or Eurocentric prepossession, and uphold a pretension to universality by accepting the study of literature of India and other oriental countries. One is now ready to reconstruct the structures of the alien value systems with reference to one's own value system and understand differences and similarities. But then what about the common reader? Is he studying Indian literature? Practically very little. He has read some Indian literature written in English to know about India rather than to enjoy it as literature. His approach is purely documentary.

Professor Anantha Murthy once spoke of this dismal situation. We in India would read the novels of Saul Bellow or Michel Tournier or William Golding as pieces of literature, but his *Samskara* or any other Indian novel would be read only as a piece of sociological or anthropological study of the Indian society. Westerners have hardly read Indian literature in English translation. They have read, as I said, a bit of Mulk Raj Anand,

R.K. Narayan, Anita Desai, and a few others. But people in India have now started questioning Indian English writing. They want to know if it has all that which makes it great literature? Let me quote Dr. Amrik Singh in this context: "All that I wish to affirm is that Indian writing in English can be of good quality, and even of some significance, but it is highly unlikely that anything like greatness in literature can be achieved through the use of this medium" (Seminar Paper).

I would not be a party to this kind of controversy but would like to point out that in one of the anthologies of Indian English poetry covering an exhaustive list of names ranging from Sri Aurobindo and Sarojini Naidu to Dom Moraes and Pritish Nandy, one finds a statement by a poet, "I am an Indian writing in English.... I write in English because there is always a consistency between a particular ethos and the language it produces. The Indian ethos is alien to me and so are the languages which express it" (Lal 56). This sort of statement confuses the image of Indian literature here and elsewhere.

There are, however, many outstanding contemporary writers like Anita Desai, Nayantara Sahgal, Arun Joshi, Vikram Seth, Shashi Deshpande, etc. who would never suggest a self-conscious distancing from their Indian situation and show lack of commitment to Indianness. "The creative choice of a language must be respected and one should judge by results rather than by dismal prophecies of what the result must fail to be" (Rajan 108). What I would like to point out is that in the West, Indian literature is generally taken to be Indian English literature which is only a minute fraction of the total literary output, but the West hardly knows it. The reason is that literature in different Indian languages is not available to the West in translation, and also no consistent effort has been made to promote Indian literature in translation. That there still stands a deafening barrier, which people call 'translation curtain,' is all very true. Attempts have been made to effect a breakthrough so as to do away with the translation curtain, but still they have not gathered the requisite momentum.

Sahitya Akademi has published a few Indian novels in English translation. UNESCO also, with its *Collection of*

Representative Works, has placed some significant modern Indian classics on the world map. As part of the celebrations of the 1985 Indian Festival in France, several Indian literary works of Manik Bandyopadhyaya, Bibhuti Bhushan Bandyopadhyaya, U.R. Anantha Murthy, Kamala Markandaya, Tarasankar Bandyopadhyaya were translated into French. But this is only a drop in the ocean. A few years ago at the Frankfurt Book Fair only a few Indian authors could sell the translation rights of their books. The verdict is clear. The West is still not interested in our creative literature. But one wonders how it could be so much interested in Garcia Marquez—a Latin American writer. The reason is not far to seek; it is because the translation was done so well that even Marquez once made a comment, 'It is better than the original' (Stavans iii). The disinterestedness of the Western reader, some Euro-American literary fanatics say, has sprung up because of lack of 'universality' in the Indian writings. The idea is so absurd that it does not need any comment. Right from the days of Aristotle one knows that the particularity of the situation of the writer determines his perception which creates its own universals. The actual problem is how to educate the Indian reading public about the wealth and variety and excellence of writing in Indian languages. On the face of it, this is a strange proposition, but then this will lead us to the right course. Unless an awareness is created for our literature at the home front we cannot think of any promotion of our literature abroad. The writers should not hesitate to give away the translation rights with all generosity and help in the translation of their works. This is now being done extensively in the West.

Years ago the translator Mr. Manguel translated Yourcenars' book on Yukio Mishima, *A Vision of the Void* in collaboration with the author. Indian authors should come forward in a big way to promote translation of their books in different Indian languages. The Indian reader is interested in the study of English or American literature or European literature in translation. He is to be educated to read Indian literature not only of his language but of other Indian languages also in translation. The use of English as a target language along with other Indian languages is obvious, but the use of English by the Indian translators in the world market has not created any requisite interest in the Western reader for our literature mainly because of stylistic reasons and the culture settings.

An English rendering of a Tamil poem may evoke joy and excitement in us but will leave most of the Western readers cold primarily because of the Indian style of English and the cultural prison in which a Westerner generally stays. But that should not deter us. Our attempts at translation of Indian literature into English will help us define the specific area of Indian literature, its drawbacks and its positive strength. Moreover, our author-translators/professionals should continue the work of translating for inter-lingual understanding within the country. In the process we shall find the foreigners who know our languages coming forward. Eventually, the Western writer will join his Indian collaborator, and from English the work of translation will spread out to other foreign languages.

There is another problem. It is true even today that a majority of the Western readers do not understand our literature. They cannot read and judge Indian literature as literature and like or dislike particular works as they like or dislike works in their own literature. Is it possible to encourage a re-tailoring and redressing of our literature to suit a different taste? Even if it were possible, it won't be wise. It would be unwise to enlarge our literary market before we are sure that there has been an enlargement of taste. The enlargement of taste is primarily a literary objective which is connected with the development of a critical apparatus that will help us place our literature alongside the literature of the West in a common perspective. The Indian interpreters and authors must help in the reconstruction of a critical standard so that the Western readers may understand our literature in a convincing way. It is a task of great magnitude. It is a task involving major affections and interests and calls for important enterprises in literary criticism.

To sum up, the role of an author in this venture will be to help the translators and interpreters in affiliating our literature to the total literary inheritance of the West. Only a greater interest in the literature of our country can bring that about and only through translations will this be possible. National pride and a passionate desire to promote a national product should not prompt the interpreters or critics to make fantastic claims for Indian writing. Only the best works need to be promoted—works which have the power of the Indian heritage, the complexity of the Indian experience and the uniqueness of the Indian voice. The West will have to be made aware of this inheritance, complexity and uniqueness. A great work of art is the expression of both the tradition and the actual. Only when it is indissolubly wedded to both the exterior landscape and the interior vision, shall we see an Eastern sensibility wholly at home in a Western scenario.

Works Cited

Forster, E.M. *A Passage to India*. London: Penguin Classics, 2005. Print.

Gilale, H.A.R. 'Literature,' *The Legacy of Islam*. Ed. Thomas Arnold and Alfred Guillaume. London: Oxford UP, 1965. Print.

Lal, P. (ed.). *Modern Indian Poetry in English*. Calcutta: Writers Workshop, 1969. Print.

Pargiter, Fredric Eden (ed.). *Centenary Volume of the Royal Asiatic Society of Great Britain and Ireland (1823-1923)*. London: 1923. Print.

Rajan, B. 'Identity and Nationality,' *Commonwealth Literature, Unity and Diversity within Common Culture*. Ed. John Press. London: Heinemann Educational, 1965. Print.

Sacy, Silvertre de. *Melenges de litterature Orientate*. Paris: n.d. Print.

Said, W. Edward. *Orientalism*. New York: Random House, 1978. Print.

Stavans, Ilan. *Gabriel Garcia Marquez: The Early Years*. New York: Palgrave Macmillan, 2010. Print.

Suresh Kumar, A.V. Paper presented in International Seminar on Indian Literature in English & English Translation. New Delhi: Sahitya Akademi, 1986. Print.

http://hansard.millbanksystems.com/lords/1909/sep/27/oriental-languages, accessed on 2-11-2014. Web.

5

Multiculturalism and the Problem of 'Representation' in Indian English Literature

B. Yadava Raju

Multiculturalism is a perspective on or a way of viewing human. Its central insights, according to Bhikhu Parekh, are three, each of which is sometimes misinterpreted by its advocates and needs to be carefully reformulated if it is to carry conviction.

First, human beings are culturally embedded in the sense that they grow up and live within a culturally structured world and organize their lives and social relations in terms of a culturally derived system of meaning and significance. This does not mean that they are determined by their culture in the sense of being unable to rise above its categories of thought and critically evaluate its values and system of meaning, but rather that they are deeply shaped by it, can overcome some but not all of its influences, and necessarily view the world from within a culture, be it the one they have inherited and uncritically accepted or reflectively revised or, in rare cases, one they have consciously adopted.

Second, different cultures represent different systems of meaning and visions of good life. Since each realises a limited range of human capacities and emotions and grasps only a part of the totality of human existence, it needs other cultures to help it understand itself better, expand its intellectual and moral horizon, stretch its imagination, save it from narcissism to guard it against the obvious temptation to become absolute in its outlook. This does not mean that one cannot lead a good life within one's own culture, but rather that, other things being equal, one's way of life is likely to be richer if one also enjoys access to others, and that a culturally self-contained life is virtually impossible for most human beings in the modern and interdependent world.

Third, every culture is internally plural and reflects a continuing dialogue between its different traditions and strands of thought. This does not mean that it is devoid of coherence and identity, but that its identity is plural, fluid and open. Cultures grow out of conscious and unconscious interactions with each other, define their identity in terms of what they take to be their significant other, and are at least partially multicultural in their origins and constitution. Each carries bits of the other within itself and is never wholly *sui generis*. This does not mean that it has no powers of self-determination and inner impulses, but rather that it is porous and subject to external influences which it assimilates in its now autonomous ways.

If this give-and-take kind of enrichment of experience is taken into account, the Indian English Literature (IEL) and its representation of Indian life and reality need to be scrutinized and appreciated *vis-a-vis* the bhasha literatures of the country. In the bhasha literatures, the experience and representation of the experience relating to various issues like caste, religion and gender appears to be more authentic and convincing than in IEL. In support of this argument, it may be relevant to consider two instances—one from the Tamil and the other from Telugu novella in English translation—Bama's collection of short stories in Tamil entitled *Kisumbukkakaaran*, published in 1996 and Kesava Reddy's translation of the novella, *Athadu Adavini Jayinchadu* published in 1998.

'Bama' is the pen name of a Tamil Dalit writer who hails from a Roman Catholic family. She was born in 1958 at Puthupatti, Tamil Nadu. She teaches in a primary school in Uthiramamerur, near Chennai. In 2001, the English translation of her childhood memoir, *Karukku*, won the Crossword Prize, which established her as a distinct voice in Dalit literature. She is the author of two other acclaimed novels, *Sangathi* (1994, 2005), and *Vanmam*

(2002). Fighting impossible odds she went through school and college, was trained as a teacher imparting values aimed at building self-esteem and social consciousness. She published *Karukku* in 1992, an autobiography, *Sangathi* in 1994, a novel and *Kisumbukkakaaran* in 1996, a collection of ten short stories. All through her works and several of her articles, she hopes to focus on themes related to caste and social discrimination.

Karukku means Palmyra leaves, which, with their serrated edges on both sides, are like double-edged swords. By a felicitous pun, the Tamil word *karukku*, containing the word '*karu*', embryo or seed, also means freshness, newness. In her Foreword, Bama draws attention to the symbol, and refers to the words in Hebrew (New Testament), "For the word of God is living and active, sharper than any two-edged sword, piercing to the division of soul and spirit, of joints and marrow, and discerning the thoughts and intentions of the heart" (*Hebrews* 4: 10).

All the stories in *Kisumbukkakaaran* (*Harum-Scarum Saar & Other Stories*) are set among the Dalits of Tamil Nadu and display the full potential of the "weapons of the weak"—the dominant Brahminical order is not openly challenged, but bawdy comments and subversive intent undermine the authority of the powerful. Rustic humour takes the indignity and suffering of lower-caste life in its stride, and bristles with the raw energy and vitality that comes from living close to the ground. The English translation of the collection has been titled *Harum-Scarum Saar & Other Stories* and published in 2006 by Women Unlimited (an associate of Kali for Women, New Delhi). Harum-scarum means uncontrolled, in all directions or without thinking.

In the first story entitled "Pongal" Madasami comes to realize what his literate son, Elavarasu, tells him about the upper castes and the landlords. After many attempts at making a living, Madasami finally settles as a farmhand in the fields of Ramasami Ayya. So it has become a custom with him that would offer to the landlord whatever he produces in the leased outfields. As usual, this year also he is about to take some of these offerings to the landlord. But his only literate son tells him not to do so because these items of offer are more valuable than what the landlord returns. But still Madasami wants to go see his landlord and offer these gifts. This time the landlord does not even come to see him, and sends him away with only a bit of "pongal" like every year. On thinking about the truth in what his son says, Madasami is convinced that they need not go see him with so many offerings. He asks his wife to get rid of the "pongal" which they bring home and prepare their usual food.

In the next story entitled "annachi" the central character Ammasi does not believe in respecting the landlords and Naickers. He refuses to get up and offer a seat to the landlord while he travels standing. In a later incident in the story, he is called by the village panchayat and an explanation was sought as to why he has called the landlord "annachi." To the question raised by the headman at the panchayat, Ammasi replies as follows:

> There's nothing wrong with what I said. Did I call him *mama* or *machan*, trying to create a relationship and asking for the hand of a girl? I only called him *annachi* politely, respectfully, and you raise hell? What did you people do when I addressed Irulappan, the drain-cleanner, as *annachi* last week? Didn't you reproach me for addressing a *korava* as *annachi*? Now you ask me why I called a *naicker*, *annachi*? (14)

Saying so, Ammasi walks away. This deed of Ammasi was a deed of defiance, which no elderly person would have done. But his act is immediately approved and supported by the young boys of the village who laugh at the whole incident. This indicates the changing customs and practices in the Dalit communities.

In another story "rich girl" an eight-year-old school girl Ramayi is trapped in the choice between school and work. She is sent to school, sparing her from hard physical labour. But she is asked to take the new born baby with her to school because both her parents go to work. At the work place babies are not allowed by the *mothalli*. But at school the baby is not permitted because that will be a disturbance to all others and the baby is always in need of care. Therefore, the teacher asks her to go out of the school. Ramayi, therefore, goes to swim to the *kamma* with the baby. There she notices her father who comes to wash the buffalos of his landlord. In the process of washing, one of the buffaloes goes to the other side of the *kamma*. In an attempt to save the buffalo, Ramayi's father gets drowned in the *kamma*. The whole village witnesses this tragic event. As a compensation, the landlord pays one hundred rupees to the family of Ramayi making her richer by hundred rupees at the cost of the life of her father. The conversation between two young innocent girls in the story is worth mentioning here:

> 'Dying by drowning gets you one hundred rupees?' Pechiyamma found this difficult to digest.
>
> 'No, no, nothing like that, atha. You know nothing! Only if you drown while washing mothali's bullocks will he give you one hundred rupees.' (49)

In "half-sari" and other stories also we find similar representation of the marginalized and the underprivileged represented as being socially conscious and able to react to the type they are reduced to.

II

Kesava Reddy, born in 1946, is a doctor of medicine and has treated for the past nineteen years or more leprosy at Dichpalli in Nizambad district in Telangana. He published five novels of which *He Conquered the Jungle* is one. This work has been widely translated into fourteen Indian languages. It is translated into English by CLL Jayaprada and published by Macmillan under the Modern Classics series in 1998. The protagonist of this novella is an old man who happens to be a swineherd. One evening he notices the boy and the pigs that had been taken out to graze had not returned. Misgivings and apprehensions rise in his mind and he begins to get upset. His pigs are everything to him. They were his sole wealth. He sets out in search of the missing boy and the "sukka sow" (pig), which is pregnant and may have entered the jungle in expectation of the event looking for a safe place to give birth. He is a seventy-year-old-man, but still determined to find the sow and her litter. He must seek them out and protect them from the wild animals of the forest. Armed with no more than a spear and a knife, the old man falls back on his huntsman's skills and unconquerable will.

In the forest, it is time for the wild animals to emerge from their lairs. After a long and arduous search he tracks the sow to a bush, and finds that she has just given birth to ten young ones there. The old man tells himself: "I should be cautious. If the sow is in there and senses my presence she will attack like a tigress. She might grip a leg or arm and crunch it off. She might even kill me. She is a brute and cannot distinguish between enemies and well-wishers" (11). In his eagerness to have a look at the piglets, he is chased and attacked by the ferocious mother. Lacerations bleeding, the old man shins up a tree to save himself. His wounds and pains are swiftly forgotten and remain submerged by his ecstatic and excited mood. His euphoria lay in the sight of the ten beautiful piglets. He now decides to stand guard over the mother and her litter to protect them from wild animals. As the night progresses, a lone jackal first sneaks in but the mother tears it to pieces. Soon a pack of four jackals approach the bush. The mother-pig kills one; the old man spears another from his perch on the tree, while the other two jackals run away with a piglet each. A little later a large pack of jackals are seen coming towards the bush. Now, the old man quickly realizes that the sow, being one against many, cannot protect her litter. He must come down from his perch to drive the jackals away, but for this he has to first kill the sow. He is reluctant to kill her but decides to do so in order to save the remaining eight piglets. He quickly spears the sow and succeeds in driving the jackals away. Eventually he makes a basket to carry the eight piglets. When weariness overtakes him, he drops off, and wakes to find that vultures have pecked to death the already starving piglets. He feels utterly defeated.

This battle of the old man is punctuated by his reflections and remembrance of things past that add depth and richness to the novella, enlarging its significance. It is a tale of endurance and of man's archetypal struggle. From this point of view, the narrative seems to suggest that to survive is to have struggled. As if to underscore this view Kesava Reddy creates in the novel conditions of frontier existence. Nothing seems to accentuate this better than a man living on the edge. To the millions of people in India who live below the poverty line, like the old man in the novel, making both ends meet is itself a heroic struggle and in most of his novels Kesava Reddy focuses on their lives. But it must be said to Kesava Reddy's credit that he never sentimentalizes poverty nor does he explicitly draw our attention to it, for the struggle of his characters in this strata of society, poverty merely provides an unobtrusive setting. It is no coincidence that the old man in *He Conquered the Jungle* is invaded by thoughts of suicide in his moment of utter defeat and despair; that is, just when he is about to find the piglets dead in his basket, after a long desperate struggle to save them, he unwittingly recollects how, in the past, a shepherd in the jungle had hanged himself on discovering the death of his whole herd. If the old man did not end up like the shepherd it would only be because of stoicism born of mature years. He survives although he is driven to desperation, and his survival is his triumph.

To many discerning readers, Kesava Reddy's novel *He Conquered the Jungle* readily brings to mind Hemingway's *The Old Man and the Sea*. It is true that in both the novels the old men go too far out and have only their courage, determination and endurance to fall back on in their lone, heroic, unequal fights. Fighting with their backs to the wall, both display dignity. Both are stoic and reflective. Both are losers in the end but enjoy moral victory for daring the impossible with extraordinary grit and tenacity. But the difference is that Hemingway's heroes seek out death in order to live life with unusual intensity, whereas for Kesava Reddy's protagonist it is an inseparable part of his daily struggle for existence—the life lived by the humblest folks in India. It is significant to note that Kesava Reddy leaves his protagonist in the novel unnamed, referring to him throughout the novel in the third person. That way he could be anybody whoever dares and challenges life in the game of survival.

Such representations are common in bhasha literatures, and Indian English Literature (IEL) remains incomplete to this extent of life either lived or represented in it, if there is no multiculturalism among the writers of various languages and literary cultures across the country.

Works Cited

Bama. *Harum-Scarum Saar & Other Stories.* New Delhi: Women Unlimited, 2006. Print.

Hebrews 4: 10. Print.

Parekh, Bhikhu. Multiculturalism? www.india.seminar.com/1994/484/20 parekh.htm. dated, Nov. 29, 2012 4.25p.m. Web.

Reddy, Kesava. *Athadu Adavini Jayinchadu.* Translated from the Telugu original by CLL. Jayaprada. *He Conquered the Jungle.* Chennai: Macmillan Indian Limited, 1998. Print.

6

Socio-cultural Significance of Nativism: An Overview

M. Rajagopalachary and *B. Krishnaiah*

Nativism is an offshoot of the crisis in the present postmodern culture. It emerged as a concept to check the Eurocentric modernism and internationalism. It opposes criticism that compares every literary text with some Euro-American creation. Satchidanandan says "nativism is post-colonial in its battle against the invasion of alien sensibilities and modes of feeling and articulation, while it is post-modernist in its emphasis on cultural difference" (17). It looks for modernity in its own roots, traditions, cultures and realities with a notion of belongingness. In other words, in its progressive attitude is a performance of the pluralism of Indian culture. It imparts authenticity to the writing as Shashi Tharoor confesses:

> I grew up in this country (India) and a lot of who I am has been shaped and formed by growing up here. And so I do feel very much that my roots are here.... At the same time I'll be foolish to write about India if I didn't feel I understood it if I didn't feel instinctively that I was writing from a sense of roots and *a* sense of being anchored to this place and to the preoccupations of Indians. (xi)

Balachandra Nemade and G.N. Devy are the initiators of the movement of Nativism. Nemade is a Tagore Professor of comparative literature, Bombay University and Marathi novelist, poet and critic. Devy, Professor of English, M.S. University, Baroda, is a translator, literary historian, bibliographer and critic. Nemade and Devy have been conferred Sahitya Akademi awards for their critical work pursued for decades. They are deeply rooted in our *bhasha* traditions and dedicated to the cause of freeing Indian literary criticism from the shackles of Euro-American dominance. They wish to make "Indian criticism more responsible, self-respecting, and Indo-centric activity...and have brought the agenda of decolonisation to Indian literary criticism" (Paranjape xi).

Nativism, however, does not have a set definition of its own. It has multiple identities and diversified opinions for it is language-specific or community-specific or region-specific. It is not a specified theory. Some of its concepts and attitudes contradict each other. On the one hand, Nativism can refer to specific styles, genres, linguistics, and formal features of a work, "on the other, it can encompass the whole socio-cultural and psycho-spiritual outlook of an author or even a society" (Paranjape 172). American cultural anthropologist, Ralph Linton identifies 'Nativism' as a "strategic way of protest" by the community which is threatened by the other dominant community. For instance, nineteenth century India witnessed many protests as a result of the British domination. To mention a few, Gandhiji's freedom struggle through satyagraha and non-violence, farmers' revolts and other tribal uprisings can be cited as striking examples of political Nativism.

Nativism has been discussed from different perspectives in *Nativism: Essays in Criticism* edited by Makarand Paranjape. Nemade published Marathi essay "Sahityateel Deshiyatam" in 1983 which was later translated into English as "Nativism in Literature" by Arvind Dixit and edited by Makarand Paranjape. In the essay "The Concept of Nativism," Nemade replaces the word *Desivad* by the term Nativism. He says, "the English term Nativism is used as the equivalent of Indian term *deshi*" (Qtd in Paranjape 164). In the Indian context, *Desivad* is used as a synonym for the term 'Nativism.' It triggered an active discourse and has become a crucial treatise in post-independent Indian literary criticism.

It appears Nemade has borrowed the term Nativism from the American anthropologist Ralph Linton. He refers to Linton in his essay on Marathi novel in 1980. "The nineteenth century gave rise to feeling that the native culture was being suppressed by the cultural encounter of a victor-victim character. Anthropologists called this phenomenon 'Nativism'" (Qtd in Paranjape 160). Nemade explains the nature of Nativism as follows:

> The present generation must have an unfailing nativistic awareness that the novel in Marathi is a creation of Marathi writers, who, in turn, are product of the Marathi society. Further formalistic unintelligent practice of picking up all and sundry works of art from languages all over the world for a comparative assessment of artifacts in Marathi—a tendency rife in our criticism—has to be avoided. It is dangerous for criticism to enter the comparative field without making a deep study of both cultures compared. Culture is not a hothouse, but a soil bound process; literature is not a theoretical construct but a living phenomenon. (193)

G.N. Devy upholds Nemade's essay and his concept of Nativism in his book *After Amnesia* for opening the possibility of rooting criticism in the *bhasha* tradition. It shows a way out of the tripartite *(deshi, marga and videshi)* division that has kept Indian literary criticism fragmented and abstract (123). He feels literary activity should take place within the rules of a specific language of its origin. It has to maintain some ethical sense and avoid the "concept-specific" way of 'universal' criticism. He defines Nativism stressing its language-specific activity.

Nativism views literature as an activity taking place 'within' a specific language, such as Marathi or Gujarati and bound by the rules of discourse native to the language of its origin. It understands writing as a social act, and expects on the part of it an ethical sense of commitment to the society within which it is born. It rules out the colonial standard of literary history as a series of epochs and the *marga* claim of the mainstream literature as being only the authentic literature. Nativism is a language-specific way of looking at literature. It rejects the concept-specific method of 'universal' criticism. As such, it gathers its main critical issues and themes from within the tradition of the literature it examines, instead of approaching it with preconceived notions of good and bad literature. At the same time, it refuses to glorify history, tradition, and values of realism.

Devy opines that the Indian literary criticism is facing the identity crisis. He says that Indian literary criticism exhibits the models of the tripartite relation of the *bhasha* (vernacular/indigenous/local), the *marga* (Sanskritic/traditional/mainstream/national) and the *videshi* (colonial) tradition and that it is conditioned by a cultural laxity which still remains a fragmented discourse. He advocates that Indian critics should begin their work with the knowledge of *bhasha* traditions which help the growth of literary culture thereby enabling literary criticism to gain a tremendous momentum with nativistic recognition.

A peculiar kind of colonialist internationalism emerged in different parts of the colonial world as a consequence of the hundred years of bondage to the European rule. Nemade castigates the despicable situation prevailing in India due to this false internationalism. He ironically says:

> No matter if we lack drinking water, but we must enjoy tid bits from the world over on colour television; no matter if our promising young sportsmen and women from remote corners of the country get no milk to drink, but Delhi must host extravagant Asiads. In a period when such fads have become prestigious, it is but natural that being aware of poor, narrow nativism is automatically to be labelled a revivalist or nationalist. In order to foster such a grand internationalism, it follows that our children need not know their mother tongue but must be educated through the English medium. And then, if our scholars do not read Dnyandev or Tukaram nothing much is lost, but they must study in-depth some insignificant English or American authors. How can a great international consciousness be nourished otherwise! (Nemade 1996: 234)

Nemade holds that a human being or a literature can survive only in its own native land and linguistic group. It does not require any foreign or international dimensions. He continues that a popular writer intends to write basically for his own community and time. If anybody receives international acclamation, it is purely incidental and secondary. The innate ability of a writer makes him universal. Any piece of art or a literary work, music, painting, sculpture is a part of its milieu, place and time; and its stylistic values, forms and structures sustain indisputable mark of its locality and period. Wole Soyinka also suggests that the writers should be local and universal to refrain from the danger of being overwhelmed by the incongruous globalization (10).

A cursory view of Universalism and Internationalism shows that it is not against Nativism. Universalism appreciates the variety of native styles of various regions in their particular context as it is. A product of art is primarily native and it can be universal in its appeal while Internationalism is an artificial and dependent concept. It is not possible without Nativism as its basis, because Nativism is a "multi-cultural, descriptive and real concept" (Nemade 246). It looks for the homogeneity in the works of different areas. While Nativism identifies uniqueness in the works of different regions, Universalism and Internationalism rely very much on comparative means.

A society makes use of its culture as a fabric for its mutual interacting system. Every existing and efficient culture consists of the innate capacity to transform and absorb alien influences into its native methods. This process of absorption can be called nativisation. The same process takes place uninterruptedly in literary tradition too. Every writer is aware of his native or local traditions in which he is profoundly rooted. The classics of literature actually establish their primary right to Nativism. The smothered cultures utilize Nativism as a weapon to throw away the oppressive systems of alien methods which deteriorate efficient native culture or structure.

Both Nemade and Devy intend to make Indian literary criticism independent. They are not for Sanskritic or Brahmanical revivalism. Nemade and Devy are aware of the suppressive nature of the traditional Indian society and hence plead for cultural self-respect and freedom that emerge from the Bahujan Samaj who knit the plurality of Indian civilization. It attempts to debunk the mythical assumptions and provides room for the actual. Nativism places the culture of the mass in opposition to that of the elite. Language thus assumes a cultural significance.

Besides Nemade and Devy, many critics and writers interpret the concept of Nativism based on their outlook towards culture, community, language, traditions, region and society. K. Satchidanandan, a Malayali poet and critic, interprets Nativism as a literary cultural theory, spatial and verbal, and presents the language with its dialectical varieties of *a* "place or a community along the ways of life and thought and the structure of feeling peculiar to that community and its space" (17). It acquires its political content from the circumstances from which it operates and in the methods in which it is adopted. "In Dalit literature", Satchidanandan says, "for example, we find Nativism put to a class, caste use, while it can also go beyond class distinctions as in the lines of *a* language-based struggle like that of the restoration of the old script in Manipur or the resistance to Hindi in Tamilnadu" (17). Satchidanandan explains that classes are like gender divisions and tend to be subdivided on the basis of economic and communal factors in a multi-religious country like us which cannot be away from the divisions of communal lines.

Satchidanandan distinguishes between national identity and Nativism. For him, national identity is more extensive than the idea implicit in Nativism. He asserts that national identity "requires, besides a language and territory, common myths, and historical memories, a common mass public culture and common legal rights and duties for all members" (18). Nationalism is a political ideology with a cultural doctrine at its center while Nativism is primarily cultural-linguistic (18). He further differentiates 'nativistic ideology' and the ideology of 'the state.' There is no single state that shares "a single ethnic culture." The people living in various communities, religions and races communicate in different languages. Nativism forms ethnic and linguistic ties that look for literary expression in a particular region. However, there is a possibility for Nativism developing into a "full-fledged political ideology" when it is connected with the regional movements like the Jharkhand, Uttarakhand, Goorkhaland and Telangana movements in India. Democracy can allow the demand for the creation of separate state within the federal polity, but it hardly tolerates "demand for outright independence" as in the case of the Khalistan movement in Punjab. Such extreme ideology of Nativism "will cease to be a positive literary ideology" and lead to ruin and disintegration of India (19). Satchidanandan warns that there is a possibility of coming up of evil effects such as revivalism, parochialism and disintegration from Nativism if it falls in the hands of narrow-minded persons. He says that Nativism, in its attempt at deconstruction of Indian tradition, should play a role of "greater secular and egalitarian project of constructing unity at a higher and more realistic conceptual level, of heteroglossia, cultural plurality within the nation's boundaries and intertextuality within culture" (Satchidanandan 27).

Avadesh Kumar Singh views *desivad* (Nativism) as an able alternative to neo-colonialism. He defines Nativism as "a strategy that with its insistence on identity, specificity and authenticity resists direct or indirect invasion or encroachment by 'other' or alien homogenizing forces" (Singh 76). He compares Nativism (Deshivad) with Gandhi's *swadeshi* movement during freedom struggle. He argues that the issue of *swadeshi* versus *paradeshi* is over. In the post-Independence era we have to make a choice between *kudeshivad* and *sudeshivad.* And our choice should fall on *sudeshivad*—positive, progressive, inclusive, *swastha sudeshivad* whose alternative there is none" (Singh 77).

Culture has its own way of interacting with the other cultures and religious systems and absorbing their positive aspects into a native system which can be termed Nativisation. Therefore, its significance is multiple. Nativism being progressive fights the Hindu revivalism (promoting hindutva) which cuts at the very basis of our inherent multiplicity. The multi-religious system of India is "democratic enough" to absorb the ideology of atheism and materialism of Internationalism. The developments which took place after modernism made possible the movements like Dalit Movement, Women and Ecological Movements to cross its borders. The true nature of Indian Nativism is revealed as a combination of the *marga, desi* and *videshi* critical idioms, working against "derivative and debilitating traditions and practices" (Paranjape xv). In its positive aspects, Nativism endeavours to indigenise modernism.

Indra Nath Choudhuri asserts that India is seeking to evolve its own modernity by assimilating its traditional values and creations. He explains the terms *Kula* and *Shila* to understand it better in the Indian context. He says, "*Kula* is hereditary, inheritance, tradition. *Shila* is the making of a man, his demeanour and personality which, however, are conditioned by his *Kula.*" *Shila* goes on discarding elements of *Kula* and thereby ensures the continuity of a culture. Hence a great work of art, in the Indian context, is the expression of both the traditional and the actual (2). He argues that for us both the *Kula* and *Shila* are important.

Rajee Seth, a Hindi novelist and poet, defines Nativism as a return to the roots. "This is the call of the self-awareness of a country that remained a colony for a long time. The histories of civilizations tell us that the human race has a tendency to go far away from its social and cultural axes and return to its centres again. It is an emotional need of the human race" (102).

Nativism is not only a movement for the authority and self-assertion of the marginalised, regional, subaltern groups and people but also a supporting movement of broader confederate nationalist movement against outsider's domination as it is against the bogus Internationalism. Therefore Paranjape aptly suggests that Nativism must be "flexible and plastic enough" to resist multiple articulations and "specific enough to assert its own identity in a particular cultural context" (xv).

Works Cited

Choudhuri, Indra Nath. "Seminar on Nativism: Welcome Speech." *Nativism: Essays in Criticism.* Trans. from Marathi by Arvind Dixit. Ed. Makarand Paranjape. New Delhi: Sahitya Akademi, 1996: 1-4. Print.

Devy, G.N. "Deshivad: Keynote Address." Makarand Paranjape. Ed. *Nativism: Essays in Criticism*: 5-13. Print.

———. *After Amnesia*. Bombay: Orient Longman, 1992. Print.

Nemade, Balachandra. "The Marathi Novel 1950-1975 (1981)." Trans. from Marathi by G.N. Devy. *Indian Literary Criticism: Theory and*

Interpretation. Ed. G.N. Devy. Hyderabad: Orient Blackswan, 2002. 192-219. Print.

———. "Nativism in Literature." Makarand Paranjape, Ed. *Nativism: Essays in Criticism*. 233-54. Print.

Paranjape, Makarand. "Preface" in his ed. *Nativism: Essays in Criticism*: ix-xvi. Print.

———. "Beyond Nativism: Towards a Contemporary Indian Tradition in Criticism." in his ed. *Nativism: Essays in Criticism*. 153-76. Print.

Satchidanandan, K. "Defining the Premises: Nativism and its Ambivalences." Makarand Paranjape. Ed. *Nativism: Essays in Criticism*: 14-27. Print.

Seth, Rajee. "Nativism: An Area of Introspection." Trans. from Hindi by Sudhir Kumar, Ed. Makarand Paranjape. *Nativism: Essays in Criticism*. 102-12. Print.

Singh, Avadesh Kumar. "Postcolonialism and Post-(In)dependent India: Images and Alternatives." *Contemporary Indian Literature, Positions and Expositions,* Ed. Santosh Gupta. Jaipur: Rawat Publications, 1996. 70-71. Print.

Soyinka, Wole. *Myth, Literature and the African World*. Cambridge: Cambridge University Press, 1976. Print.

Tharoor, Shashi. "Cultural Collisions," Interview by Suchitra Behal. *The Hindu Literary Review* (19 Aug. 2001). xi. Print.

7

Questionable Nationalisms and Chicanery of their Alternatives

T.N. Gurudutt

Reiterating that Kashmir was not an integral part of India, Arundhati Roy has accused India of launching "a protracted war" to suppress the ongoing movement in Kashmir by its military might. "I believe Kashmir is not an integral part of India. It is a historical fact" (Qtd in Wani), she opines. For her, nationalism of one kind or another was the cause of most of the genocide of the twentieth century. Flags are bits of colored cloth that governments use first to shrink-wrap people's brains and then as ceremonial shrouds to bury the dead. Though she may offer elaborate justification, her position upsets larger sections, including academic ones, of India. There are different types of nationalism like Ethnic nationalism, Civic nationalism, Expansionist nationalism, Romantic nationalism, Cultural nationalism, Postcolonial nationalism, Liberation nationalism, Left-wing nationalism, Liberal nationalism, Religious nationalism, Pan-nationalism and Diaspora nationalism. In the light of this, we have to recognize that the concept of nationalism is many a time partial and being under construction.

Similarly, Cosmopolitanism/Internationalism is not a single encompassing idea but rather comes in at least six different varieties, which have often been conflated in previous literature. The six varieties are: (1) moral cosmopolitanism, the view that all humans belong to a single moral community; political cosmopolitanism, (2) reform of the international political and legal order or (3) a strong notion of human rights; (4) cultural cosmopolitanism, which emphasizes the value of global cultural pluralism; (5) economic cosmopolitanism, which aims at establishing a global free market; and (6) the romantic ideal of humanity as united by faith and love. These six kinds of cosmopolitanism are not mutually exclusive, and the relationships among them are clarified. Are Roy's views truncated? How to account for the larger issues of History? What fits well in a multicultural country like India which inherently has many nationalistic characters and identities? What are the responsibilities of a writer that serves beyond a hit and run exercise? Venkateshan Vembu echoes a fact that is rightly accepted by many when he says that History doesn't flow in straight lines, but in contours, and in Kashmir's tortured history there are many contours to negotiate (www.dnaindia.com).

The Indian state may not always have got it right in Kashmir, but Roy's black-and-white delineation represents a colossal and intellectually questionable oversimplification of the problem without sufficient appreciation of the fanatical geopolitical forces at work. It also takes her farther down the slippery slope of shrill and decidedly dangerous sloganeering which has enormous lethal consequences in the real world. Perhaps she should break the spell that her own hypnotic prose appears to have on herself and her increasingly fanatical flock of followers.

Postcolonial literature attempts to examine the effects of decolonisation. One of the major themes of postcolonial literature is nationalism and its failures. Post-nationalists still cling to the nationalist politics of the anti-imperialist struggle and because they cling to nationalism and in some way to its producer, capitalism, they often cannot fully imagine an alternative. Or, a resistor of degenerated nationalism too fails to contrive a useful alternative and this inability, perhaps as in Roy, tends to undo the newly founded independence without a final vision. Any abstraction or ideal has to be framed in reality howsoever rude it is, failing which, 'the centre cannot hold'. The chicanery of poor alternatives renders the older things harmless or a kind of necessity.

However, on other count, we need to be alive to the freedom of expression of any person. In his classic defense of free speech, "On Liberty," John Stuart Mill laid down what is known as the 'harm principle.' It postulates that the only justification for silencing a person against his will is to prevent him from causing harm to others. It is to this powerful libertarian mid-nineteenth century principle that we owe the idea that free speech cannot be proscribed merely because we find it disagreeable, and that curbs may be imposed only if such expression constitutes a direct, explicit, and unequivocal incitement to violence. There is no such nexus in Ms Roy's statements on Kashmir, which are shaped around the theme of gross human rights violations. To recognize that there is also a dispute about the constitutional future of Kashmir is recognition of the reality there. To say that the status of Kashmir is a bone of contention between different groups who live there is also a matter of fact. Perhaps a solution would then emerge over time. Still, the question is whether it is correct to make Kashmir independent. Does it help the country or Kashmir? What is the role of nationalism around these choices? Again, the answer to these could be just an illusion.

But then, what about national integration? If national integration is a major value under the umbrella of a state, comprising the nuances and questions of population, territory, government and sovereignty, demythification of nationalism is a minor value. If self-esteem is essential for a human being, then positive patriotism is necessary for a nation and a citizen. May be what is reasonable would be check it within its extreme points. It is a healthy identity. It is essential for at least a mass, though a few individuals can surpass it and remain normal. Free speech does not guarantee any responsible expressions. We have evidence in the media every moment. The more and more we speak about these issues, the more we complicate them. With diplomacy, dialogue or ruthless force, any effort at secession should be put down. Once economy is built, people will not have time for such divisive talk. But for that to start, we need a conducive atmosphere. Encouraged by a failed state like Pakistan, which has a bomb in one hand and a begging bowl on the other, intellectuals jumping into engagement of incomprehensive history judgments on it does not look acceptable.

It is argued that the imposition of the concept of the nation state on other parts of the world by the European colonisers, the divisions of ancient civilisations brought about by modern political boundaries have given rise to many of the enduring conflicts of the postcolonial period including Kashmir. With globalisation and the evolving global village, should we not endeavor to organise the affairs of the human society on a global scale rather than on the basis of conflicting national interests? True. But that is possible when we have peace in the state and we cannot move in the direction of truth or goodness in a war like situation. We can think of Tagore's ideas of nationalism which are really enlightening. But they remained utopian for Japanese because of the tension of war. The literary historian Sujit Mukherjee says: "When Tagore said that Western society was being dehumanized by excessive organization, it was pointed out that lack of organization had not brought happiness to India". (qtd in Pramanik 393). This can be applied to nationalism as well. Excessive and irrational nationalism is not good for the world and the lack of reasonable and healthy nationalism is not good for a nation. This would hold good till the institution of nation exists. True, Tagore's *Nationalism* and such theories have influenced many makers of modern India like Gandhi and Nehru. It is also necessary to get exposed to them. It is very relevant in the light of xenophobia, sectarianism, violence and intolerance. They are valuable. But the principles of those ideals cannot be applied in a deliberately disturbed context like Kashmir. Just think of India's role in Sri Lanka and Pakistan's role in Kashmir. Can a blanket judgment be given in one sweep in both the cases? Can we see Roy's views as well founded as Tagore's or Ambedkar's? We need to respect the broadened or undone nationalism but be practical till a proper time. It is the case of trusting one's neighbour and yet locking the door.

In Postcolonial studies, nationalism is frequently characterized as a movement that promotes the interests of a particular group while claiming to represent the whole. It is the elitist interests of the bourgeoisie that nationalism is alleged to serve, necessarily sacrificing or ignoring the interests of subaltern groups (Spivak 24-28). Anti-national nationalists such as Cabral, Cesaire, and Fanon, Tagore could not have been more concerned about the dangers of elite nationalism, nationalism that they anticipated and also witnessed coming into postcolonial power in a number of states. But these concerns could be defeated by the elements that doctor a political situation in favour of forces that have no respect for globalism or oneness. Since cosmopolitanism relates basically to human values, it is the doctrine of universal human rights which constitutes its vital core. In this value-centered conception, neither nationalism nor localism is to be considered the main antagonist of cosmopolitanism.

There are and have been alternatives to nationalism. They are the variants of cosmopolitanism which are mentioned earlier. Although many of the alternatives have their own pitfalls or appear unrealistic in the present time, they are nonetheless accepted as something to be worked on or worked towards. Forcing anything into a system untimely may cause more damage than help. Global governance and the promotion of cosmopolitan notions of coexistence should ideally replace nationalisms. An acceptance of human particularism must be incorporated into any project to foster more global cooperation. Hence, projects for more international harmony must redefine how interests are defined and how peace and security are reached as opposed to merely basing future forms of human organization on ethics alone. Till a point of time when this is achieved to a considerable measure, we should not lose the strength of nationalism nor allow it to weaken humanism. In the process, a high level of law and order problem and its containment should not become a yardstick to study the facts of nationalism or otherwise in operation in the true sense. Ideas bereft of these and attacking a particular situation like Kashmir does not render much service to any ideology.

Kashmir situation is like Khalistan movement of the eighties. Its leaders demanded for plebiscite. But what happened later? With no other option, military had to enter Golden temple; this cost the life of Indira Gandhi. Plebiscite will be only a mockery of itself if it is held in a tensed state. Any state, district may want to free itself from the national fold. However, the military activities should not cross the limit of human dignity.

Working on several related areas that address the global legacy of European nationalism and empire-building, researchers in the Nation, Identity and the Postcolonial group specialise in cultural nationalism, colonial sovereignty, multi-ethnic identities, diasporas/trans-national formations, regional postcolonial literatures, responses to war and fascism, and landscape and identity.

For Arundhati Roy, nationalism of one kind or another was the cause of most of the genocide of the twentieth century. Any sensitive person accepts this opinion. But our polity, all over the world, is still clumsy. The worst fears have come out in Wikileaks. Comparatively, India is a soft and straightforward country. It has to struggle with many failed and/or rogue states. Many a time the condition of 'failed' and 'rogue' are complex, camouflaged, full or partial. If the countries around are yet to deserve your readiness to be universal, you have to wait—may be not losing optimism. If liberalism reaches a point of gullibility, one should imagine the imminent dangers. May be a good number of countries should come forward and work towards a practical globalized identity. But it takes time to be optimistic. We all know the plight of the UN. When Cosmopolitanism is an illusion to a great measure, at global level at present time, we cannot reciprocate it with real antinationalism. True, someone must begin with the ideology. Honestly, we are not big enough to lead such a mechanism putting our interests at stake. A moderate nationalism that is bereft of aggressive attitudes and which accommodates cosmopolitan concerns should be strength of a country in practical terms.

Works Cited

Anderson, Benedict. *Imagined Communities: Reflections on the Origin and Spread of Nationalism*, London, Verso, 1983. www.ijird.com. Web.

Brubaker, Rogers. *Nationalism Reframed: Nationhood and the National Question in the New Europe*. Cambridge: Cambridge UP, 1996. Print.

Greenfeld, Liah. *Nationalism: Five Roads to Modernity*. Harvard UP, 1992. Print.

Hobsbawm, Eric J. *Nations and Nationalism Since 1780: Programme, Myth, Reality.* Cambridge: Cambridge UP, 1992. Print.

http://www.dnaindia.com/.../column-arundhati-roy-is-dangerously-wrong-on-kashmir-1458329). Web.

http://www.greaterkashmir.com/news/2010/Oct/25/kashmir-not-india-s-integral-part arundhati-36.asp. Web.

Ignatieff, Michael. *Blood and Belonging*, London: Vintage, 1994. Print.

Malesevic, Sinisa. *Identity as Ideology: Understanding Ethnicity and Nationalism.* New York: Palgrave, 2006. Print.

Mill, J.S. *On Liberty*, edited by Alburey Castell, New York: Appleton-Century Crofts, Inc., 1947. Print.

Ozkirimli, Umut. *Theories of Nationalism: A Critical Introduction.* New York: Palgrave, 2010. Print.

Pramanik, Ramachandra. "Rabindranath Tagore: An Advocate of Humanism." *International Journal of Innovative Research and Development* (Online). 2. 8 (August 2013): 393. Print.

Spivak, Gayatri Chakravorty. "Can the Subalterns Speak?" in *The Postcolonial Studies Reader.* Ed. Bill Ashcroft, Gareth Griffiths, and Helen Tiffin. London and New York: Routledge, 1995. 24-28. Print.

Wani, Arif Shafi. "Kashmir not India's integral part: 'High Time To Set Goals For Azadi and Achieve Them'": Arundhati Roy in *Greater Kashmir.* 25-10-2010. Print.

8

Persian Contribution to Indian Multiculturalism: Focus on Parsi Fiction

Rajeshwar Mittapalli

If we take multiculturalism to mean the peaceful coexistence of the adherents of several cultures within the geographical boundaries of a nation, preserving their identities and professing pride in their ancestry, India has been a multicultural society all the time, but especially since it came into contact with different cultures across the border. India is now the home to countless cultures, ethnic groups and religious minorities—some homegrown and some of foreign origin. The curious fact about Indian multiculturalism is that India has not practiced multiculturalism as a state policy to begin with—the way the USA, Canada and Australia have done, for example—but by consensus evolved over a period of hundreds of years. This is the single most important reason why minorities feel a lot more comfortable and secure in this country than even in the developed West in spite of the so-called liberal state policies.

Among the foreign contributions to Indian multiculturalism the Persian contribution is perhaps the most significant. Traces of Persian culture can be discerned in almost every aspect of Indian life—cuisine, architecture, language, literature, music, etc. Persia has a long and glorious history of civilization and cultural advancement. Will Durant and Ariel Durant in their book *The Story of Civilization* describe how, in terms of civilization, Persia was like before AD 7th century.

> They [the Persians] had beautiful homes and luxuriant gardens, which sometimes became hunting-parks or zoological collections; they had costly furniture—tables plated or inlaid with silver or gold, couches spread with exotic coverlets, floors carpeted with rugs resilient in texture and rich in all the colors of earth and sky; they drank from golden goblets, and adorned their tables or their shelves with vases turned by foreign hands; they liked song and dance, and the playing of the harp, the flute, the drum and the tambourine. Jewelry abounded, from tiaras and ear-rings to golden anklets and shoes; even the men flaunted jewels on necks and ears and arms. Pearls, rubies, emeralds and lapis lazuli came from abroad, but turquoise came from the Persian mines, and contributed the customary material for the aristocrat's signet-ring. Gems of monstrous and grotesque form copied the supposed features of favorite devils. The king sat on a golden throne covered with golden canopies upheld with pillars of gold. (413-14)

In many ways the Persian culture was far advanced for the time. Added to this was the geographical proximity with India so that the cultural exuberance of Persia eventually percolated into India by means of people to people contact as well as political alliances.

The earliest Persian contact with India occurred about 1200 years prior to the period mentioned above—during the reign of Cyrus II of Persia (600-530 BCE), better known as Cyrus the Great, who treated his subjects humanly and their customs, practices and religions with tolerance. At the zenith of his power his empire extended to the edge of India. One of his successors Darius I (550-486 BCE), son of Hystaspes, expanded the Persian Empire beyond the Indus river and well into India, and reorganized it into satrapies. The Indian part of the empire formed the twentieth satrapy. The Greek historian Herodotus writes in his book *The Histories* that the Indians were the most important contributors to the treasury of Darius I.

> The Indians, who are more numerous than any other nation with which we are acquainted, paid a tribute

> exceeding that of every other people, to wit, three hundred and sixty talents of gold-dust. (103)

During these ancient times much cultural exchange, especially in terms of culinary arts, was said to have taken place between the Persians and the Indians. Prerna Uppal, a well-known commentator on culinary matters, thinks that the Persian rulers "brought with them their culture and ingredients like spinach, pistachio, almond, pomegranate, saffron and rosewater. It is interesting to note that during this time they were introduced to rice, a grain indigenous to India, which soon became and still is an Iranian staple. It is such an important part of their food culture that the skills of a cook are judged on how well he or she cooks rice." Many centuries later, during the Mughal period, these 'culinary ties' were further cemented between Persia and India. The Mughals had great admiration for everything Persian. Madhur Jaffrey, film actress and food writer, writes in the Introduction to her famous cookbook *An Invitation to Indian Cooking* that the Mughals had passed Persia on their way to India and had been "awed by the glitter of courtly robes and the delicacy of the miniature paintings, and by the exquisite food they had been served. Much of it they introduced into their own courts, sending off to Persia and Afghanistan regularly for melons, pomegranates, plums, grapes, dates, and nuts" (22-23).

The second Persian contact with India took place in the 10th century when a large number of Zoroastrians, known today as the Parsis, migrated to India. [The term 'Parsi' needs a little elaboration. Iran (Persia) was once called Paras and the language spoken by its people was known as Parsi. The Arabs, who eventually subdued Persia, replaced the 'P' in Paras with 'F' since they had no corresponding sound in their language represented by the letter 'p'. Parsi thus became Fārsi which is how it is known in India and elsewhere today. The Parsi speaking Zoroastrians who migrated to India before this event retained the original term Parsi to refer to their language as well as to them as a community, although now they speak mostly Gujarati. Incidentally, Fārsi is only one of the three Persian dialects spoken today. The other dialects, or groups of dialects, are Dari (spoken mostly in Afghanistan) and Tajik (spoken in Central Asia).]

These Zoroastrians were under siege and were being persecuted by the Arab invaders at that time. After offering resistance to the invaders for nearly two centuries, often described as the "Two Centuries of Silence," they finally gave it up and a big number of them migrated to India where, after some initial hesitation, they were offered asylum. Ever since, they have lived in India and immensely contributed to its economic, social and cultural life. A few prominent Parsis may be mentioned in this context: Homi Jehangir Bhabha (nuclear scientist), Ardeshir Godrej (co-founder of the Godrej industrial empire), J.R.D. Tata (industrialist and Bharat Ratna laureate), Homi K. Bhabha (cultural-studies theorist), Aruna Irani (Bollywood actress), Ardeshir Irani (filmmaker), Bejan Daruwalla (astrologer), Farrukh Dhondy (novelist and screenwriter), Firdaus Kanga (author, actor and screenwriter), R.K. Karanjia (journalist and founder of India's first tabloid, *Blitz*), Persis Khambatta (Miss India, 1965), Meher Baba (mystic), Zubin Mehta (conductor of western classical music), Sohrab Modi (film actor, director and producer), Bapsi Sidhwa (author and screenwriter), Keki N. Daruwalla (poet and short story writer), Dadabhai Naoroji (economist and political activist), Pherozeshah Mehta (political leader and activist), Madame Cama (freedom fighter), Soli Sorabjee (former Attorney-General of India), Sam Manekshaw (former Indian Army Chief and the second Indian Field Marshal) and the most popular of them all, Freddie Mercury (stage performer and lead singer of the British rock band, *Queen*) who is often bracketed with Frank Sinatra and Michael Jackson. (Freddie Mercury's birth name was Farrokh Bulsara. He is best known for his hits "Bohemian Rhapsody," "Killer Queen," "Somebody to Love," "Don't Stop Me Now," "Crazy Little Thing Called Love" and "We Are the Champions"). The range of contribution of these men and women to the enrichment of the cultural life of India is not difficult to guess, because it is enormous by any count and it is there for everyone to see.

The third important Persian contact with India took place during the reign of the second Mughal emperor Humayun. History texts inform us that Humayun sought the help of Shah Tahmasp of Persia in 1540 when he lost his throne and crown to his enemies, chiefly to Sher Shah Suri and his own half-brother Kamran Mirza. The Shah of Persia was generous in offering military and logistic support to Humayun and with that he not only regained his lost territories but also built a vast empire. Humayun returned from Persia with not just military aid from the Shah but with a large contingent of Persian noblemen. In the wake of his triumphant return to India many poets, artists, architects and scholars also migrated to India. This brought about an important change in the Mughal court culture. Persian art, architecture, language and literature made their presence increasingly felt in India and in course of time they almost replaced the Central Asian cultural heritage of the Mughals. Especially the Persian language became the language of the court and lingua franca of India and continued to be so till English replaced it in 1839 at the instance of Macaulay. It was also the default language of creative and literary expression. At one point during the Mughal era there were more Persian manuscripts in India than in any other language of India or in Persia itself for that matter. Persian also loaned about 70 per cent of the words and expressions of the Urdu language which is the only truly pan-Indian language, or has been so up until recently. Apart from vocabulary Persian gifted to Urdu several beautiful forms of poetry such as *ghazal* (series of rhymed couplets), *qasida* (lyric), *marsia* (elegy) and *nazm* (poem dealing with a single subject/thought). Persian also enriched, by means of loan words as well as a few grammatical patterns, the linguistic repertoire of a number of other Indian languages, notably Punjabi, Sindhi, Hindi, Kashmiri and even a Dravidian language such as Telugu. And if this comes as a surprise, here is a short list of Persian words which form part of the common Telugu parlance: *ājamaishī* (from *āzmāish*; tentative, management); *chekumuki* rayi (from *chaqmaq*; flint); *darjā* (rank, grade, position); *farārī* (from *farār*; run away, abscond); *firyādu* (from *faryād*; petition, complaint); *jīnu* (from *zīn*; saddle); *julapālu* (from *zulf*; long hair); *khātaru* (from *khātir*; count, sake); *māfi* (from *muaf*; pardon, excusing); *manzūru* (from *manzūr*; approval, agreement); *nāzūku* (from *nāzuk*; delicate, nice); *rawānā* (from *rawānah*; send, dispatch); *rusumu* (from *rusum*; fees, dues, custom); *sanjāishi* (from *sanjāish*; explanation, conciliation); *sifārasu* (from *sifārish*; recommendation); *tarafu* (from *tarf*; side) and *wasūlu* (from *wasūl*; payment, collection).

A number of Persian tales and legends also travelled to India with Humayun: for example, *Rustam and Sohrab*, *Shirin-Farhad* and *One Thousand and One Nights* which have since become part of the popular imagination of the Indians and gained as much currency as the stories of the epics such as the *Mahabharata* and the *Ramayana* having been made into films, performed on stage and told and retold as bedtime stories for centuries.

However, it has not always been a one-way traffic. India too enriched Persian language, literature and culture in significant ways. In this context we are reminded of the famous 'cross-over' Indian poets Amir Khusro Dehlavi, Abu al-Faraj Runi and Masud Sad Salman, and the more recent poets such as Mirza Ghalib and Muhammad Iqbal who made an important contribution to Persian literature. These latter poets were greatly admired in Iran too since Persian literature there stagnated in the post-Safavid period. Near at home, the Asaf Jahi rulers of Hyderabad patronized Persian language and literature so much that they retained Persian (or Fārsi, as they preferred to call it) as the court language for about fifty years after it was replaced by English elsewhere in India. They also encouraged the migration of a large number of Iranians to Hyderabad. These Iranians went chiefly into the restaurant business and added to the multicultural ethos of Hyderabad. The Irani cafés have become so much a part of the life of Hyderabad that it is often said that every Hyderabadi visits an Irani café at least once in a day.

Mughal emperor Shah Jahan's son Dara Shikoh (1615-59) translated 50 Upanishads from the original Sanskrit into Persian in 1657 under the title *Sirr-e-Akbar* (The Greatest Mystery) with the aim of exploring common ground and establishing the affinities between the Hindu and Islamic holy scriptures. He wrote the following about the genesis of this book, referring to himself in the third person in the fashion of a religious mendicant:

> And the *summum bonum* of these four books [the four Vedas], which contain all of the secrets of the Path and

> the contemplative exercises of pure monotheism, are called the *Upanekhats* [Upanishads].... And whereas this unsolicitous seeker after the Truth [Dara Shikoh] had in view the principle of the fundamental unity of the personality and not Arabic, Syriac, Hebrew and Sanskrit languages, he wanted to make without any worldly motive, in a clear style, an exact and literal translation of the *Upanekhat* into Persian. (Quoted in Stein 172)

It might be interesting to note here that the library which Dara Shikoh established in the 17th century still stands on the campus of Guru Gobind Singh Indraprastha University, Delhi. It is now a museum run by the Archeological Survey of India.

The tradition of the Persians making an important contribution to the culture of India still continues mainly in the form of Indian fiction in English by Parsi writers, although there are several Parsi poets writing in English as well. Given the fact that the modern literary world is dominated by fiction, only the Parsi novelists and short story writers in English are discussed briefly here. In spite of being a minuscule minority the Parsis constitute the single largest ethnic group of Indian novelists in English. Important among them, in terms of history as well as quantity and quality of fiction, are: Cornelia Sorabji, Perin Barucha, Dina Mehta, Rohinton Mistry, Bapsi Sidhwa, Firdous Kanga, Farrukh Dhondy, Boman Desai and Nergis Dalal.

Cornelia Sorabji published three volumes of short stories and sketches under the titles, *Love and Life behind the Purdah* (1901), *Between the Twilights* (1908) and *Sun Babies* (1918) which, as the titles suggest, deal with the problems of *purda nasheen* women. Perin Barucha's *The Fire Worshippers* (1968) addresses the problems of the Parsi community in India, especially their ethnic identity and inter-faith marriages. Boman Desai's *The Memory of Elephants* is a fantasy tale rooted in culture and designed in such a way that it records the history of the Parsi exodus from Persia. Firdaus Kanga's autobiographical novel *Trying to Grow* traces the growth of a physically challenged boy into manhood facing identity crisis all along. Rohinton Mistry's *Family Matters* tells the story of a middle-class Parsi family undergoing a domestic crisis. Focusing on a single Parsi family, Mistry conveys not just the dilemmas among the Parsis but a variety of concerns including corruption and communalism. A similar attempt is made in his *A Fine Balance*. This novel, in spite of its mandatory focus on Parsi life, qualifies as a modern Indian classic in that it treats a range of issues facing India during the 1970s. Mistry unequivocally condemns the evil practices, misuse of power by the politicians and atrocities committed by the state on the hapless citizens of India during the Emergency of 1975-77. Similarly, Bapsi Sidhwa's *Ice-Candy Man*, though centred on a Parsi family, portrays the trauma experienced by helpless people on the Pakistani side of the boarder.

The distinction and special contribution of the Parsi novelists to Indian fiction in English is best summed up in the words of Narendra Kumar whose book *Parsee Novel* is a pioneering work on the subject.

> Parsee novel in English...is a potent index of the Zoroastrian ethos. It voices the ambivalence, the nostalgia and the dilemma of the endangered Parsee community. In Parsee novel in English, the 'operative sensibility' is Zoroastrian. The Parsee novelists have forged a dialect, which has a distinct ethnic character. The tempo of Parsee life is fused into their English expression just as the tempo of Jewish life has gone into the best works of Saul Bellow and Bernard Malamud. The triumph of the Parsee novelists in the use of English language is largely due to westernization and exposure to English culture. Their prose is interspersed with Persian words and Gujarati expressions. Besides being innovative, the Parsee novelists describe in detail, the esoteric rituals, and the Zoroastrian customs such as Navjote. Thus, Parsee novel in English gives us a peep into the turbulent Parsee mind of today. (17-18)

The Parsis did not culturally hybridize with the Indians and melt away into the vast Indian population the way the Greeks perhaps did in the years following Alexander's military expedition. They remained firmly rooted in their culture and maintained their distinction all along and that way strengthened the multicultural fabric of India. The Parsis were certainly one of the best things to have happened to India from the cultural perspective as well as in terms of contribution to the modernization of India. This is just one instance of the advantages of multiculturalism and India is a unique beneficiary of it.

Works Cited

Durant, Will and Ariel Durant. "Persia, 'Science and Art,'" *The Story of Civilization: Our Oriental Heritage 1935*, Volume One, Chapter XIII, Electronically Enhanced Text (World Library, Inc., 1991). Print.

Hasrat. "Dara Shikoh," *Sources of Indian Tradition*, comp. William Theodore de Bary et al. New York: Columbia UP, 1958. 446-68. Quoted in Burton Stein, "Early Modern India," *A History of India*. Ed. David Arnold. Oxford: John Wiley & Sons, 2010. Print.

Herodotus. *The Histories of Herodotus of Halicarnassus*, Book Three, trans. George Rawlinson. Ames, Iowa: Omphaloskepsis, 2000. Print.

Jaffrey, Madhur. Introduction, *An Invitation to Indian Cooking* 1973; New York: Alfred A. Knopf, 2011. Print.

Narendra Kumar, V.L.V.N. *Parsee Novel*. New Delhi: Prestige, 2002.

Uppal, Prerna. "Indian Kitchen Tales: The Persian Connection," *Express News Service*, 17 Feb 2012. <http://expressbuzz.com/search/indian-kitchen-tales-the-persian-connection/364189.html>. Web.

9

Contribution of Persian Sufism to Indian Literature

Anita Ahmadi

The Sufi School of spirituality emanated from Islam. Although the people who propagated this doctrine belonged basically to Muslim background, they were not intent on floating a new religion or establish a new priestly order. They followed Islamic religious tenets and used the Quran as their holy scripture. They lived and worshipped within the framework of Islam. Their contribution lies in transforming Islam into a mystical entity, and then cloth it in the spiritual garb embellished with passionate love for God.

The Sufis claimed a rich spiritual territory to all human beings—a territory which is free from external obligations and inner compulsions. They guided the human heart towards God visualizing Him as a divine beloved. They emphasized purification of human spirit and acquisition of spiritual wealth rather than material wealth. Sufi saints preferred to wear coarse garments made of wool which symbolized their scant regard for worldly comforts.

Although it is difficult to document the Sufi life and literature, it is clear that Sufi mysticism spread from Persia all over the vast Islamic world, thanks to the efforts of such pioneers as the Egyptian Sufi saint Dhul-Nun al-Misri and the Arab Andalusian Sufi mystic and philosopher Ibn Arab, and easily won the hearts of people there. Sufism freely explored the possibility of interaction among religious streams in the East and the West which led to the idea that there is a fundamental unity among them.

Sufi mysticism is primarily framed by soul-stirring poetry. It is enriched by religious fervour and spiritual love. This is clearly evident in the mystical romance of Yusuf and Zuleikha which has been beautifully rendered into Persian by Nur ad-Din Abd ar-Rahman Jami (1414-92) in his *Haft Awrang* (Seven Thrones). The names of the great Persian Sufi poets such as, Jalal al-Din "Rumi", Farid al-Din 'Attar, Saadi Shirazi, Nur ad-Din Abd ar-Rahman Jami, Khwajeh Shams al-Din Muhammad Hafez-e Shirazi, Mansur al-Hallaj and also Hakim San and Mahmud Shabistari and the prose writers, Hazrat Ali Hujwiri and Abu Nasr al-Sarraj, Najm al-Din Razi also need to be specially mentioned in this context.

Thus while in the ancient past Persia dominated much of the civilized world under the leadership of the emperors Cyrus, Darius and Xerxes, during the medieval period Persia established a spiritual empire across the world through the Sufi saints.

II

Apart from the Islamic world, Persian Sufi missionaries went to India, China, Japan and other countries in the East. This paper, however, is limited to the contribution of the Persian Sufism to Indian literature.

Persia's interaction with India dates back to the hoary past. It concerned many aspects of political, cultural, and religious life of that time. Perhaps Persian culture influenced Indian life, customs and values as no foreign culture has ever done before. Its influence on the literary traditions and spirituality of India via Sufism thus comes as no big surprise.

India was the cradle of pantheistic philosophy when Sufi mysticism came to India around eleventh century, in the wake of the establishment of Islamic rule. The psychological resistance to Islamic rule was largely blunted as Persian Sufi spirituality spread in India by means of the poetry of love and accommodation. Sufi ideology focused on the moral and ethical aspects of Islam and

Sufi saints of India would often quote the verses of the Persian Sufi poet Saadi Shirazi to make their point. Indeed Persian poetry played an important role in the cultivation and propagation of Indian Sufi mysticism and in the production of much of the Indian literature of that time.

The great Persian literary figure Hafiz profoundly influenced Indian literary traditions with his ghazals imbued with spiritual and ethical values which form part of the Sufi ideology. The poets of Bengal and Kashmir were in constant literary dialogue with Hafiz in order to derive inspiration for their literary works. Acknowledging the appreciation of his poetry by the people of Kashmir, Hafiz said:

> *be shere hafeze shiraz miraghsand o minazand*
> *siah chashmane kashmiri o torkane samarghandi*
> (http://peacefulrivers.homestead.com/Hafiz)

This verse means that the black-eyed Kashmiri and Turks of Samarkhand love the verses of Hafiz of Shiraz and dance in tune.

Similarly, the Persian poet Nizami Aruzi's ethical and philosophical ideas had a tremendous impact on the literary and Sufi doctrines of India. Prominent Indian Sufi mystics such as Shaikh Farid al Din Ganji Shakar and Shaikh Nizam al Din Awliya frequently quoted verses of Nizami to elaborate and sketch the manifestations of emotion and mystical impressions.

The Persian Sufi poet Molana Jalal ad Din Muhammad Balki (Rumi) was known for his advocacy of the integration of the individual with the universal. Indian poets recognized Rumi's spiritual purpose and wrote a lot of poetry under his influence. It did not go unnoticed by Rumi himself since he fondly refers to India in his Mathnawi. Rumi's thoughts disseminated throughout India.

Another seminal Persian figure who influenced Indian Sufi poetry was Mansur al-Hallaj. He was born in Persia but often visited India and his religious thought pervaded Indian mystical poetry. Ali Hujwiri, the Persian Sufi and scholar was deeply impressed by Hallaj. His work *Kashf al Mahjoob* was extremely popular in medieval India. Hallaj presented a magnificent exposition of the spirit of sacrifice for permanent values.

Imam Ghazali was another Sufi figure who influenced South Asia through his masterpiece *Kimiya e Saadat*. This work included psycho-ethical analysis of the basic religious ideology. *Kimiya e Saadat* became an invariable reference work for the Indo-Muslim population. Imam Ghazali's approach attracted those people who believed in the authority of reason.

The last Persian Sufi figure I would like to mention is Ibn Arabi who was favourably disposed towards pantheism. The ideology of Ibn Arabi attracted the Indian Sufis. Indeed, from the sixteenth century onward countless literary works were woven in India around the mystical concepts of Ibn Arabi.

III

Having sketched the influence of Persian Sufis and Sufi poets on Indian literature, I would like to briefly discuss some Indian poets whose works bear indelible marks of Persian Sufism.

The first of them is Amir Khusrau Dehlavi, an Indian Sufi mystic, musician, scholar and poet of Persian descent. He was an iconic figure in the cultural history of the Indian subcontinent. He wrote poetry primarily in Persian, and also in Hindavi. Amir Khusrau was as prolific in tender lyrics as in highly involved prose and could easily emulate all styles of Persian poetry which had developed in medieval Persia, from his forceful qasidas to Nezm's khamsa. His most famous poem is "Zehaal-e-Miskeen." This poem is written in Persian and Brij Bhasha. Brij Bhasha is a Dehaati Zabaan. In the first verse, the first line is in Persian, the second in Brij Bhasha, the third in Persian again, and the fourth in Brij Bhasha. Let me quote a couple of verses from this poem.

Zehaal-e-miskeen makun taghaful,
Duraye naina banaye batiyan.

Do not overlook my misery,
by blandishing your eyes and weaving tales,

Ke taab-e-hijran nadaram ay jaan,
Na leho kahe lagaye chatiyan.

My patience has over-brimmed, O sweetheart!
why do you not take me to your bosom.
(http://sufipoetry.wordpress.com)

Kabir comes next and he brought through his poetry often-clashing religious cultures of Islam and Hinduism together. He was equally disdainful of professional piety in any form. His prominent works are: The *Bijak* of Kabir translated by Linda Hess and *One Hundred Poems of Kabir* translated by Rabindranath Tagore.

Bulleh Shah is considered to be one of the greatest mystic poets of the Punjab region, India-Pakistan. Bulleh Shah was a respected scholar, but he longed for true inner realization. Later he became a disciple of Inayat Shah, a famous master of the Qadiri Sufi lineage, who ultimately guided his student to deep mystical awakening. His prominent works are: *Bulleh Shah: A Selection Rendered into English Verse* and some of his famous poems are: "One Thread Only," and "Remove duality and do away with all disputes."

Abdul-Qadir Bidel wrote extensively—poetry, philosophy, and wisdom stories. I would like to present a short poem by this poet:

Creation's Witness
At time's beginning
that beauty
which polished creation's mirror
caressed every atom
with a hundred thousand suns.

But this glory
was never witnessed
When the human eye emerged,
only then was he known. (Fideler, trans. From Persian)

Mirza Ghalib was a court poet who often wrote in the courtly language of Persian, but he is best known for his couplets written in the popular local tongue of Urdu. His poetry spoke to Muslims and Hindus alike. His mystical love poetry makes him a favourite of Sufis. Some of his most famous poems are:

"Let the ascetics sing of the garden of Paradise," "The Candle Flame" and "The Footprint." Let me quote a few lines from the first of these poems.

> Let the ascetics sing of the garden of Paradise
> Let the ascetics sing of the garden of Paradise—
> We who dwell in the true ecstasy can forget their vase-tamed bouquet.
>
> In our hall of mirrors, the map of the one Face appears
> As the sun's splendor would spangle a world made of dew.
>
> Hidden in this image is also its end,
> As peasants' lives harbor revolt and unthreshed corn sparks with fire.
>
> Hidden in my silence are a thousand abandoned longings:
> My words the darkened oil lamp on a stranger's unspeaking grave.
>
> Ghalib, the road of change is before you always:
> The only line stitching this world's scattered parts.
> (Traslated into English by Jane Hirshfield from Urdu; http://allpoetry.com)

Allama Muhammad Iqbal is considered one of the finest poets from the Indian subcontinent. He wrote in Urdu, Persian and English with equal ease. His prominent works are: *Poems from Iqbal: Renderings in English Verse* translated by V.G. Kiernan and Bang-e-Dara (Urdu). His Persian poetical works are: *Asrar-i-Khudi, Rumuz-i-Bekhudi, Payam-i-Mashriq, Zabur-i-Ajam, Javid Nama and Armughan-e-Hijaz.*

From the foregoing discussion of the Indian poets it should be clear that the currents of Sufi thought emanating from Persia profoundly influenced and pervaded the minds of the Indian poets and immensely contributed to the development of poetry of the first order in India as attested by the fact that it is still read, sung and enjoyed by all.

Works Cited

Fideler, David and Sabrineh Fideler, Trans. *Love's Alchemy: Poems from the Sufi Tradition.* n.p.: New World Library, 2006. Print.

http://allpoetry.com/Let-the-ascetics-sing-of-the-garden-of-Paradise by Mirza Ghalib/accessed on 1-11-2014. Web.

http://peacefulrivers.homestead.com/Hafiz.html./accessed on 1-11-2014. Web.

http://sufipoetry.wordpress.com/2009/11/06/zehaal-e-miskeen-amir-khusro/accessed on 1-11-2014. Web.

10

Memoirs as *Afsaanas*: Life and Times of Ismat Chughtai

K. Damodar Rao

With the publication of English translations of her works, *The Quilt and Other Stories* and the novels, *The Crooked Line*, *A Very Strange Man*, Ismat Chughtai (1915-91), the celebrated Urdu writer, came to be known to the rest of the literary world as the forerunner of liberation aesthetics. *Lihaaf* has remained the most controversial of her works as it dealt with the theme of alternate sexuality in the 1940s. She was far ahead of her times in dealing with subjects that were considered a taboo in mainstream literature. She is hailed as one of the four pillars of Urdu fiction along with Sadat Hasan Manto, Rajinder Singh Bedi, and Krishan Chander. She is a great story-teller in the first instance and then a woman writer who concentrated on woman-centred issues. A reference point for feminist perspective in Urdu literature for long, with the publication of English translations of a few of her works, Ismat assumed a powerful voice in gender studies in Indian literatures. Besides, as Tahira Naqvi, the translator of *A Very Strange Man* and her non-fictional work, *My Friend, My Enemy* notes, Ismat Chughtai has now become a "major South Asian woman writer in Western academic circles...where South Asian Studies, Women's Studies, Feminist/Gender Studies are taught, Ismat's work draws as much attention as her Western peers" (Naqvi 5). An important aspect of her fictional substance is that at the time when she began writing in the 1940s there was hardly any feminist writing proper in the West. Margaret

Atwood, Simone de Beauvoir, the icons of Western feminism appeared much later.

Any discussion of 'gendering Indian narratives' would be incomplete without an analysis of Ismat Chughtai's work. She grew up in the face of many constraints: She was a woman, a Muslim, and a writer with a penchant for uninhibited portrayal of feelings. It was no mean achievement for a Muslim woman of that period to move freely in society and be a writer true to oneself what with the many taboos that were imposed by a conservative culture, and an orthodox family. Important thing to note is that Ismat is not merely a woman writer but 'a writer' who moved beyond the problems of women and dealt with issues like corruption and injustice: "Her writing is ironic, caustic, frank, bold, and yes, irreverent if the occasion merits it. She is merciless in her depiction of corruption, deceit, injustice and hypocrisy" (Naqvi 5).

Ismat's non-fictional work, *My Friend, My Enemy* (2001), comprising three parts—essays, reminiscences and portraits—provides glimpses of her childhood, formative influences, her rebellious spirit and minutiae of the notorious Lahore trial for obscenity. It offers an authentic resource for a study of the socio-political and artistic milieu of her times. Commenting on the degrees of difference between autobiography and fictional representation in respect of constructing the self, Jasbir Jain comments:

> The degrees of difference between autobiography, imaginative and literary biographical reconstructions, fictional representation are of significance as multiple ways of 'writing-the-self' surface. The act of writing is simultaneously a reading—of the self, the past, history, experience, others and of political contexts. (Jain 78)

The present paper focuses on the four chapters included in the second part, "Reminiscences." While evocatively capturing the essence of the people and feel of places, these memoirs offer interesting observations, associations, reminiscences and anecdotes; and coupled with her inimitable style these read like *afsaanas*. This might be because:

> Fictionalizing is always present in the confessional mode, whether it is autobiography, memoirs or letters. The writer shows only what he/she wants to show... the intrusion of the present self is there in the selection, sequence and discreet interpretive signatures of the details. (Parameshwaran 53-54)

While tracing her childhood and ancestry in the first essay, "We People" (*Humlog*) written in 1970, she does not sound apologetic in any way for her being impressionable and stubborn, for having a sharp, biting tongue. She recounts that her ancestors were descendents of Changez Khan and her childhood was spent playing gulli danda, football and hockey with her many brothers. She reminisces: "Come to think of it, the real culprits were my brothers, it was their company that enabled me to think freely" (Ismat Chughtai 101). When the family moved to Agra after her father's retirement, what she found was 'stifling, oppressive atmosphere' (101). The elderly women there were horrified to see her 'leaping across rooftops.' Her mother, Nusrat Begum, was often embarrassed by the many complaints she used to receive. But Ismat, after witnessing many cruelties perpetrated against women, regretted for the first time being a girl:

> What was the purpose of this dejected, helpless, captive being? The washerwoman was beaten every night, the sweeperess received a walloping from her husband every other day, and in the adjacent neighbourhoods, husbands often thrashed their wives. (102)

For her, childhood was another name for innumerable 'constraints and deprivations' (118). With the loving affection of a considerate and open-minded father and eight older brothers and sisters, she says 'she awaited adulthood eagerly' (118). She remembers how she was surrounded by her brothers and confesses "I had been greedy in my struggle to be like them" (120). Her mother did not approve of her actions as she was worried about her future. In her teenage, she provided quite a contrast to her older sisters. She recollects:

> My sisters were extremely well-mannered and possessed all the necessary social graces. Along with being proficient in Urdu, Farsi and the Quran, they were

> experts in sewing, needlework, and cooking. I was a failure at everything. All I was interested in was climbing trees and riding a bicycle like my brothers. (119)

As a result, her clever friends used to warn her no man would passionately love a girl like her. But she is firm in her views that as long as the women remained weak and helpless, the country would be 'preyed upon by a sense of economic and political inadequacy' (121).

When one finds strong influences in formative years, it is difficult to shrug them off as such influences are likely to remain for the rest of a person's life. Ismat recounts two major influences that shaped her personality, her brother Azim Bhai and the fiery Rashid Jahan. She recalls how she became increasingly conscious of her brother, Azim Bhai, in shaping her sensibility when the family moved to Aligarh. He taught her many things, especially the virtue of reading classics. Ismat was considered, during this period, 'an echo of his (her brother's) voice' (104), not only that, her disposition, 'obstinate and headstrong' (104) was also attributed to the encouragement she received from him. He took unusual interest in her as he was studying law and working in a factory at the same time. He also wrote *afsaanas* and Ismat recalls it was from him that she derived inspiration to read the *afsaanas* of Hijab Ismail, Manjun Gorakhpuri, and Niaz Fatepuri. As is the wont of young adolescents, she imagined herself as the heroine of such stories and began writing 'exciting ones' (105) herself. In the imagined stories the first hero was always a doctor—'because perhaps in those days the only male outsider who could come into your house and feel your pulse was the doctor' (105) who used to be, invariably of course, very handsome. He would sit by her bedside all night and weep when her condition deteriorated and 'wail uncontrollably at her youthful death, or, better still, commit suicide' (105).

Ismat Chughtai notes that writing such stories was as much fun as reading them. But she tore up the stories for fear of being punished. She recollects an incident when one of her elder brothers, Shamim, came to her room and stumbled upon one of her stories and wondered how she could write such 'filthy stuff.'

She got away with it because the boy was known to be a liar and no one took his 'allegations' seriously.

Another decisive influence on her was the dynamic personality of Rashid Apa who was known for her smoldering words. "Was there anyone alive who could meet Rashid Apa of the bright eyes and smiling, fresh face and not be influenced by her?" (107), she ruminates. The doctor hero of her stories is gone, disappeared forever as life appeared before her in all its harshness: "The Rashid Apa who was cast in clay destroyed all my marble statues" (107). She learned many things from Rashid Jahan in formulating her views on womanhood, loyalty, passionate love, honesty and social realities:

> ...when I think carefully about my stories I realize that I have only been able to seize Rashid Apa's boldness and candour. Her rich, overwhelmingly impressive personality has evaded my grasp. I always hated the griping, weeping, whining womanhood that bore bastards. I regard as a curse that loyalty that exists for the sake of loyalty alone and loathe all those other qualities that are considered to be an eastern woman's adornment. I am exasperated by sentimentalism. (108)

While recounting other influences in the next chapter, "The Dust of the Caravan" (*Ghuber-e-Karavvan*) Ismat says that books have affected her more than anything else as they were 'the closest of friends' (124). To begin with, it was Hardy, then the Bronte sisters, and then Bernard Shaw. But she says it was the Russian writers who impelled her most as 'Russian literature seeped into every corner of my mind' (124). She fondly says, 'I still read Chekhov for luck, for guidance' (124). In addition to reading, conversation was a big passion with Ismat; and she fondly remembers that the streak was there in the family. Outside the family, she says, talking to Manto sharpened her sensibilities; found discussions with Sardar Jafri entertaining, and Fazlur Rahman, then pro vice-chancellor of Aligarh University, was encyclopedic from whom she learnt many things. She valued the opinion of her husband, Shahid Latif, a budding Hindi film director, greatly and their 'friendship stubbornly stood its ground'

(127) despite their marriage. Writing was another passion that sustained her in moments of happiness and anguish. She wonders, 'How many burdens it has helped me relinquish, how many burdens it has placed upon me' (126). She asserts that somehow she developed an intense hatred for Farsi, maybe because of the punishing attitude of the tutor. The language spoken at home was 'so dynamic' (126) that she never had to grope for the right words when she was writing fiction.

Ismat's observations on culture and religion are noteworthy because these point to a personality that is liberal in outlook, secular in faith, all-embracing in temperament, and visionary in attitude. As one of her childhood friends, Soshi, placed a tiny brass image of the crawling infant Krishna on her palm she could not refuse it. She observes:

> I'm a Muslim. Idol worship is sacrilegious. But the *devmala* is part of my homeland's heritage. Centuries of culture and philosophy are imbued in it. Faith is one thing, the culture of one's homeland is another.... Will my faith falter if I splash coloured water on holi, or light lamps at Diwali? Are my beliefs and my judgment so shallow, so defective that they would be shattered into tiny fragments? (129)

Ismat was cultured enough to distinguish between her faith and the culture of her land. In the same vein she recollects that she 'was greatly affected by Buddhism' (128) during her college days.

In the chapter, "From Here to There" (*Yahaan se Wahaan Tak*) she recounts her journey to Karachi in 1976 nearly after twenty-eight years. She was a celebrity in India and Pakistan and her works were widely known there; and in many meetings the question that was posed to her was regarding the health of Krishan Chander. The people there would be satisfied only on hearing that he was recovering from an illness. She says that she anticipated this question in many meetings and so started her speeches narrating the well-being of the noted Urdu writer. Another person about whom questions were posed, she recalls, was Ainee (Qurratulin Hyder), another noted Urdu writer. They felt happy knowing that her much awaited new novel had been published. Ismat avers, "Although we are physically apart, we occupy an immeasurable space in each other's hearts" (154). With her tone of wry humour she recounts how journalists asked her regarding the fate of Progressive literature and whether Urdu was finished in India. Ismat's replies are characteristic of her personality: "If progressive literature were not still alive so many of you would not be asking me about Krishan Chander. Literature is kept alive not by writers but by readers" (151). Regarding the well-being of Urdu, she says, "Even now there are more people in Hindustan who speak and understand Urdu than here in Pakistan" (151). The implication is clear that a language cannot be the monopoly of a community, or a country. Transcending all barriers is in the very nature of a language.

Ismat notes with satisfaction that in Pakistan Urdu is increasingly used in combination with Sindhi, Balochi and Punjabi dialects which was having a good effect on Pakistan's literature. In Hindustan, Urdu was influenced by Braj and Poorbi but in order to spread further, she thinks it must utilize Sindhi, Marathi and other regional languages while she feels happy that Hyderabadi writers have succeeded in making use of Deccani. She observes that Urdu in Hindustan 'is picking up musical words from Hindi while in Pakistan Urdu is becoming increasingly Arabic and Persian in character' (163).

Ismat recollects how Karachi held a special aura for her and how the people treated her with love and respect at meetings, dinners and luncheons with which "Pakistanis are obsessed" (150). She met many celebrity writers, Josh Sahib, Faiz Ahmed Faiz, for instance, and recollects many impromptu *mushairas*. She evokes the place and people of Lahore with same gusto and passion in another of her memoirs "The 'Lihaaf' Trial" that took place in pre-independence days, in 1944 to be precise. The stubborn self of Ismat comes out to the fore in this piece of reminiscences.

Ismat had been charged with a case of obscenity for her story "Lihaaf" (Quilt) and was ordered to appear in the Lahore High Court in January 1945. She refused to take the orders in the first instance. Her husband Shahid had great difficulty in convincing her that the summons had to be taken, otherwise she would be jailed. Having agreed, she was released on bail, then they came home, and fought bitterly with one another, and again they 'came to the point of divorce' (134). Ismat received a phone call from Sadat Hasan Manto who informed her that he too had been charged with obscenity and his case was also scheduled for the same day. Manto appeared very jubilant 'as if he had been awarded the Victoria Cross' (135) and she was comforted by his exuberance. She wrote the disputed story when she was living with her brothers. When she read it to her sister-in-law she didn't comment that it was an obscene story. She had sent the story to the journal *Adab-e-Latif* and the editor published it right away. About the same time Shahid Ahmed Dehlavi included the story in a collection of her stories to be published. It was a period when her friendship with Shahid was culminating in marriage. He expressed his dislike for the story, after which an argument followed, one of the many that were to take place.

In Lahore, though they came for the trial, they were enjoying themselves attending one reception after another, most of the hosts being Manto's friends. Ismat remembers how beautiful Lahore was: "Still invigorating, full of laughter, its arms spread out in welcome, embracing all those who arrive here, the city of cheerful people who love unconditionally, without reserve, the 'heart of the Punjab'" (137). In fact, she thanked the case that has afforded the golden opportunity of having a festive time in Lahore.

The second hearing of the case was posted in the pleasant month of November 1946 for which Ismat waited eagerly. Aslam Sahib was their host who urged her to offer an apology for writing the story. Ismat stood her ground arguing vehemently that he too gave explicit details of sex act in his story, "Nights of Sin." She exhibited a rare verve and spirit that day in forwarding a case of conniving with the so-called elite of Lahore in implicating her in the case.

On the designated day, the witnesses were to prove that the stories in question were obscene. In the case of Manto, which came first for hearing, to a question of the judge, the witness replied that the word "Bossom" was obscene. In the story of Ismat the sentence that was pointed as obscene was "She was collecting *ashiqs*." Arguments followed, and a few friends suggested that they should offer an apology. But Manto turned it down bluntly for both of them. The case which was already losing its interest was finally closed without any punishment. The judge, in fact, greeted her in his chambers saying he had read all her stories and they were not obscene, nor is 'Lihaaf.'

The remarkable contribution of Ismat to an aesthetics of resistance could be gauged from the fact that she lived and wrote at a point of time characterized by modernity which, in the given context, appears hegemonic in many respects. In a perceptive essay, "Being Indian: An Essay on Image/Text/Man" Srivatsan comments that "the archive of Indian modernity functions through three modes of Man: Europeanness, Masculinity and BrahManism. Man is the sense of identity, agency and authorship/ authority that results in the coalescence of the modern individual, and this triad of Man is the singular feature of our Indianness today" (149). Each of these modern modes, he continues, has its 'characteristic foundation of disciplining of the self, and of the oppression of the other' (150). Ismat's co-ordinates in her fiction run quite contrary to these paradigms of modernity: Indianness, *counter-femininity*, and a minority ethos.

It has been rightly pointed out that "writing about women was never the same after Ismat appeared on the scene. She was a major force in creating new trends in writing by and about women..." (Naqvi 5). Who else could have made the following observations about politics except a writer-visionary endowed with sharp acumen and remarkable foresight?

> Politics, which is the world's most profitable profession, is god in this world. The blood of innocent washes the black stains of defeat formed in the field of politics. Human beings are compelled to fight with one another like dogs so that politicians can prove their superiority over each other. (130)

Works Cited

Chughtai, Ismat. *My Friend, My Enemy: Essays, Reminiscences, Portraits.* Tr. Tahira Naqvi. New Delhi: Kali for Women, 2001. Print.

Jain, Jasbir. "The Difficulty of Writing/Reading the Self", *Literary Constructs of the Self: Socio-Cultural Contexts.* Eds. Santosh Gupta, Mini Nanda. Jaipur: Rawat, 2010. 63-80. Print.

Naqvi, Tahir. "Ismat Never Minced Words" Tahira Naqvi in conversation with Ziya Us Salam, *The Hindu.* Sunday (September 30, 2007). Print.

Parameshwaran, Uma. "Writing the Self that Isn't, Or writing the Self that Is, Boils Down to the Same", *Literary Constructs of the Self: Socio-Cultural Contexts.* Eds. Santosh Gupta, Mini Nanda. Jaipur: Rawat, 2010. 53-62. Print.

Srivatsan, R. "Being Indian: An Essay on Image/Text/Man." *Re-figuring Culture: History, Theory and the Aesthetic in Contemporary India.* Ed. Satish Poduval. New Delhi: Sahitya Akademi, 2005. 1-16. Print.

11

Dr. B.R. Ambedkar and Dalit Literature

B. Krishnaiah

The social and literary struggles of the epoch-maker Bharata Ratna Babasaheb Dr. B.R. Ambedkar have brought about revolutionary changes in the social structure of India. They led to the emergence of two important movements in the second half of the twentieth century, namely—Dalit literature and Dalit Panthers Movement. The phenomenal stream of Dalit literature started during 1960s and a social organisation called Dalit Panthers Movement was formed in 1972 in Bombay by young Dalit writers like Namdeo Dhasal, Arjun Dangle, Daya Pawar, J.V. Pawar, Umakant Randhir. Both the movements were born out of the battles of consolidating discourses and protest activities of Dalits. Dalit Panthers Movement has made the term 'Dalit' popular and acceptable in every part of India. In the words of Gail Omvedt, "It was a defining moment of the post-Ambedkar Dalit Movement in India, a moment that was an upsurge giving inspiration to all of India" (2002, 301). Indeed, it marked a massive stirring of the Dalit poor in cities and village streets throughout the country. Though the identity of Dalits is established in many parts of India after Dalit Panthers Movement, its application is not the same all over India. Dalit Panthers consider scheduled castes, scheduled tribes, and other Backward Castes including women, minorities, agriculture and industrial labour as Dalits. But, presently its usage is narrowed down only to scheduled castes. Other identity movements such as 'Adivasi' and 'Bahujan' are used in the same fashion referring to scheduled tribes (STs) and other backward castes (OBCs) respectively. It resulted in the coinage of new phrases such as Dalit-Bahujan and Dalit-Adivasi-Bahujan.

Dr. B.R. Ambedkar has led social movements relentlessly in his life for the emancipation and empowerment of Dalits whose lives were imprisoned. He had to fight at all levels simultaneously in life while opposing all traditional values. His thoughts contained the graph of the progress of the people at the grass roots level of the society. For this, Dr. Ambedkar's life itself has become a guiding surge of revolution. This revolution has changed the consciousness of the Dalits as well as other privileged sections. Many derived inspiration and direction from this movement. That is why, it could be said that Dr. B.R. Ambedkar and his philosophy provided direction and inspiration to Dalit literature. Commenting on the impact of the philosophy of Dr. B.R. Ambedkar on Dalit literature, Gail Omvedt asserts that "it was Ambedkar's spirit of revolt, his modernism (identified in this speech with the French Revolution) and his rationalism which provide the philosophical context of the new Marathi Dalit literature" (2009, x). In the words of Arjun Dangle, "Dr. Ambedkar shaped the transition of revolutionary thinking of almost a generation of Dalits, who can today hold their heads high, thanks to him. The literary manifestation of this social awareness is Dalit literature" (xxiv). In spite of Dr. B.R. Ambedkar's revolutionary scholarship and fighting spirit, he called himself an untouchable Dalit. This is the reason why "writers of today as well as of tomorrow—whose works have the potential to be placed in the tradition of great literature of the world, call themselves Dalit writers" (Bagul 28).

Dr. B.R. Ambedkar is the most influential thinker of our times. His unique contribution to the Indian philosophy lies in his vision of a just society which is underlined by the principles of liberty, equality, and fraternity. He aims at reconstructing a moral society distinguished from the hierarchical exploitative caste-ridden Indian society. Dr. Ambedkar asserts that the rights are protected not by law but by social and moral conscience of society and the democracy as a form of society of a more associated living and the social conscience is the only safeguard of all rights. The roots of democracy are to be traced in social relationships in terms of associated life among the people who form a society. For him, social relationships are the basis for democracy. Ambedkar is a social democrat in spirit and practice.

The revolutionary work and speeches of Dr. Ambedkar in 1927 and his call to the Dalits to 'educate, organize and agitate' roused tremendous self-respect among the Dalits. He established Siddhartha College in Mumbai in 1947, Milind Mahavidyalaya in Aurangabad in 1949 and many schools and colleges later to bring about the social awakening. Thousands of educated Dalit boys and girls joined the mainstream society and evaluated it critically from the perspective of Dalit culture. This Cultural Revolution among the Dalits has not taken much time for them to comprehend that they were deprived of the opportunities in all walks of society down the centuries on the pretext of God and His creation of human society based on *chaturvarna*. They also felt that the mainstream literature or the literature of the elite was not dealing with their life problems.

The knowledge and consciousness, self-respect and dignity generated in them by Dr. B.R. Ambedkar led them to initiate a revolt against the mainstream literature. He challenged the existing social order, turned the state of appeal into a sense of deprivation of rights and deserved status. It was the turning point in the rise of Dalit consciousness. Explaining the discriminating and exploitative nature of the Brahminical ideology, Dr. Ambedkar elucidates that "Dalithood is a kind of life condition that characterizes the exploitation, suppression and marginalization of Dalits by the social, economic, cultural and political domination of the upper castes' Brahminical ideology" (204). The rebellious and revolutionary spirit has graduated into an increasing confidence and consolidation of Dalit consciousness. Dalit literature reflects vigour and aggressiveness claiming the rightful owners of social and economic resources, demanding a radical change on Ambedkarite model i.e. social justice in the existing social order. A human being is not a Dalit inherently or by birth, but it is the system of *karma* theory or the system of *chaturvarna* that was cleverly infused into the psyche of the human mind by the ideology of upper castes justifying the degradation of the human society. Revealing the conspiracy behind the theory of *karma*, Eleanor Zelliot says that "in the term and concept Dalit, there is an inherent denial of dignity, a sense of pollution and an acceptance of the *karma* theory that justifies the caste hierarchy" (267).

Starting in Maharastra, Dalit literature has spread to all corners of the country giving impetus to the Dalit writers. The consciousness disseminated by the writings and movements of Dr. Ambedkar has enabled the Dalit communities to shun their servile status inflicted on them by the Hindu social order. It has attempted to erase the Brahminical hegemony from literature and inspired the educated Dalits to protest. Waman Nimbalkar explains that "After studying the rejection, acceptance, protest, struggle, anger, inspiration, tendency, role and nature of Dalit literature, it is seen that the philosophy of social democracy of Dr. Babasaheb Ambedkar forms the crux. Dalit literature stands against the background of Dr. Babasaheb Ambedkar's life, revolution and struggle" (39). It stirred up thinking in Dalit intellectuals and inspired creative zeal in them. The counter-cultural movement and ideology propagated by Dalit intellectuals contained a critique and negation of Brahminical Hinduism and undermined the cultural tradition of caste-Hindus. They asserted the idea that they were the original sons of the soil.

Dalit literature reveals a pattern in it—from that of accepting the identity given by the dominant groups to the stage of finding their own identity and redefining their cultural position in such a way as to sever links with the so-called Brahminical culture, and develop an alternative way of living and thinking defying their authority. Dr. Ambedkar reveals that the root-cause of untouchability is the Brahminical religion and the political power. He explains, "The root cause of untouchability is the caste system; the root of the caste system is the religion attached to *varnashram*; and the root of *varnashram* is Brahminical religion; and the root of Brahminical religion is authoritarianism or political power" (www.ambedkar.org). Therefore, the

Ambedkarite phase questions the Brahminical religion and attempts to replace the present political set up and the social constructs of the oppressors by Dalit ethos and, most importantly, the empowerment of Dalits. Dalit writers of this period began the process of de-Sanskritisation pleading for complete transformation of society and emerged with their own self-image as Dalit intellectual community. In the words of K. Satyanarayana and Susie Tharu "Dalit Scholars re-read Ambedkar and proposed an alternative anti-caste intellectual tradition in Indian history: Buddha, Jyotirao Phule and Ambedkar: The public presence of Ambedkar as a scholar and thinker contributed immensely to the self-image of the dalit community as intellectuals" (8). The cultural revolutionary movement set off by Phule in nineteenth century and Dr. Ambedkar in twentieth century paved the way for the emancipation of Indian society from the hold of Brahminism.

Many a Dalit writer such as Om Prakash Valmiki, M.D. Namishray, Bandhumadav, Namdev Dhasal, Baburao Bagul, Arjun Dangle, Yendluri Chinnaiah, Bojja Tarakam, Kolakaluri Enoch, Shiva Sagar, Shikhamani, Kathi Padma Rao, Yendluri Sudhakar, Laksman Mane, Banna Ailaiah, Bama, Sivakami, Urmila Pawar, Sushila Takbhoure, Gogu Shyamala, Vinodini, Jupaka Subhadra, etc. have produced significant literary works identifying themselves with pride for being Dalit. With gradual passage of time, they have influenced all walks of life demonstrating their magnificence. The word 'Dalit' has acquired a different connotation in the recent past by shunning the inferior and humiliating wound attached to it. They have brought about a revolution by connecting their life with struggle, protest and liberation movement. Thus, it has acquired a new meaning of change, reformation and revolution. In a letter addressed to Eleanor Zelliot, Gangadhar Pantawane, Professor of Marathi, underlines this changing scenario of Dalit literature as follows:

> To me, Dalit is not the caste. He is man exploited by the social and economic traditions of this country. He does not believe in God, rebirth, soul, holy books teaching

> separatism, fate and heaven because they have made him a slave. He does believe in humanism. Dalit is a symbol of change and revolution. (Quoted in Zelliot 267)

Dalit literature demands proper implementation of the constitutional rights to the Dalits so that they can progress on a par with other privileged communities of the society. It demands equal rights and opportunities as a matter of right but not as a matter of charity. It is "about assertion of human rights, self-pride, revolt against social injustice, chronicles of personal and collective suffering, and hopes and aspirations for a new and just society devoid of discrimination" (Dasan 17). In a wider perspective, it is a counter movement, an anti-thesis to fight against philosophical and theological aspects of the *Vedas*, *Upanishads*, *Puranas* and *Tantras*. It supports the rationalistic and scientific approach in literature. It is a source for the oppressed society to assert their survival. In the words of James Massey, "The Dalit School of literature represents a new level of pride, military and sophisticated creativity. It is essentially a label to help the Dalits to achieve a sense of cultural identity. 'Dalitness' is a source of confrontation and is a matter of appreciating the probability of one's total being" (7). Contemporary Dalit literature is not mere expression of anger and suffering but a serious contestation of the hegemonic cultural systems from Dalit theoretical vantage point.

Dalit literature explores the lives of the neglected subaltern communities. It is based on the life experiences of the Dalits, hence, authenticity and reality are the important characteristics of Dalit literature. Explaining the distinctiveness of Dalit literature J.K. Lele and R. Singh say:

> The distinctiveness of Dalit literature lies in its authentic unity of Dalit language and content. In it, the disillusionment and disgust of young Dalits, often accompanied by desire of revenge, come alive. It revives the memory of the pain and suffering of past generations. It confronts centuries of hypocrisy, deceit and violence sustained in the name of tradition. (Quoted in Adapa Satyanarayana 79)

Making use of the language of the depressed, the Dalit writers portray their humiliation, anger, grief and unflinching hope for a bright future. Commenting on the indomitable spirit of Dalit literature, Jugal Kishore Mishra says:

> Dalit literature is experience based. This '*anubhava*' (experience) takes precedence over '*anumana*' (speculation). Thus to Dalit writers, history is not illusionary or unreal as Hindu metaphysical theory may make one to believe. That is why authenticity and liveliness have become hallmarks of Dalit literature. These writers make use of the language of the out-castes and underprivileged in Indian society. Shame, anger, sorrow and indomitable hope are the stuff of Dalit literature. Because of the anger against the age-old oppression, the expressions of the Dalit writers have become sharp. (Quoted in www.ambedkar.org)

Thus, Dr. Ambedkar's movement revitalised Dalit community and turned it towards self-respect. They have rejected the dark and death-like life and have been marching ahead towards bright life through their writing and struggles.

Works Cited

Ambedkar, B.R. *The Ostracised India (Bahiskrit Bharat)*. New Delhi: Bharat Bhushan Printing Press, 1927. Print.

Bagul, Baburao. "Dalit Literature is but Human Literature." *Journal of Literature and Aesthetics* 8. 1. (2008). Print.

Dangle, Arjun. "Introduction: Dalit Literature Past, Present and Future." Poisoned Bread. Ed. Arjun Dangle. New Delhi: Orient Blackswan, 2009. Print.

Dasan, M. "Dalit Movements and Literature in the Post-Ambedkar Era: Emerging Issues and Challenges." *Dalit Movements and Literature*. Ed. B. Krishnaiah. New Delhi: Prestige Books, 2011. Print.

Massey, James. *Indigenous People: Dalits*. Deluxe Universal Traders, 1998: 7. Print.

Mishra, Jugul Kishore. "A Critical Study of Dalit Literature in India." www.sasnet. Lu.se/EASASpapers/4JugalKishore.pdf. Web.

Nimbalkar, Waman. "Inspiration of Dalit Literature." Dalit Literature: Nature and Role. Nagpur: Prabodhan Prakashan, 2006. Print.

Omvedt, Gail. "Literature of Revolt: Prefatory Note." *Poisoned Bread*. Ed. Arjun Dangle. New Delhi: Orient Blackswan, 2009. Print.

———. "Ambedkar and After: The Dalit Movement in India." *Social Movements and the State*. Ed. Ghanshyam Shah. New Delhi: Sage Publications, 2002. Print.

Satyanarayana, Adapa. "Dalit Protest Literature in Telugu: A Historical Perspective." *Dalits and Upper Castes: Essays in Social History*. New Delhi: Kanishka Publishers, 2005. Print.

Satyanarayana, K. and Susie Tharu. Ed. "Introduction." *No Alphabet in Sight*. New Delhi: Penguin, 2011. Print.

Zelliot, Eleanor. *From Untouchable to Dalit*. New Delhi: Manohar, 1992. Print.

www.ambedkar.org/research/optimism_Master_key.htm. Web.

12

Portrayal of Social Inequality and Quest for Unity among Dalits in Gurram Joshua's Poetry

M. Suresh Kumar

Gurram Joshua is one of the eminent Telugu Dalit poets. He deals with a number of issues like political, social background, historical facts, caste, gender discrimination and social reforms in his writings. Joshua, born on 28th September, 1895 in Vinukonda of Guntur District to Veeraiah and Lingamamb, is a poet of rare excellence. In his poetry, he combines the beauty of craftsmanship with the undying urge for human dignity. He is a reformer by nature and temperament and this sensibility is evident in all his writings. He fought, through his poetry, all forms of exploitation in society. He pleaded for humanism, equality and progress. He criticized the rituals that were devoid of purpose. He revolted against the social evils and superstitions, as they perpetuated the social inequalities. With a universal outlook, his poetry creates a world of freedom without sectarianism. Deep compassion for the suffering humanity with probing intellect defines his artistic interest. A profound and bright sense of logic and "reason" breaks away the clouds of ignorance of tradition. He was awarded "Padma Bhushan" in 1970. This paper deals with Gurram Joshua's poetry with special reference to the poem "The Graveyard" to explore how the form of poetry is used as a weapon to eradicate the social evils of the day. It also shows how his authorial voice shakes the evil social practices in this part of Andhra region as was done by Ramaswamy Periyar in Tamil Nadu.

Joshua tried to reveal the 'myths' which are strongly framed by the privileged upper castes who kept the underprivileged sections like women and dalits under their control on the pretext of sacredness and traditions. In fact, the travails of dalits have not yet ended and they have yet to voice them. Joshua's ideology is to bring about a change in the thought processes of all sections of the society. He wants to create awareness among the upper caste communities about the travails of the victims of the society. Some of his ideals in his own words:

> For the terrorized and oppressed masses a poet's word should give a ray of hope. It should show them the levelling of the ups and downs. It should give voice to the mute tears of the tormented people and make them raise their lives. (Qtd in Mahesh 2)
>
> ...Life has taught me many lessons. I have two teachers—Poetry and disparity of caste and religion. One has taught me "tolerance" whereas the other has developed in me the "power to protest" but hasn't made me a slave. I have decided to expose poverty and caste disparities and prove myself to be a man. I raised my sword against them. But my sword is poetry. My sword has no hatred against the society. But its hatred is against the policy of the society. (Qtd in Mahesh 2)

Joshua who has experienced inequalities and discrimination since his childhood, is shaped as a poet by a sense of suffering and protest. A humanist to the core, he writes:

> A man from my country spoke to the world
> Assembly of religions and they approved,
> A merchant from my land defied the power
> of five continents with a spindle.
> A scholar from my home sat on the highest
> teacher's chair in the land of the whites.
> A poet of my people won the honour
> of all the world, the Nobel prize.

It was our man who told you trees have feelings
and proved it all with scientific evidence.

I was counted out,
But to tell the truth
We were all sons of the same mother. (Mahesh 2)

Joshua told his daughter Hemalatha Lavanam how terrible was the poverty he had experienced in his childhood days. One day, Hemalatha Lavanam was about to throw away leftover sweetmeats prepared in her house. Joshua prevented her from doing so and said, "Don't waste them, Give them to somebody. They eat them." Then he narrated to her one of his childhood experiences.

> That was Christmas day. Joshua's companions wear wearing new dresses and were enjoying sweetmeats. Joshua and his brother Israel were pleading with their mother that they too wanted new dress and sweetmeats. Mother had not even single paisa on her hand. There were no provisions in their house. She was pained to see her children asking her in such a way and she was on her way to the grocer's shop to request him to give some provisions on loan. Meanwhile, on the way while a girl was taking plateful of sweets, some of them fell on the ground due to the force of wind. The girl left fallen sweets there itself and went away. On seeing that, Joshua ran there and took those sweets from the ground and ate them. Mother who had seen that was at a loss for words. (Mahesh 2)

This incident reflecting their utter poverty left an indelible influence on him. That's why he said, "While poverty taught me tolerance, caste disparity developed in me the energy to protest." He steadfastly faced those painful experiences. These unbearable incidents became the seeds of emotion for his poetry of suffering.

Don't feel that I'm heckling these things
They worried me greatly by pricking into my mind like spears
They became the seeds of emotion for my poetry. (Mahesh 2)

These experiences ignited his poetic imagination that resulted in a fine sensibility and a fine poetic idiom and poetic emotion. The disparities in the Christian religion are the main reason for his dislike of the Christian organization though he liked Christ. In those days when Christianity was being propagated, it greatly spread mainly among the two groups of dalits—Mala and Madiga. Even before the advent of Christian religion, there was the feeling of 'superior' and 'inferior' in these two dalits groups. The missionaries had failed to inculcate the philosophy of Christ—love and equality—in their minds. They failed to unite these two groups into one. Joshua had severely condemned the Dalit groups for not having mutual love. He also condemned them for developing contempt and failing to become one. Joshua expresses his contempt in the poem "*Inti Guttu*" ("The Secret of Home"):

> I'm a Madiga in panchamas
> He is Mala in panchamas
> Both of us embraced Christianity
> But brotherhood hasn't suited us.
>
> God is one for us, but churches are two
> We are one for country, but we are of two tribes
> For world's sake we say ours is one religion
> But on caste issues we fight among ourselves.
>
> We won't tolerate if we comment on each other
> If others abuse we don't care
> We can even give our religion
> If anybody speaks of treaty between us
> Mala Jesus Christ is not Madiga's
> Madiga's Christ is not ours
> One sprinkles and gives both
> Where is the path for us to become one?
> The crow that alights on his hut
> should not alight on mine
> The mala crow and the madiga crow
> in crows prove our enmity
> On seeing Hindus we laugh at them
> But we don't hate the dirt in our house

We can't tolerate others' faults but
We are not severe about our own faults.
In religion we have some amity of word
But we have neither "amity" nor "nearness"
It has become inevitable for us
To fight for low and high shamelessly. (Mahesh 3)

In a poem entitled "*Gusagusalu*" (Whispers), Joshua delineated Dalit psychology. Joshua impartially portrayed the dichotomy that existed among the Panchama race. Joshua observed the religious strife between Malas and Madigas and went into despair with the feeling that the union between these two groups is impossible.

> It is a shame to speak of untouchability practised by the untouchable Mala and Madigas. Neither Shiva nor Krishnas nor many Christs can unite these castes, I say, despite their prestigious B.A. and M.A. degrees. Their rivalries increase but not compromise. Of what use are religious teachings to them? Evil people, affected by caste factionalism.... (Mahesh 3)

Joshua was distressed about religious disputes. Religion should do good to the mankind but not develop hatred. Religion should be reformative but not retrogressive. Joshua who had understood Jesus Christ's philosophy of love and reformation, moulded his poetry as his weapon for equality. Hence, he questioned,

Why these useless studies without equality?
Why there are thousand religions?
Why there are hundred vows?
Proclaim in your gospel that these
Crore and crores of humans are

God's children and friends
Life will be profitable with love and equality. (Mahesh 3)

Thus, he professes equality of all human beings.

II

Joshua's poem, "The Graveyard" is an elegy describing the temporary nature of human existence. Compassion and deep love for humanity permeates through this poem. All forms of glory and triumphs as well as sorrows are only transitory. This poem can be compared with "An Elegy Written in a Country Churchyard" by Thomas Gray. It is elegiac in its tone and mood. The poem, in its somber quality, is meditative, without being sentimental about the "history" of man and his "glorious" civilization.

Following is the poem translated by me from Telugu into English as follows:

Years've passed; yet of those hapless myriad
None has risen from this funeral ground.
Alas! is this stupor an everlasting one?
Many a woe-begone mother has bemoaned her loss
And made the marble hot with her tears.

Dark clouds are gathering menacingly,
Hooting owls are fighting with ghosts.
The night-birds close in from around,
But not a leaf stirs; what a secluded spot!
The bard's sweet pen to ashes was reduced.
Scepter and crown have gone beyond recall.
Into the waters of Ganges was thrown
The sacred string of a woman newly-wed
Here was lost, once forever,
The swift moving of a renowned artist.
This is the dreaded stage where presides
The God of Death with awful spirits,
This is the throne of ashes wherein sit
Death's minions frowning furiously on the Earth
Like a glowing fire-fly flickers a lamp
From that new grave amidst the gathering gloom;
It burns on, though the oil ran out.
Is it an earthen cresset?
No, it is the flutter of some bereaved mother's bosom
Lingering there in anguish still
Pens of poets and voices of singers
Can hardly help visiting these grim regions;
Mortal remains of mighty poets
Of the line of Kalidasa and Bharavi

Have mingled with the clay of potter's wheel.
Our hearts melt away
When we look on those little graves.
What tender cheeks are consumed by dust,
What darling kisses lost in sleep eternal?
What flames of grief rage in the mother's heart,
What great arts and promising lore
Lie here languishing, nipped in the bud?
Here is no place for distinctions, no high and low,
No room for touch-me-nots;
Here's the leveller annulling all differences
That thrives in the masquerade of life.
Here are rocked in a single cradle
Both the wild tiger and mild lamb
Here beside the glistening marble mausoleum
Reigns supreme the Spirit of one
Who rolled in untold wealth;
There lies the neglected corpse in rags
Of someone swallowed by the scorching flames
Of penurious pangs of hunger.
None sheds a tear for the forlorn,
Even the grave ignores that departed soul.

The poem, in its scope and range, describes all forms of human existence, the 'poor' and the 'rich', the 'saint' and the 'sinner', the 'scholar' and the 'ignorant', the 'poet' and the 'ordinary'. Within these contrasting images of human life and desire for excellence, Time is eternal and unfaltering. If everything that is born in the world is bound to die, only *Time* as an 'invisible overseer' forever exists. All our agonizing subjective moments disappear into the world of eternal objective reality, that is "Time." Here, Joshua is neither "apologetic" nor "sorrowful" about this inevitable passage of 'Time' from the 'temporal' to the 'eternal.' His images are natural, even as the symbols are rendered with a restrained ardour. Though deeply interested in the pleasure and fulfilment of life's moments, the poet is objective and well-orchestrated with a classical restraint. There is enough grandeur in his portrayal of human life, as his vision is not nihilistic. Life is grand and sublime, though it is turned temporary due to Death, the ultimate destiny of life. In this poem the poet is not glorifying the destructive nature of Death. He suggests the "triumphs" and 'adventures of man' are beyond the destructive action of Death. Joshua projects many evocative images which show the "richness" and "variety of life."

A structural analysis of the poem shows that death is projected as the everlasting stupor; it is a mysterious unknown dark world. The world is filled with mother's tears of sorrow. In this world of Death, "the dark clouds of loss" and "misery of separation" and "longing for the lost" can be observed in the first two stanzas. It betrays the feelings of the world and projects the emptiness of life. Later in the third and fourth stanzas, Joshua projects some wonderful images which show the denied human glories. It equals all. Death treats everyone equally whether he is the poet "Kalidasa" or "Bharavi" or a "potter." So Death is a universal leveller. It is "the leveller annulling all differences." In the cradle of Death "both the wild tiger and mild lamb" are similar. It is an irony of life that Death not only destroys all forms of living but also makes the world ignore and forgive those departed souls. The poet feels that Death is an "untold wealth." Finally the poet shows and says that Death is "an involved outsider" in all the processes of life. The poet ends the poem with an optimistic note that we have to continue to live as if there is no Death and we must continue our efforts to achieve glories in life. Thus the poem is an elegy which shows a perfect balance of the contrasting elements of 'pathos' and 'ethos', 'eerie silence' and 'eternal voice', 'love for living' and 'empathy for Death.' As a common leveler, Death brings home the lesson of equality of all human beings.

Works Cited

Daiches, David. *Critical History of English Literature*. Vol. 3. Hyderabad: Allied, 1989. Print.

Joshua, Gurram. *Gurram Joshua Jeevitam, Rachanalu*. Vol. 2. Hyderabad: Visalandhra, 1998. Print.

Mahesh, P.N.V.D. and Suresh Kumar. "Gurram Joshua's Dalit Concept." *Deccan Literary Journal* 2. 4. 1-5. Print.

13

Urmila Pawar's *The Autobiography of a Dalit Woman*: An Exploration

Simran Luthra

The dalit autobiography is distinct from the Western autobiography as Poitevin points out that the "...context, perspectives and characteristic of that historical trend differentially qualify the concept of autobiography itself vis-à-vis the Western definition of the genre." More significantly, he points out that the dalit autobiography is not "originally and essentially a literary exercise..." and does not have aesthetic pleasure as its aim. On the other hand, "It serves purposes of social intervention and accordingly carries strong militant connotations." By describing their lived experiences in such rich detail, the subaltern finds a voice and established the perspective of the 'other.'

Autobiographies of this nature help examine how social and political institutions influence people's lives at the everyday level. Urmila Pawar's *Aaydan—The Autobiography of a Dalit Woman* articulates the relationship between caste and gender. This paper attempts to examine this relationship with a special focus on her schooling experience embedded in a larger discourse of gender theory.

Vasantha and Kalpana Kannabiran make two very important assertions: "The caste question and gender question are intermeshed and that you can understand one only if you understand the other" and "The social relations of caste and gender are based on the exercise of power through the use of force" (2130-33). These two assertions come out very clearly in Pawar's autobiography. Pawar's work describes her life from her earliest childhood memory up to the point when she has two grown daughters. The autobiography, which has been rightly recognized and felicitated with several awards and recognition, is a progressive and emancipatory text since it also shows how Pawar is able to engage with the politics of her identity as a woman and as a Dalit and negotiate meanings for herself. It is towards the end of the book when she is married and also becomes a mother, through her involvement with women's groups and Dalit women's groups, activism and writing, that she is able to bring together her life experiences and understand her position better. Her activism and writing both are at the heart of her exploring this identity politics. In fact, the sections which describe her work and closeness with the women of the groups that she worked with resonate the idea of the lesbian continuum (*Wikepedia* on Homosociality) and make her stance even more radical (It is precisely this broad spectrum of women's homo-social loyalties that Adrienne Rich has referred to and celebrated as the "lesbian continuum").

The importance of education for Dalits and in particular for women is a recurring theme of the book and is most poignantly articulated in the words of Pawar's elder daughter who says: "The real change came when Aai began to educate herself.... After she passed her M.A., the change was still more pronounced. Education made her a feminist." Pawar's father who was able to gain some kind of social mobility for himself through education by becoming a teacher and a priest understood the value of education and wanted all in his family to get educated. The initial part of the book contains stories of how he used to thrash his nephews for not going to school insisting that girls must be educated, be independent and stand on their own feet. Even on his death-bed he made his wife promise him that she would ensure that the children would be educated—a promise which Pawar's mother took very seriously.

Dalits in general believed that education was a means for upward social mobility: As Paik says, "They believed that 'education was a magic wand' which would bring about their advancement. They believed in the human-capital approach to education: that is, 'if they invested in education, they would be investing in techniques which would help them to better their life chances.' In the parents' view, education is a valuable asset and, of course, part and parcel of the modernising process" (175). She goes on to say that "Many Dalit parents had imbibed the prevailing high-caste attitude towards learning, seeing it as something to be forced on reluctant children through strict discipline, including physical beating to make them memorise their lessons" (175). Something which is true for Pawar as well—in fourth grade when she fails, her brother Shahu and mother are extremely upset and shout at her, after which her mother beats her with a stick. Or the amusing story of one of her father's nephew's mother, who tired of Pawar's father thrashing her son, uses the pulp of a red fruit and smears it on his buttocks and complains to the relatives that owing to the uncle's beating, her son had shat blood! Paik concludes in her essay that "Caste and the education system have worked ruthlessly to discourage Dalit entrants but Dalits have set great store by education" (175).

This point about caste and the education system working ruthlessly to discourage Dalit entrants is amply illustrated in the book too. So, not that Dalit children are denied admission, but the way in which the curriculum is designed, or the way the school is arranged, the hidden curriculum of the school cater to the upper castes/classes and comes across in interesting ways. In the first place, as Paik points out, "Many Dalit parents were illiterate and lacking experience in school culture, so they were unable to provide much useful help to their children in their studies" (175). Perhaps it was for this reason that Pawar says "Aaye had given the teachers full permission to beat me up because she firmly believed in the principle, 'spare the rod and spoil the child.' Baba had taught her that education was impossible without punishment."

However, the practices within the school itself were discriminatory and reinforced the caste roles that the Dalits were fighting to get out of through education. Herlekar Guruji, Pawar's fourth grade teacher used to make her "do the dirty work, like cleaning the board, the class, collecting the dirt and disposing it off." And also cleaning the verandah where the cows made nuisance. On one occasion when she refused for being consistently singled out to clean up, she was slapped hard by the teacher so that her cheek became red and swelled up. On going home and narrating the incident to her mother, her mother decided to speak to the guruji. This was an occasion when a widowed Dalit woman stood up for her daughter against an upper caste male teacher, and is one of the most amusing and heartening incidents in the book. Aaye also mumbles to herself in anger that "Everybody else can get education, but when it's the turn of my child, it turns out to be a big problem." And when she confronts the guruji, speaking to him in her dialect, threatening: "Let me see you laying a finger on my girl again and I'll show you! Let me see how you can pass this road if you do so." This threat of palpable violence in her own dialect asserts power over the teacher, who Pawar reports never troubled her again. Such instances indicate how force coming from unexpected quarters can help a situation, and that articulation of anger at the appropriate moment is needed to counter injustice. Pawar adds, "And most important of all, I started considering my mother as a great support." This act of standing up for her daughter must indeed have had an important psychological impact on Pawar's young mind, as did several other pleasant and not so pleasant incidents at school and outside.

The mental makeup of a child is affected by all sorts of experiences. As an untouchable from the Mahar community, even outside the school she faced typical discrimination, such as when she used to go to the Brahmin Pandit family to buy pickle, she had to stand outside like a beggar and shout for someone to come and give her pickle, which then used to be kept on the third or fourth step, while she had to be careful not to let even her shadow fall on the person giving her the pickle. And then she had to leave the money on the step which would first be sprinkled with water to get rid of the impurity and only then collected.

Uma Chakravarti says: "Caste oppression is far more dehumanizing than economic exploitation. It denies subjectivity to the dalits by depriving them of personhood and dignity" (579-85). This is certainly true; however, it is the reality of caste that leads to their poor economic status as well. Deprived from knowledge, owning property or other means of earning well, relegated to menial tasks, poverty is a huge reality for the Dalits. So while other girls in her school used to dress up their hair with nice satin or plastic ribbons, Pawar's mother used to tie her well-oiled hair into a plait with a piece of her torn sari. Further, she had only two sets of clothes which she used to wear alternately. Neither did they have the 'custom' of washing their clothes every day. Being pointed out or feeling like the odd one out would thus be a natural consequence. Her older siblings who had been schooled into cleanliness, used to reprimand her for spitting, also a habit that she had which was considered a marker of low social status.

Food is another site where caste and status differences play out. In the first place, her family faced deprivation of food at a very basic level. Fancy preparations which her upper caste classmates brought to school or spoke about, were thus a far cry away: "We were aware, without anybody telling us, that we were born in a particular caste and in poverty, and that we had to live accordingly.... I was born in a backward caste in a backward region, that too a girl!" The sort of frugal and mostly tasteless meals that they used to eat have been described in great detail. She also tells us of stories that their mother used to tell them so that they would eat the food either out of amusement or guilt.

It is later through friends that she and her siblings got exposed to delicacies which they had never had as children. She says of her sister, used to go to the house of a friend of hers—Prabha Godbole, whose father used to offer English tuitions: "I am not sure how much English she learnt, but she certainly picked up their Brahmin habits very fast." These habits were mainly to do with language and food. She tells us of an occasion when her classmates and she decided to cook a meal. On asking enthusiastically what she should bring, she was told—nothing, but money. The cooking was done at a certain friend's house: "They did not allow me to touch anything though we all ate together. I really enjoyed the meal. The next day I was horrified to hear that my eating had become the hottest topic for juicy gossip. Girls were whispering about how much I had eaten. 'She ate like a monster,' someone said. Another endorsed it, 'God, she ate like a goat.' 'She ate so much of everything! Awful!' it was so humiliating that I died a thousand deaths that day!"

Thus the 'chhadi' that Shailaja Paik speaks of in her paper entitled 'Chhadi Lage Chham Chham, Vidya Yeyi Gham Gham (The Harder the Stick Beats, the Faster the Flow of Knowledge)' which works against the Dalit students seeking education and staying on in school works at several levels—being discriminated against by teachers at the academic as well as social level, and also being discriminated against by one's classmates. There is immense psychological pressure on Dalit children then, which stems both from economic deprivation as well as being from a polluting caste. The upper-caste children, mimicking the adults soon learn how to talk and behave with lower caste children, asserting power over them through the cultural capital they bring from home.

One of the hurdles she faced was in learning English and she describes what a painful process it was with her trying to learn by rote for the exams. Some other things are not explicitly mentioned in the book, but we can take for granted the curriculum not relating to Dalit culture and society, etc. Pawar changed schools in grade eight and joined her brother's school called Shirke High School in Ratnagiri. Adolescence was the stage of life she was passing through, and she speaks of her interest in boys at school. She laments that she hardly used to receive the sort of attention from boys that other girls of her class would: "I do not know how I had offended the boys. I felt so left out. I was so different from all those traditional girls! I was very active! I participated in every programme that the school organized. I had resolved not to remain behind in anything." The comment 'I was very active!' stands out. The passivity of women is something that patriarchy considers desirable. An active woman, particularly in the time that Pawar was young, was certainly not an attractive woman, despite being talented. She hits bull's eye, when she remarks that she didn't know how she had 'offended' the boys. She had indeed offended them by being active and entering their domain. It was for this reason that she was teased by the nick-name 'Aga' also the name of a famous Hindi film comedian. And on one such occasion of being teased, she screamed back at the boys saying: "I don't give a damn for you, May someone shit in your mouth for you!" following this outburst, she no longer was teased.

Perhaps in this case it was the lack of the baggage of being lady-like and refined that allowed her to use such language and vent her anger on the boys. Perhaps a Brahmin or upper-caste girl would have been unable to react like this owing to notions of acceptable behaviour. Urmila Pawar's experiences certainly do reflect the reality of Dalit women. However, there is also a difference—she has chosen to react in ways which are different from the normal ways that Dalit women would have responded to the caste and gender issues. And it is because of reacting differently that she has been able to experience some shift in her own dignity and personhood.

In the above instance and through the whole exercise of her activism and writing she has made the subaltern speak like Paik: "...the matrix of social structures and cultural forces interacted with the system of education to constrain the thoughts and actions of Dalit girls. Despite these impediments, many Dalit girls successfully completed their education at various levels" (175). Urmila Pawar is certainly one of those resilient women who did not allow the hurdles to overwhelm her. Padma Velaskar speaks of: "...the double burden for the rural girl child as against the boy child. The burden of poverty is borne through hard work on farms or elsewhere, and that of patriarchy through relegation to the lesser occupation, survival on less food, less clothing, and more household work in a general atmosphere of subservience, restriction and oppression" (131-45). Pawar was lucky to have been born in a family which focused on girls' education and escaped hard labour; however she could not escape the poverty, deprivation and discrimination. In fact schooling came with its own burden of psychological and social pressures.

The end however, is hopeful—her resilience, support from her family in whatever ways, and the basic skill of writing Marathi which she had picked up at school and later started taking seriously as a writer, became what weaving—*Aaydan* had become to her Aaye: an escape, and an expression, which is where the title of the book comes from as well. But her writing goes way beyond just a personal escape or expression—it is leading the way as Paik says to "an alternative construction of Dalit reality" and subsequently may, and should influence pedagogy as well (175).

Works Cited

Chakravarti, U. "Conceptualising Brahmanical Patriarchy in Early India: Gender, Caste, Class and State." *Economic and Political Weekly* 28.14 (1993): 579-85. Print.

http://en.wikipedia.org/wiki/Homosociality. Web.

Kannabiran, K. and V. Kannabiran. "Caste and Gender: Understanding Dynamics of Power and Violence." *Economic and Political Weekly* 26.37 (September 14, 1991). 2130-33. Print.

Paik, S. "Chhadi Lage Chham Chham, Vidya Yeyi Gham Gham (The Harder the Stick Beats, the Faster the Flow of Knowledge: Dalit Women's Struggle for Education)." *Indian Journal of Gender Studies* 16 (2009). 175.

Poitevin, Guy. "Dalit Autobiographical Narratives: Figures of Subaltern Consciousness, Assertion and Identity" http://aune.lpl.univ-aix.fr/~belbernard/misc/ccrss/dalitautobio.htm. Accessed on 17th April, 2012. Web.

Velaskar, P. "Unequal Schooling As a Factor in the Reproduction of Social Inequality in India." *Sociological Bulletin*, 39.1 and 2 (March and September 1990). 131-45.

14

'Inventing a Poetics of Suffering and Resistance': Narrative Strategies in Mahasveta Devi's Story, "Dhouli"

K. Damodar Rao and *D. Vijaya Prakash*

As the dominant cultures occupy centre stage and tend to obliterate the voices of the lesser privileged sections, Mahasveta attempts to provide a voice and visibility to these neglected masses. Though frail and in her mid-eighties now, the sites of her activism include Singur, Nandigram in her home state and the far away, strife-torn Godhra in Gujarat. That is, frail she is in appearance but unbending in spirit. And the tribal areas of Jharkhand, Orissa and West Bengal such as Palamau, Chhotanagpur, Birbhum have become famous as areas of her activism and resistance. She becomes one among the tribals of these regions, listens to them, speaks their language, and makes representations to the government authorities at various levels including the PMO to redress their grievances. She records their travails in her activist writings, and then gives their lives a fictional form as only she can. This is all a part of her relentless crusade against the establishment for its indifference to the subhuman conditions of the exploited masses, starving millions, dispossessed communities, which she records in her fictional and non-fictional writings.

Mahasveta targets exploitative machinery that she confronts and brings to light any injustice in any form and manifestation. Her fiction is a demonstration of the harsh realities the underprivileged sections had to contend with on a daily basis. Although Mahasveta does not give importance to labels and categorizations, her commitment and portrayal of marginalized classes have invited descriptions such as "Chronicles of the Oppressed", "Aesthetics of Liberation" and "Poetics of Resistance." The four stories included in *Outcast* provide a case in point. All the four stories have women protagonists, three of them being adivasis; and rape happens to be the trope in all the four stories. Besides, the translator has included two essays by Mahasveta at the end as if to prove the point that her stories are not weird figments of imagination, but rather re-creation in fictional form of what really is happening out there. As many of her activist writings reveal with documentary realism, one wonders whether fact is stranger than fiction. In fact, the situation in these parts of the country is so inhumanly bizarre that Mahasveta has to invent new narrative techniques becoming in the process, "the originator of the hybrid book in Bengali that mixes history, myth, melodrama and fiction with documentary reality" (Asaduddin, 236). She has developed a fictional form which is unique in many ways. Mahasveta's multiple story telling techniques include, for instance, minute attention to detail, matter-of-fact narration interspersed with ironic observations, time-frames freely seaming into each other, occasional conjuring up of the classical and the romantic strains, juxtaposition of the earnest and the satirical, the real bordering on the grotesque, the fictional giving a feel of the fantastic, the absurd giving way to the practical, what with the oral element playing dominant role in different narratives, and sometimes within the same story at different points. Out of the four stories included in *Outcast*, the first story, "Dhouli" is taken up here for a closer examination of the narrative strategies Mahasveta employed in depicting her fictional concerns.

Mahasveta has the storyteller's rare genius of transporting her audience into her world of creation in no time, here a world of suffering, unrelenting suffering. One feels the atmosphere of the setting, as for instance, when she describes the opening scene in the story, "Dhouli": "Rohatgi's Company's bus was the only link between Taharr and the rest of the world.... They used poor, rundown buses for poor, rundown places like Taharr, Palani or Burudhia" (Mahasveta Devi, 1). The buses do not ply during the rainy season and Taharr is completely cut off from the rest of world during that season. Rundown places like these inhabit rundown people who become victims of the machinations of the privileged ones. The tinge of suffering, introduced in the atmospheric setting, takes a human shape in the form of Dhouli who waits near the bus stop near Parasnath's tea-stall-cum-grocery shop at eight in the night, the last bus service to the village. The object of her waiting, the cause of her suffering happens to be one Misrilal, a Brahmin youth, who doesn't turn up that day even. In his conversation with his wife while commenting on the plight of Dhouli, Parasnath observes that it was nearly four months since Misrilal has left the village. He is a *deota* (literally, god or brahmin), they wonder, and there is no possibility of redemption or redress for the girl that is implied in the simple statement: 'The girl's here again today' (2) and the overt observation: 'she's finished now' (2).

Having created the locale, the atmosphere and introduced the protagonist, the narrator proceeds to give enough hints, while holding back something at the same time, as to what has happened and the reader is now ready to pick up the threads. In the next scene Dhouli is seen crying by the side of her mother's bed: "Tears seeped from her eyes. Tears of deep despair. Her mother could hear; she understood everything...her mother finally said, 'They'll throw us of out of here'": Dhouli's mother has been a witness to the earlier proceedings and therefore gives a judgment, but the readers wait in anticipation to know the whole truth. The fact that Dhouli has been victimized is made clear. In the course of the conversation between Dhouli and her mother we come to know that Dhouli is a 19-year old girl, that she is pregnant, and that she does not accept the proposal of her mother 'to get rid of the thorn' in her womb. The man responsible for this is Misras' son, Misrilal, while Dhouli, in her idealistic romantic vision, still thinks that he would come back and look after the child, whereas her mother's practical knowledge born of age and experience prompts her to think that this is a routine for the privileged Brahmins to exploit the innocent *dusad* (outcast) girls. She says: "They always make such promises. You're not the first *dusad* girl the Misras have ruined. *Dusad, ganju, dhobi*—who have they spared?" (4). Dhouli's innocence comes forth as a sharp contrast to the worldly wisdom of her mother when Dhouli replies "He loves me" (4).

Dhouli's mother could also understand why she has lost the job of a cattle-grazer. She explains the same to Dhouli. It has got something to do with her daughter's involvement with Misrilal: "You fell in love, and I had to lose my cattle-grazing job. A wolf stole one of their lambs and they put the blame on me. Is that fair?" (4). With her sense of foreboding she warns Dhouli what was in store for her saying that if Misrilal takes care of her and the baby, no one will raise a voice, otherwise she would be torn to pieces. Various thoughts cross the mind of the vulnerable Dhouli. Mahasveta's narrative, at this point, focuses on a part of Dhouli's past as she thinks for a while that she would have been better off at her in-laws' place but immediately corrects herself when she remembers that her elder brother-in-law wouldn't have spared her. "And Misrilal did?" (5), the question is shot like an arrow by her mother. The atmosphere of suffering born of personal guilt and tragedy is unrelenting: "Her eyelids felt dry from crying endlessly. She shut them" (5). Since Misrilal had left the village four months ago like a thief, Dhouli spent sleepless nights with different thoughts overwhelming her including that of suicide. It was one such night.

II

Mahasveta proceeds with her narration of capturing the different time-frames in Dhouli's life. The love story of Misrilal and Dhouli, narrated in an earnest tone devoid of any note of irony, is quite interesting. The narration, in a matter-of-fact fashion, follows the familiar seduction-submission-betrayal pattern which has got great visual impact with the description of 'primordial, langourous' afternoons, pristine forests and waterfalls, a bathing scene with a wet sari, a perfect setting for romance. While grazing goats in the forest the Brahman youth makes overtures which eventually Dhouli could not resist. At this level, the narrative offers glimpses of vintage romantic cinema especially of the nineteen sixties and seventies. The technique here follows the classical, even if melodramatic presentation of the romantic (p)air. The overtures of the Brahmin boy are initially resisted, but Dhouli inwardly takes pride in attracting the attention of a *deota* ('She, Dhouli, a *dusad* girl, had driven a brahman's son crazy', 11).

A flashback within flashback shows Dhouli recollecting her past: she does not exactly remember her marriage but remembers how she was sent to her in-laws' place at a tender age, how her father had to borrow from the Misras for her wedding, and subsequently died as a bonded labourer repaying that loan. Her husband used to beat her, but soon he died of fever. She used to work hard in the fields and road construction work for one square meal a day, but when her elder brother-in-law from Bhalatore began to eye her, Dhouli returned to her mother. In Taharr, she had not encouraged any *dusad* men. Life was devoid of any bright patch: "The same poverty and hunger. The same back-breaking labour" (8).

It was during this phase, 'an enchanted dream' (11) followed her for two months in the form of Misrilal in the lap of forest and 'all caution was swept away in a flood of passion. Nineteen and twenty-three' (11). Misrilal makes promises to her as one would only expect of him in that moment of frenzy: "I only want you" (11), "I don't care about things like caste and untouchability" (12), "We'll go to Dhanbad via Bhalatore and from there to Patna. We'll open a shop and earn our living" (12). But he was unable to utter a word when the head of the family, Hanuman Misra came to Taharr. When he musters enough courage and informs his mother that Dhouli was carrying his child, she dismisses him with characteristic disdain as if it was all part of the routine of their males: "So what? The men of our family have planted their seed in so many *dusad* and *ganju* girls.... Even Jhalo has three sons by Kundan." She hurls curses at Dhouli: "She has sinned. She'll suffer for it. They'll both starve to death, mother and daughter" (13). It was, according to her, Dhouli's sin, not her son's: "It's always the fault of the woman. For not considering a brahman's honour, she's even more to blame" (13).

In return for his going away from the village, Misrilal is able to extract a promise from his mother that they would provide for the *dusadin* and see that they don't starve to death.

Having shed light on the upper caste community's stand on morals and illicit relationships, Mahasveta, then, moves the focus on the reaction of Dhouli's community which holds no hope for the hapless woman. The community's stand is intriguing, even illogical, because of the strange reasoning with which it views the relationship. It finds fault with her because 'she had fallen in love' (14). If Misrilal had forcibly taken her, they would have been sympathetic to her plight but not when it was known that 'Dhouli had been willing' (14) partner in the affair. They consider it an 'unforgivable offence.' The seemingly casual statement of the narrator puts the irrational situation in its ironic context: 'If Misrilal had used force, they would not have spurned her. There were several illegitimate Misra children growing up in the *dusad-ganju-dhobi* quarters' (14).

As Dhouli was overwhelmed with fear and sorrow Nature looked like empathizing with her. The forest lost all its charm, 'the trees were ghostly sentries,' and she 'waited in vain near the waterfall' (15). Misrilal finally appears one day and again utters the same promises assuring her that he would come back within a month. Four months passed, and everyday Dhouli would return home after waiting for the bus. That night, somehow she began to feel, Misrilal and his love seemed as unreal as a fairytale. Dhouli gives birth to a male child. Misrilal had earlier said if it was a boy, he would name him Murari.

Mahasveta assigns an important role here to a character called Shanichari, introduced earlier in passing remarks by Dhouli's mother when she pleads with her daughter to seek her help in removing the child from her womb. Shanichari is a midwife, also the village gossip and medicine woman. As soon Dhouli gives birth to a male child, she comments, "It's Dhouli's (one who is fair) child, that's why he's so fair." She gives an assurance to Dhouli's mother that she would give a potion that would make Dhouli infertile ('I gave the same medicine to Kundan Misra's wife. She didn't die, did she?' 18) and also informs her that Misrilal's marriage was fixed and after marriage they would be sent to Dhanbad to set up a cycle shop there. One is here reminded of the earlier promise of Misrilal to Dhouli that together they would go to a place and set up a shop. Here shop is the constant, woman in his life is different. Shanichari is moved by the story of hapless Dhouli and decides to mobilize the 'public opinion in the girl's favour' (19). No better place than the house of the Misras to begin her campaign. She goes to treat Misrilal's mother for rheumatic pain and informs that Dhouli has given birth to a son who looks exactly like her son. Shanichari's attempts at extracting something from the Misras as compensation to Dhouli are negated by Kundan Misra, the elder son.

The transformation of Dhouli from a docile, young widow trapped by a Brahmin youth into a decisive, protesting woman is effected by Mahasveta not as a sudden, miraculous happening, but as part of a natural, evolutionary transformation. Dhouli begins to view her former love with a note of disbelief and then aversion. She thinks:

> Had it really happened? Had a *deota* really kissed the feet of a *dusadin* after extracting a thorn from it one day? No, it couldn't have been. It was all a fantasy! Only the child sleeping in her lap was real. (21)

As the ostentatious wedding of Misrilal takes place in the village, Dhouli sends message through Shanichari that if he doesn't come to her place she would take his son to his wife even risking her life. This was the first gesture of assertion on the part of Dhouli. When he finally comes to her and mentions that he still loved her she is no position to swallow it all. On the contrary, she expresses her contempt for him, also for her own self for having loved him:

> '*Thuu*! To hell with your love! If you had taken me by force, I could have got an acre of land. But you're not even a man! Your brother's a man! He gave Jhalo sons and he also gave her a house and land. What did you do for me?' (23)

He promises her to send money to look after the child which he never keeps. She tries everything to keep both ends meet, but nothing works for her in the village. Dhouli's decision to take to prostitution is aimed at redeeming her family from starvation and also a protest against the injustice meted out to her not only by the upper caste people but also by her own community members. Her taking to prostitution as a last resort, implicitly, has the two-pronged gesture of defence and offence; survival and retaliation. Dhouli is now able to provide two square meals a day to her mother and son, and in addition, is able to insult the Misras family. Kundan watches all this: 'Dhouli had learnt to survive, had bested his attempt at vengeance' (28). He goes to Dhanbad and accuses his younger brother of bringing shame to his community in the village. Mahasveta here establishes Kundan as an unscrupulous, cunning upper caste youth. He is already adept at the ways of the world, who knows the pulse of the people, hence the methods of manipulating them come easy to him. He has destroyed the lives of many young *dusad* girls but provides them the means to survive:

> Otherwise how would Kundan manage it all? So many fields, orchards, illegitimate offspring, sexy, lowcaste females! Such bliss! How else would he manage his empire? (29)

In fact, by establishing the credentials of Kundan, Mahasveta implicitly raises the question as to who is better of the two brothers: Because Kundan thinks if he had been his younger brother he would not have given up that woman 'on the say-so of Hanuman Misra' (29). Kundan asks his brother sternly to provide some land or some money to her because they had to contend with a whore in the village. Showing off his superiority, and a worldly wise man's condescending attitude, he spews contempt on the *dusad* girl when he says: 'the door through which the lion entered is being visited by rats and swine' (30). In the process of establishing his big brother superiority, Kundan unabashedly exhibits the streak of jealousy at his brother's 'catch.'

Misrilal, in a fit of anger, comes to Taharr that evening. As he knocks on Dhouli's door, 'draped in a red sari with green bangles, hair smoothly oiled and braided, *a Dhouli* opened the door to him' (30, italics mine). Mahasveta presents the defiant posture of Dhouli in no uncertain terms as she confronts him by pointing out how he had left her after having his fun and how his brother tried to kill them by denying food: "I had to save *your* son and myself" (31, italics mine). To his pointed question why she had not killed herself, Dhouli answer is sharp and poignant: "I tried to kill myself. But then I thought, why should I? You can get married, run a shop, see movies with your wife, and I have to kill myself? Why? Why? Why?" (31).

Within a few days a panchayat meeting is convened in the village and without seeking the opinions of the aggrieved ones, Hanuman Misra gives his judgment that Dhouli can no longer practice prostitution in the village, she can leave the place, go to any place, Ranchi, for instance, and practice it there. If not, her house would be set on fire and the inmates would be burnt to death. A final gesture of resistance on the part of Dhouli is shown when she asks the gathering why is it that the Brahmins never thought of providing for the upbringing of one of their own offspring. But she is a lone individual, a woman, a *dusad* whose voice will not be heard. The next morning, she hands over the child to her mother who weeps inconsolably and prepares to become a professional *randi*. As she begins her bus journey to Ranchi, a long way off, the bus driver and the contractor could not look at her face as if they were carrying the collective guilt of the village.

III

The transition of Dhouli from a young, suffering widow to a dreamy, loving woman to a wronged prostitute marking a process of suffering, protest and endurance is narrated by Mahasveta using different strategies. In other stories as well, such as "Doulati", "Sanichari", and "Fairytale of Rajabasha" women succumb to male exploitation, sometimes are sold for money by their fathers (Douloti). It has been pointed out that "Prostitution becomes their meagre means of livelihood, which perpetuates the brutality and routinizes the indignity of their sexual exploitation" (Nivedita Sen, 20). Using different strategies such as subversion of myth Mahasveta Devi has created strong willed female characters like Dopdi Mejhen in "Draupadi" who refuses to clothe herself, who turns her body into a weapon whereas Mary Oraon in "The Hunt" exhibit a different form of resistance in thwarting the attempts of the male aggressor and by actually killing him. Dhouli's taking to prostitution at the end is in contrast with the gullible, innocent woman portrayed in the beginning. Not only is the transformation important, but the process of transformation, and the narrative strategies are equally noteworthy.

Works Cited

Asaduddin, M. "Of Rape and Marginalization" Review of *Outcast: Four Stories*, *The Book Review*, 26.11.2002 rpt. *Mahasveta Devi: An Anthology of Recent Criticism*. Ed. Nivedita Sen and Nikhil Yadav. New Delhi: Pencraft International, 2008. 236-41. Print.

Devi, Mahasveta. *Outcast: Four Stories*. Tr. Sarmistha Dutta Gupta. Calcutta: Seagull Books, 2002. Print.

Sen, Nivedita and Nikhil Yadav. ed. *Mahasveta Devi: An Anthology of Recent Criticism*. New Delhi: Pencraft International, 2008.

15

Multiculturalism and the Modern Indian Novel: An Analysis of U.R. Ananthamurthy's *Bharatipura*

Shikha Bhatnagar

U.R. Ananthamurthy's writings include short stories, poems, novels and plays. The Navya literary movement in Kannada began in the 1960s and 70s and Ananthamurthy was one of its leading exponents, deeply rooted in the existential reality of experience. *Bharatipura* was written in a small village named Heggodu in Malenad where the novelist stayed with a dramatist called Subbanna. The impact of history is clearly evident. The novel is set in the hilly regions of Malenad in Karnataka. The village remains a mute witness to the traumatic experiences of post-Independent India and the history of the village depicts at micro-level what happened to rural India in the wake of independence. Socialism was facing a grave threat from Marxism. The title of the novel is very apt, highly evocative and symbolic. Bhartipura symbolises India with its multi-cultural, multi-lingual, multiracial, cosmopolitan identity.

In the novel *Bharatipura* the narrative shifts from England to a South Indian village in Karnataka, from macrocosm to a microcosmic permeation of reality. Jagannatha Rao, the central character of the novel, believes that he is incapable of action, and strives to become a man of action by inspiring the untouchables to break the shackles of bondage and superstition that bind them, and become strong and free human beings by crossing the threshold of the Manjunatha temple. This perceptual point of view permeates the entire text. Jagannatha wants to make his life a meaningful one.

In his unfinished letter to Margaret he writes that he is not yet a man, and after the completion of his task he would become a man. He had not yet recovered from the disease of self-analysis and had been amusing himself standing before mirrors, and that he cannot be real to himself without mirrors. Therefore, the mirror becomes an image of his self-conscience, a mirror of reflection of his thoughts and actions. He confesses that there was a wide chasm between his real self and the mask which he wore in society. While working for his Bachelor's degree in Mysore, Nehru's idealism was his mirror, and his speech patterns, gestures and demeanour were tricks with which he made his personality more attractive.

Jagannatha Rao's rebellion does not arise out of sheer organic necessity. He is driven by a deeper desire to establish a more humane relationship with the world. Gandhian praxis is also a product of ontological necessity and the approach of Gandhian ideology to the question of untouchability is shaped by such an impulse. He confesses: "I have never engaged in action that would lead to exertion, that would exercise me, melt my fat, ignite it and burn it up" (Anantamurthy 28).

The narrative is infused with myth, history, and politics as it attempts to come to terms with social inequality by fighting against racial prejudice. Jagannatha Rao creates social awareness among the dalits by educating them about human rights. The symbol of the temple stands for the old world order, an image of orthodoxy ridden with superstition, illiteracy and exploitation of the weak, culminating in the need of the protagonist to change the social hierarchy of the village. The narrative is imbued with a historical past which blends with the political present of the village. The irony as an undercurrent cuts across these distinctions making it possible for a revolutionary change in the village asleep for centuries in the lap of Manjunatha's glory. The theme of a political revolution is a distant dream which Jagannatha Rao wants to transform into an illuminating reality.

The single event of the entry of the untouchables into the Manjunatha temple and the dislodging of the lingam by Ganesha in Chapter XIV acts as the fulcrum of the entire novel. Jagannatha Rao is driven by socio-moralistic intellectual challenges and upholds a liberal humanistic creed in his demand for social equality. However, he is a flat character since there is no significant development or progression in his personality. His problem is a psychological and socio-political one and indecisiveness is a major flaw in his character. The dalits are portrayed as weak-willed, subservient individuals ready to don the garb of slavery at the slightest opportunity. The narrator's point-of-view reinforces such an opinion. The crux of Jagannatha Rao's evolutionary impasse can be seen in Chapter XII of *Bharatipura.* Jagannatha is an atheist who does not believe in Lord Manjunatha's glory while the entire village of Bharatipura is enthralled by the Lord for generations. It is also not so easy to erase such a portentous belief according to Sripathi Rao who cites the Russian example thereby linking the theme of a political revolution against despotism to the situation of Bharatipura. In the conversation, Sripathi Rao says: "It won't go, Jaganna. In Russia they killed god, but what happened? Stalin himself became god didn't he?" (118). This argument with the question tag at the end serves as an effective contrast in highlighting two different ideological points of view in the novel. Subraya Adiga continues:

> What I finally say is this, without intensity living means death-in-life. When Paramahamsa touched Vivekananda with his feet, the latter felt that the ground under his feet was sinking, when we are in the hands of god, we burn, we shake to our roots. If we don't experience terror at least once in life, it is all a waste. True terror strikes us at such a moment, everything seems to detach itself from everything else. We horripilate. The thought that I am distinct has to vanish thus and that is really tough.... If Jaganna has intensity now and if at least in his hate, Manjunatha fills his mind, he is a lucky man, that's what I say: Acceptance or rejection of Manjunatha is not important. That terror, that struggle Jagannatha will experience and thus ego will have to be annihilated. (118-19)

Thus the entire meaning of the novel, its message comes out in the voice of Adiga, the philosopher. His philosophic treatise paves a new way of examining life. The entire '*advaitha*' doctrine is compressed in one paragraph and brought out beautifully by Ananthamurthy in the following lines:

> One is born a shudra.
> One's karma makes him a twice-born.
> One's reading of the vedas makes him a vipra.
> One's knowledge of the Brahman makes him a Brahmana. (119)

Distinctions of caste, creed, religion and race fade away, but the underlying superstition of a hierarchical, caste ridden society is unmistakably seen here, while by birth one becomes an untouchable or shudra, it is one's action or *karma* which makes him a twice-born, the first birth being a physical one while the second birth is a spiritual birth. The reading of the vedas imparts wisdom but in order to attain a higher state it is an individual's knowledge about Brahman or ultimate reality which makes him a true brahmin, who sees his image in every human being, who though being apart, is in the philosophical sense a part of the whole dynamics of creation. Adiga says that this is because we are still 'dwijas' in the second stage, struggling from the physicality of being and moving towards another plane of spiritual growth.

It is a master-stroke on the part of Ananthamurthy that the entire panorama of an individual is methodically, philosophically and majestically analysed in vivid detail, so that ultimately a multi-dimensional view is put forth in the narrative. This dialogue continues and Adiga says: Meditation, self-integration, and study might have made Jagannatha a vipra, a wise man in the third stage, he is set on changing the relationship between the people and Lord Manjunatha through the philosophy of collective action. He will understand everything during the process of change. To put it succinctly, "something within him is struggling to liberate itself. Just as an embryo in a mother's womb kicks her, Jagannatha is kicking Manjunatha, you see, he is not a dead embryo. Let him kick, Manjunatha is sure to feel tickled all over by this kind of service. That's the truth" (119).

The focalisation of the entire novel is on this aspect. And it is in such a handling and presentation of the theme that Ananthamurthy breaks new ground in the field of the modern Indian novel. The dramatic dialogue between the three characters brings out his excellence as a master craftsman. The tone becomes sarcastic further on "If you are not familiar with the pains and pleasures of family life, why should you rebel, and for whom? Look, what rotten people have come to power through Gandhi's revolution" which is a direct attack on the political situation of the post-colonial era. The political overtones are clearly evident in the following dialogue between Jagannatha and Sripathi Rao: "Jaganna, see, Gurappa Gowda has not issued any kind of statement, scoundrel, he cannot see openly, no untouchables in the temple. After all, he is a Congressman. He cannot also say, let the untouchables in, because he will then lose his upper caste votes" (135).

The caste system asserts its superiority and power when an attempt is made to take the untouchables inside the Manjunatha temple because the brahmins and other upper caste people think that such an action would pollute the temple. Similarly the dilemma of the untouchables over such an undertaking points to the linguistic fact that in a structurally caste-dominated society necessarily involves a grasp on the social structuring of hierarchies. Individuals inherit these concepts and are inducted thus into caste-based forms of thought in their ordinary language acquisition. The linguistic differences, like most other behavioral differences, are entirely the result of learned behaviour. People speak as they do, due to the acquisition of linguistic characteristics which are culture-specific and also class-specific. Thus the cultural concepts tend to mould the understanding, perceptions and relations with members of all social groups.

These caste-based differences go beyond life and affect one even in death. For instance, a small untouchable boy Chouda dies while eating bananas. His death evokes no social sympathy. Jagannatha raged in anger as he listened to Adiga's tranquil voice. He said, "Aren't you ashamed to speak Advaitha at this moment?" Adiga replied, "That a child died while eating bananas should make you sad, not angry." Jagannatha retorted, "What if a brahmin boy died?" Adiga said coolly, "Jaganna, no arguments please. Think of your immediate responsibilities." Jagannatha could not contain himself from saying, "your mysticism, asceticism, spirituality, your Shankaracharya everything is a ploy to uphold the existing system. That's all" (186).

This question of untouchability and casteism becomes a burning issue further on in the narrative. Adiga says "The untouchables had come to terms with their conditions and lived their lives quietly. They went on adjusting themselves to their environment" (186-87). Jagannatha thinks "who knew how many centuries of conspiracy were behind Adiga's way of thinking." Jagannatha was really put off. Ananthamurthy succeeds in making us sympathise with Jagannatha Rao's problems as a failed revolutionary with his insights into his own deficiencies. He tries to cover up his indecisiveness by wearing a mask of action. We begin to view his inner self as it unravels itself in the narrative in relation to his environment, the village and the nation. "He had vaguely decided to go back to Bharatipura to become authentic as a human being. He would have to shift to Bangalore and become an absentee landlord..." (35).

In this novel, the narration is from the first person point of view of Jagannatha Rao. He is the reflector of the narrative. Thus we can apply Bakhtin's view and predict that the depicting authorial language lies on the same plane as the depicted language of the hero and may enter into dialogic relations and hybrid combinations with it (28). This principle is applicable because the narrative of *Bharatipura* proceeds in a straight horizontal axis. On a single plane whose vantage point rests on the character of Jagannatha Rao, the entire thematic framework of the novel rests on one single action, the entry of the dalits inside the Manjunatha temple. Hence,

> A letter that attacked his position stated that his deliberate move to hurt the feelings of upper caste people was far from Gandhi's philosophy. Another had analysed in big words the difference between a believer, full of love for the untouchables wanting them to enter the temple and a westernised athiest's intent to destroy

> Hinduism. Communist Dikshit had issued a statement saying that this projected action born of the idealism of a member of the landed gentry was bound to fail, and that only through an economic revolution could casteism be destroyed. (132)

The clash and conflict of ideologies is apparent here. Different sets of ideologies seem to cluster and give rise to a multiplicity of voices each striving for a supremacy over the other. These include Gandhian ideology, Socialism, Feudalism, Nehruvian idealism, etc. The author thus creates a plurality of voices and points-of-view and the meaning of the narrative emerges from the intersection of these viewpoints.

Works Cited

Ananthamurthy, U.R. *Bharatipura*. Trans. P. Sreenivasa Rao. Madras: Macmillan India Press, 1996. Print.

Bakhtin, Mikhail. *The Dialogic Imagination: Four Essays*. Trans C. Emerson and M. Holquist. Ed. M. Holquist. Austin: University of Texas Press, 1981. Print.

16

Culture as an Anti-Colonial Tool in *Kanthapura*

G. Damodar

Kanthapura (1938) portrays the participation of people from Kanthapura, a small village of South India, in the national struggle called for by Mahatma Gandhi. Imbued with nationalism, the villagers sacrifice all their material possessions in a triumph of the spirit, showing how in the Gandhian Movement people shed their narrow prejudices and united in the common cause of the non-violent civil resistance to the British Raj. The novel has been described as the most satisfying of modern Indian novels. It was an account of the non-violent resistance against the British seen from the perspective of a small village. In the style and structure of the Indian vernacular tales, a talkative old woman narrates how a village community obtains from daily life with its millennia-old worship of the local deity the strength for non-violent resistance to the British Raj. The enduring quality of the Indian village is represented as ensuring an internal tenacity that resists external crises, its relationship to past contributing a sense of unity and continuity between the present and past generations.

The village, Kanthapura, becomes a microcosm of the traditional Indian society with its entrenched caste hierarchy. In the village there are Brahmin quarters, Sudra quarters and Pariah quarters. Despite stratification into castes, the villagers are mutually bound in various economic and social functions which maintain social harmony. The village may appear isolated and removed from civilization, but it is compensated by an ever-enriching cycle of ceremonies, rituals, and festivals. In this quiet village when people live in the midst of their customs, traditions, superstitions and skirmishes, a disturbance takes place. Some young boys and girls act differently from the rest and enter the pariah quarters, when a twelve year old widow walks about without shaving her head, when young people hold secret meetings to cause revolt against the British and the like. Eventually, the entire village, including the women folk, children, Brahmins and untouchables become involved in the Freedom Movement and in their own small way, contribute to the movement.

Rao depicts the regular involvement of the villagers in *Sankara-Jayanthi, Kartik Purnima, Ganesh-Jayanthi, Dasara,* and the *Satyanarayana Puja* with the intention of conveying a sense of the natural unity and cohesion of village society. Old Ramakrishnayya reads out the *Sankara-Vijaya* day after day and the villagers discuss Vedanta with him every afternoon. Religion, imparted through discourses and *pujas* (prayers), keeps alive in the natives a sense of the presence of God. Participation in a festival brings about the solidarity among them. The local deity Kenchamma protects the villagers "through famine and disease, death and despair" (3). If the rains fail, people fall at her feet and worship as under:

> Kenchamma, Kenchamma
> Goddess benign and bounteous,
> Mother of earth, blood of life,
> Harvest-queen, rain-crowned,
> Kenchamma, Kenchamma,
> Goddess benign and bounteous. (4)

Equally sacred is the river Himavathy which flows near Kanthapura. Rao's choice of this village setting is strategic in view of his Gandhian loyalties. Gandhi locates his politics in the villages of India where the majority of Indian population resides. Rao maintains the sanctity of the village at an ideological level, but permits mobility and change to heighten the historical significance of the National Struggle Gandhi conceptualized.

The novel is set during 1920s and 1930s, when Mahatma Gandhi became the dominant figure in India's struggle for freedom. Rao treats the history of the Freedom Movement at the level of hostility between the village folk and the British colonial authority at a time when colonialism became intensely heavy-handed in its response to the Civil Disobedience Movement. The novel has the flavour of an epic as it emerges through the eyes of a delightful old woman who comments with wisdom and humour.

Rao makes a deliberate attempt to follow traditional Indian narrative technique and it is Indian sensibility that informs *Kanthapura*. In fact, both the spirit and the narrative technique of the novel are primarily those of the Indian *Puranas,* which are often described as an encyclopaedia of ancient and medieval Hinduism covering religious, philosophical, historical and social aspects. Rather than being a traditional novel with a neat linear structure and compact plot, *Kanthapura* follows the oral tradition of Indian *sthala-purana* or legendary history. As Raja Rao explains in his Foreword, "there is no village in India, however mean, that has not a rich legendary history of its own, in which some famous figure of myth or history has made an appearance" (v). The storyteller, who is linked to the past, keeps her native audience in touch with its lore and thereby allows the past to mingle with the present.

As a *sthala-purana,* one finds in the novel the blend of narration, description, philosophical reflection, and religious teaching. Rao makes a highly innovative use of the English language to make it conform to the Kannada rhythm. In keeping with his theme in *Kanthapura* he experiments with language following the oral rhythms and narrative techniques of traditional models of writing. The emotional upheaval that shook the village is expressed by breaking the formal English syntax to suit the sudden changes of mood and sharp contrasts in tone. While the intuitive borrowing from language takes place at one level, 'real' India is constructed at another interconnected level by enshrining the novel in Gandhian ideology. It is highly original in style. Rao's Foreword to the novel almost spells out the postcolonial cultural agenda:

> The telling has not been easy. One has to convey in a language that is not one's own the spirit that is one's own. One has to convey the various shades and

> omissions of a certain though-movement that looks maltreated in an alien language. I use the word 'alien', yet English is not really an alien language to us. It is the language of our intellectual make-up—like Sanskrit or Persian was before—but not of our emotional make-up. We are all instinctively bilingual, many of us writing in our own language and in English. We cannot write like the English. We should not. We cannot write only as Indians. (v)

In the Foreword, Rao set forth what was to be a lifelong literary concern: conveying the Indian experience to the larger world in a language besides his native Kannada. "We, in India, think quickly, we talk quickly, and when we move, we move quickly," he wrote. "There must be something in the sun of India that makes us rush and tumble and run on." He added:

> We have neither punctuation nor the treacherous 'ats' and 'ons' to bother us—we tell one interminable tale. Episode follows episode, and when our thoughts stop our breath stops, and we move on to another thought. This was and still is the ordinary style of our storytelling. I have tried to follow it myself in this story. (vi)

As *New York Times* remarks, 'Rao cajoles the English language into conveying the distinctive cadences of his native country' (Santha Rama Rau, 1964). The novel reveals his characteristic style—lyrical, fluid, colloquial—already firmly in place. There is more to Rao's book than a morality tale. It is written in an elegant style verging on poetry. It has all the content of an ancient Indian classic, combined with a sharp satirical wit and a clear understanding of the present. Rao's choice of this village setting is strategic in view of his Gandhian loyalties. In the last decade or so, historians, especially those centered around Subaltern Studies have attempted to demythicize the histories of the National Movement and highlighted the role of the subaltern in terms of agency, which was often neglected in the interests of a homogeneous nationalism. Gandhi, however, does not ignore the aspects of subalterneity.

Kanthapura is significant as a cultural tract which rewrites true history against the 'inauthentic' historical accounts compiled by Europeans. As it effects a cultural revival through the use of indigenous themes and motifs, Rao is also alive to the fact that religion has the potential to move people beyond dormancy—to display active political energy to the extent of sacrificing their lives. The novel evokes a sense of community and freedom, construed as a spiritual quality which overcomes all bounds and crosses all barriers.

Rao allows an easy interchange between the world of men and the world of gods, between modern world and antiquity. Accordingly, he equips his story with a protagonist whose role it is to enthuse the villagers into joining the political cause of India's struggle for freedom without reservation. The tension between these two often contradictory levels of writing—the mythic and the political—is the defining characteristic of the novel. As will be seen, this tension becomes both a source of strength as well as a weakness to the narrative. On the one hand, it enhances its sheer readability as a story, and on the other, it blurs readers' understanding of the realities of the Indian Independence Struggle.

Although *Kanthapura* was originally written in English, it is as good as a Kannada book translated into English literally. Rao has painted the most accurate picture of rural life of India during pre-Independence era. It is accurate and the nuances contained can be read but not felt or understood. If we read the novel for nuances, then we are reading the lyrics of a song but not listening to the song; we are reading descriptions of a painting without actually seeing the painting.

> The day dawned over the Ghats, the day rose over the Blue Mountain and, churning through the grey, rapt valleys, swirled up and swam across the whole air. The day rose into the air and with it rose the dust of the morning, and the carts began to creak round the bulging rocks and the coppery peaks, and the sun fell into the river and pierced it to the pebbles, while the carts of the Kanthapura Fair...rolled...around the Kenchamma Hill.... (56)

A non-Indian finds it difficult to make any sense of the novel. The novel at best gives us glimpses of things such as the way people in rural India conversed among themselves, their demeanour, disposition, mindset, social system, caste system, the state of widows in a society, the place of God in society, etc. Such a novel would, of course, deeply interest the westerners who cannot stop being fascinated by the rural life, buffaloes on roads, hungry children, customs and traditions of India.

Rao focuses on two individual leaders and their beliefs; the actual and the mythicized figure of Gandhi, and his transmutation into Moorthy, the saintly hero of the novel. As the movement reaches Kanthapura, young Moorthy, son of a Brahmin woman, Narasamma, takes up the responsibility of spreading Gandhi's message. He brings about cultural awakening among the villages by organizing *harikathas*. By a subtle subversion the *harikatha* is turned into an allegory of India's struggle for freedom wherein the Gandhian saga is inscribed. Moorthy visits the city, and returns a "Gandhi man". He has become a spokesman for Gandhi, by submitting to his beliefs and attitudes. The villagers describe him as "our own Gandhi", though he has never met Gandhi. He has only seen him in a "vision" addressing a public meeting with himself pushing his way through the crowd and joining the band of volunteers and receiving inspiration by a touch of Gandhi's hand. This enables Rao to turn the historical moment into a visionary experience, and opens a space for the possibility of assumed politics.

Moorthy preaches and practises *ahimsa,* the hallmark of Gandhi's appeal to the public, and evokes an overwhelming response among the villagers who unite in common cause, ready to break the British laws, picket toddy shops, and fight against social evils like untouchability. Moorthy has several sympathetic souls with him: Rangamma, the kind lady and a patron for *harikatha* celebrations, Ratna, the young widowed daughter of Kamalamma, Rangamma's sister, Patel Range Gowda, the Revenue Collector, and others. But there are also sceptics, like the foul mouthed Venkamma. His own mother is much concerned about Moorthy's mixing with the low caste pariahs. Indeed, when someone spreads the rumour that the Swami—the priest; upholder of dharma, has threatened the villagers with excommunication if Moorthy continues to go around with the pariahs, Narsaamma is terribly upset; she sobs and shivers and soon dies.

Moorthy has to resist orthodoxy at the social level, and at the political level he has to fight the British authority symbolized by the Skeffington Coffee Estate and the Police Inspector, Bade Khan, who is out to suppress any undercurrent of Gandhian Movement in Kanthapura. Moorthy's efforts bear fruit and the village changes. Rao is careful to point out that the transformation occurs through a complex dynamism negotiated through tradition and change, as the village affiliates itself to wider nationalistic cause.

The British find their ally in Swami, who supports them as upholders of dharma and is rewarded with "twelve hundred acres of wet land" by the Government. Meanwhile, Moorthy's message spreads far and wide and several private temples are thrown open to the untouchables. Rao does not marginalize the role of women in the Freedom Movement and highlights their individual contributions. Rangamma and Ratna form women volunteer groups despite opposition from the orthodox. Moorthy and his volunteers closely monitor the Mahatma's Dandi March and enact their own Satyagraha in Kanthapura. Their march is opposed by the police who beat them up mercilessly. The police warn them to be loyal to the British Government, but the people say they know only the Government of the Mahatma. Moorthy and several others are arrested. As a result of the police atrocities the entire village is desolate and, in the end, there remains neither man nor mosquito in Kanthapura.

Kanthapura becomes an enchanting story of how the Independence movement becomes a tragic reality in a tiny and secluded village in South India. It depicts the village life, their beliefs, their rituals in a lucid and transparent manner. It illustrates very simple happenings of a village in a lively manner. In his writing a clear picture of villagers becomes prominent. In his village religion imparted through discourses and *poojas* keeps alive in the natives a sense of presence of God. In the whole story a serenity flows in a simple harmonic motion which makes the story worth-reading.

The work was highly praised by E.M. Forster, whose masterwork, *A Passage to India* (1924), criticized British imperialism. However, Rao's India is not a certain geographical or historical entity, but more of a philosophical concept and a symbol of spiritual calling. Like Nabokov, Rao used the metaphor of the chess game to animate philosophical and psychological ideas. In the story Sivaram Sastri, an Indian mathematician in Paris, meets Proust, and recounts his love affairs and friendships. Rao has confessed: "I am no scholar. I am a creative writer. I love to play with ideas. It is like a chess game with horses, elephants, chamberlains and kings which might fight with one another. The game is not for winning. It is for rasa-delight" (Assisi).

Benedict Anderson has argued that novel is partly responsible for a community to imagine itself as a nation. The novels written in nineteenth century and even beyond in India may be used to support this claim. While in *Kanthapura*, the action is restricted to the village itself with none of the characters venturing too far out, yet the village is not insulated against the happenings in other places. In fact, the stimulation for action is not local. The grand events that form the focal points of the novel take place in response to events elsewhere—Lahore, Bengal, Gujarat, etc. The village community moves from an insulated identity towards a national identity. In one sense, *Kanthapura* chronicles the formation of a national identity within a remote village. This thematic is also supported by the manner in which the village becomes a kind of a microcosm of the nation.

The process of imagining a community—of imagining nationhood—also underlines the homogenising tendency of nationalism. The congress workers, who so vehemently are 'swadeshi' and give up anything foreign, unwittingly embrace the European model of nation. This notion requires a nation state to have a singular form. A nation is a community of people who have a common language, etc. Thus in Kanthapura, Congressmen including Moorthy follow the same model of the nation-state. Sankaru epitomises this: his insistence on speaking Hindi even to his mother instead of the local language Kannada; his fanatic resistance to the use of English and so on. This conception of the nation informs that of everyone: e.g. the narrator visualises

Moorthy (when in prison) to be wearing *kurta pyjama* instead of *dhoti.* The Hindi teacher is not from any Hindi speaking region but a Malayali (Surya Menon). Thus, the very conception of 'Nation', which is conceived after the European model of the nation-state, undermines the 'Swadeshi' spirit of nationalism. Any pure form of nationhood untouched by colonialism is seriously questioned.

Another problem arises when this novel is read as a record of a nation-in-the-making. It would seem to exemplify Jameson's argument that third world literature is necessarily a national allegory. When we keep in mind that Benedict Anderson's thesis about the emergence of nation-state is a work on the emergence of nation-state in Europe, Jameson's argument seems to put third world literature in the past of European literature. This only re-enacts the familiar theme that comes across in the colonialist historiography of Indian nationalism: that Indian nationalism is a learning process as has been pointed out by Ranjit Guha. This particular view of nationalism characterizes Indian nationalism as a response to the stimulus of colonial administration. The view of the history of the colonised society as a march towards the teleological goal of becoming ultimately 'Europe' places them always at a past time in relation to the coloniser's present time. The denial of coevalness of time is a necessity in the discourse of colonialism.

This view of India's history being bound to Europe takes us to Dipesh Chakravarthy's thesis that as far as history as a discourse is concerned, Europe remains the sovereign theoretical subject of all histories, including the one we call Indian. Further, he says, as opposed to other narratives of self and community, history is the meta-narrative that looks to the state/citizen bind as the ultimate construction of sociality. Other constructions of self and community speak an anti-historical consciousness. With modernity, history becomes the site where the struggle goes on to appropriate other collocations of memory. In *Kanthapura*, the narrative in the beginning reflects an ahistorical consciousness. The description of the village life is as a timeless continuum in the form of *sthala-purana* or *harikatha* wherein nationalist figures become mythical, whereas, colonialism disrupts the narratives of the community and introduces 'history.' In as far as the change in the narrative technique is concerned which becomes more linear while narrating the Freedom Struggle in Kanthapura, history really begins with Europe inhabiting the village. This is most clearly suggested in the loss of mythicizing tendency of the narrative in the later part when the arrival of newspapers, novels and pamphlets has exposed the first person narrator to techniques of historicizing.

This whole reading of the novel harps back upon the exchange between the coloniser and the colonised. The interesting insights offered by the novel are about the immense complications and violence that attend the arrival of colonial modernity in India. The novel highlights with no subtlety the collusion between colonialism and Brahmanism. The manner in which Moorthy becomes an outcaste in the Brahmin quarters with his campaign against untouchability indicates the tension between Brahmanism and nationalism. For Brahmanism, the colonial ruler is not the enemy but Gandhi's anti-untouchable movement is. The collusion between Brahmanism and colonialism is suggested through the alliance between Bhatta, Bade Khan the policeman and the Sahib of the Estate. Swami, who is waging a war against 'caste pollution due to this pariah business,' sees British rulers as protectors of the ancient ways of Dharma. Swami receives a large amount from the government as Rajadakshina and is promised that he would receive moral and material support in his war against caste pollution.

Moorthy's politics in the village aims at assimilating the lower castes into the nationalist movement. This may also operate as a move towards containment. For example, the discourse of nationalism meets the discourse of religion at different levels in the novel. While Bhatta, Swami and their followers (who have often material motives such as Venkamma) resist Gandhism in the name of religion, in *Kanthapura*, the nationalists increasingly employ the religious discourse and customs and symbols for nationalist purposes. Religious resources are mobilised for the politicisation of the people. But the customs, rituals and symbols that become tools of nationalist mobilisation are primarily Brahminic: *arthi, puja*, conches, bells, Vedanta, *bhajan,* etc. They do not include the cultural practices of the lower castes though their participation is prominent.

Kanthapura enacts some of the motifs of postcolonialism. Rao critiques the simple position that the discourse of colonialism instituted a notion of the natural superiority of the colonising race and this was internalised by the colonized. The novel problematizes viewing colonial modernity as having had a liberating impact on the Indian society. The problematising potential of the novel extends to anti-colonial nationalism too.

Works Cited

Anderson, Benedict. *Imagined Communities: Reflections on the Origin and Spread of Nationalism* (revised and enlarged edition). London: Verso, 1991. Print.

Assisi, Francis C. *Breathing India in America: A Tribute to Raja Rao*, retrieved at www.indolink.com. Web.

Book Review by Santha Rama Rau, *New York Times*, 1964, retrieved at www.nytimes.com/2006/07/15/arts/15rao.html. Web.

Chakravarthy, Dipesh. *Provincialising Europe*. New Delhi: Oxford UP, 2001. Print.

Forster, E.M. quoted by T.J. Abraham. "Flawed Gandhism or Hindu Fundamentalism? No Cheers to Kanthapura," *Indian Literature*. 47.4 (July-August 2003). Print.

Guha, Ranajit, *A Subaltern Studies Reader*. Minneapolis: University of Minneapolis Press, 1997. Print.

Rao, Raja. *Kanthapura*. Madras: Oxford UP, 1974. Page numbers refer to this edition. Print.

Sethi, Rumina. *Myths of the Nation*. USA: Oxford UP, 1999. Print.

17

Anti-Hero in Upamanyu Chatterjee's *English, August: An Indian Story*

Alapati Rama Naga Hanuman

Upamanyu Chatterjee has emerged as one of the most compelling new voices in the domain of Indian novel in English. His debut novel *English, August: An Indian Story* is a fascinating metaphor of contemporary English educated Indian urban youth's failed quest for self-realization. The novel can be read at two levels. On the surface level, this novel is a commentary on the administrative services of India: the corruption in high bureaucratic places, high-handedness, inefficiency, oppressive routine of the system, utter indifference of the administration to the eradication of poverty and social evils, acute class and rank consciousness among the IAS hierarchy, and the little snobberies and petty jealousies of the so-called public servants—all these form the surface texture of this novel.

But at the deeper level, it is a frank discussion of the predicament in which an intelligent and educated modern youth finds himself. There is a hovering sense of dislocation from all traditions and conventions which he finds meaningless. The novel describes a journey, sometimes pathetic, sometimes humorous, and even ridiculous—a Journey from rootlessness to attempted but failed maturity, a struggle to come to terms with oneself. The novel, at the end, gives a feeble impression of success in the attempt at maturity by experience, but its sequel *The Mammaries of the Welfare State* (2000) does loudly proclaim that even after experiences of almost a decade, Agastya Sen, who likes to be called August by his friends, does not change. He fails to gain maturity of spirit because he is not capable of any positive change. He is powerless in action; his only power lies in fantasy. He is an antihero because he lacks the usual qualities associated with heroism. He is an average man, something of a bungler. We know that the term anti-hero refers to the small, good-hearted rebel protesting against his society with clownish gestures.

The post-1950 English novelists repeatedly presented antiheroes in their fiction as protagonists. The crux of anti-heroism lies in the fact that its representative is not clear about what is precisely wrong with his society, always feeling that it is full of humbug and deception. A closer study of the novel *English, August: An Indian Story* reveals that through his antiheroic protagonist, Chatterjee gives the message that today's English educated Indian urban youth, steeped in careerism, is a victim of the breakdown of meaningful communication and relationship with his society. There is no assurance here that outward action reveals any significant fact about the doer, nor is any claim that the public gestures provided by society can achieve any real communication between individuals. It is remarkable that the antiheroic protagonist represents his antiheroic milieu. As Thorslev writes 'The hero gives one the broader, and deeper perspective of the spirit of the age which he represents' (Thorslev 20).

Robert E. Spiller in his much discussed article titled "Literary History" posits the idea of 'the peak of a literary movement' (Spiller 55-68) represented by literary production of a single or closely related kind in a comparatively short period of time and space. The decade of 1980s, in the context of Indian fiction in English, marks just such a peak. What we may call the common thread binding them all is the individual at the centre, struggling against the ugliness of life and the socio-political system. His sensibility is modern; he knows the provisional quality of life deviod of the old ideals. He is insecure, anxious, tense and sceptical. He sits on the edge of the world, waiting to be thrown into the painful vortex of agonising experiences because of the tremendous power of the political systems which he belongs to.

Agastya Sen, the antiheroic protagonist of the novel *English, August: An Indian Story,* is a victim of the bureaucratic system he comes to join. Coupled with it is his selfish careerism which again attests to the excessive power exercised by an impersonal culture of comfort-lovingness and material advancement in life. As against that, the protagonists of the novels of authors like Raja Rao and R.K. Narayan had belonged to a secure world where eternal reality stood by to ultimately dominate the temporary vicissitudes of life. But what one finds in *English, August* is the human beings buffeted helplessly by the unfeeling social world which they encounter. These novels lack the staidness, solemnity and self-consciousness that once characterised the Indian English novel. This reflects the changes which have come about in the life of Indians. They are uninhibited; they are neither idealistic nor sentimental. They express the deep urge of the protagonist to speak out, unfettered by restraints. The shaking off of the traditional hiccups about materialistic enjoyment marks the life of the period of 1980s of which Upamanyu Chatterjee's Agastya Sen is a prominent representative. Spiller rightly thinks that fiction represents 'the controlling temper and ideas of (its) time and place' (Spiller 56). Meenakshi Mukherjee, the noted Indian English critic, in her *Twice-Born Fiction* argues in the same vein that the 1930s Indian English novels show concern with national and social problems, and 1960s is preoccupied with the individual's quest for a personal meaning in life. One can proceed into the chronology and argue in tandem that the decade of 1980s represents the individual's predicament of finding himself painfully close to losing his freedom.

The novel *English, August*: *An Indian Story* reflects, through the characters of Agastya Sen, Dhrubo, Madan, Govind, etc. the image of that India which sees cities as the heaven where her rising aspirations will find fulfilment. This is the India of the young which is at the centre of the creative efforts of Upamanyu Chatterjee whose chief concern is to hold a mirror up to this class. It is impatient, mobile, far more willing to break out of the confines of tradition in its search for opportunities to make good. Fewer of Indians today live in joint families and many more women, traditionally kept out of the labour market, work in a variety of occupations. Agastya's disregard for the advice of his father reveals an accentuated version of the crumbling structure of the institution of the Indian family. Likewise, the situation of Agastya's girlfriend Neera reflects the liberation of the Indian urban woman.

In an attempt to highlight the rootedness in the time of creation of the Indian English novels of the 1980s, a critic rightly remarks that 'Politics—national and international—is their most important theme, and the displaced, marginal modern man their favourite protagonist' (Kirpal xvi). The novel *English, August: An Indian Story,* with its antiheroic protagonist Agastya Sen, fits in quite well with this assessment, as this work is a fine representative creative document of that decade. In this novel politics is particularised in its power over the individual in the form of the insensitive and corrupt bureaucracy. Agastya Sen joins it as a highly placed official. Through the corrupt and depraved bureaucracy is cogently reflected that moment in the Indian history when the relationship between the government and the people at large gets ruptured and this rupture tragically tilts against the latter. Repression and insensitivity become the hallmarks of the politico-bureaucratic system. The purpose of public service, formally enshrined in the structure of the bureaucracy becomes an empty slogan devoid of any human touch. It turns into a world of babudom which drowns in a deluge of forms and files. Here one finds an obscure hierarchy of officialdom making it impossible ever to find the man authorized to deal with a particular case. Here officials work overtime and yet gets nowhere. Numberless interviews take place but never reaching to the situation which can be said to be to the point. In fact, the readers who are in the know of the way the Indian bureaucracy operates itself, feel that it is an excruciatingly familiar world, but reproduced by a creative intelligence which turns the tale of the insipid bureaucracy into a work of highly readable fiction. The theme of the Indian bureaucracy dehumanising its members is distinctly visible in the work of Upamanyu Chatterjee. It fascinates him because he was compelled to write a sequel *The Mammaries of the Welfare State* in order to give a fuller treatment to the theme. On being asked about his novel being autobiographical (we know that the author is a serving IAS officer) he replied significantly, 'That depends on what you mean by autobiography. But some of it is certainly my own experience, and there is a large part that has been inspired by the things that I have been told, read about, etc.' (Chatterjee 1). It shows that in grappling with an impersonal theme like the bureaucracy, the novelist does not depend on his personal experiences only, though he is a part of the higher echelon of it. He keeps himself open and receptive to the views and assessments of others.

What is obvious is that at the thematic centre of the twin novels lies the predicament of their protagonist. It is his antiheroic life which forms the hub of the entire sprawl of the novels. It can be said that the novel *English, August* is a close link in the chain of those artistic works of the 1980s which concern themselves with the protagonist's inability to communicate. This inability to communicate is a reflection of the impotence they suffer from in the face of the power of the system they belong to. It is a feeling, on the part of the antiheroes like Agastya Sen that they are impotent vis-a-vis the bureaucratic world they do not want to live in. It is a crippling despair at having lost to forces too powerful to combat. They are little men lost in the web of petty interests and concerns. They prove the point that the hero, as once understood in classical literature, has disappeared from modern realistic literature, conspicuously so from the literature which has dominated the literary world since the middle half of the last century. His place has been taken by the entity popularly called the antihero who is obverse of the image of the hero. It is the antihero who dominates the novel; he is at the centre of the actions that take place in the novel. Taking the two novels *English, August* and *The Mammaries* as a single corpus devoted to the exploration of the antiheroic protagonist and his morally grey, airless and cheerless world, the novelist remarks, 'According to me, Agastya Sen is the tapeworm...the linking factor in the book' (Chatterjee). It is sufficient to prove the point that though on the surface it is the cold impersonal world of the outward politics which seems to be visible all over, the core of the novel is constituted by the sufferings and agony of the antihero, the agony sometimes felt but often remaining unfelt. This dimension represents the modern mind, seemingly self-sufficient, intelligent, sceptical and splendidly trained through modern education.

All Agastya Sen does is to envy in utter incomprehension the easy-going, free of care approach to life evinced by those people who are not so educated and rich. He does not understand the existential fact that happiness comes through the door of the commitment to a purpose, not from being highly placed in the bureaucratic hierarchy or having much wealth. But in one corner of his mind he feels envious of those who are happy, but finds himself simultaneously restrained from falling to an 'inappropriate' level. The following authorial comment sums up his plight he finds himself in when coming face to face with an ordinary salesman of medicines in his doctor friend's clinic: 'He was suddenly ashamed of himself, looking at the salesman, talking about medicines for twelve hours a day; his restlessness seemed awfully frivolous. The salesman made him feel both eerie and guilty—be happy you are not him, and how dare you behave so cheaply when you have the chance not to be him' (224). Likewise, in the remote backward village which he visits as a government official, the tribal simplicity and bravery in the face of hardships of life 'make him feel, yet again, absurd, or guilty. They irritated him, almost to the point of anger;...' (259).

The inability to comprehend makes communication impossible. Agastya Sen is a person who understands neither himself nor the world and the people around him. He is alienated from everyone he is required to deal with. He cannot connect himself with anyone at a meaningful level of relationship. In fact, he is not one person, but plays the roles of different persons at different places and situations. His personality reflects that class of anglicised Indian urban youth who, owing to their educational training, have become aliens in their own land. They are the people who have been unhinged from their roots and, consequently, rendered unhappy and restless. This unhappiness and restlessness is born out of the unrestrained desire for materialistic progress which has taken the youth under its grip, depriving them of all moving ideals of morality and service. In their inexorable thrust for material advancement they philosophise that in the world '...there is nothing such as absolute honesty, there are only degrees of dishonesty' (138). It vividly reflects the amoral temper of the times.

It is not without significance that Agastya Sen, despite being a student of English literature, decides to follow the fashion of the prevailing societal preference for the job in the Indian Administrative Service. The concept of anti-hero as we find in Chatterjee's *English, August: An Indian Story* reflects very sharply on the pathological careerism of modern Indian youth. This careerism appears basically as a feudal preference for positions of power and control over those compatriots who are ill-fated to live a life of dependence on the *mai-baap* style of administrative dispensation by the government machinery. The ideals of public service and commitment to duty are things as unimaginable as fish on a metalled road. In fact, the bureaucratic world, as very satirically portrayed in this novel, is an outward extension of the anti-heroic restless predicament of the rootless and alienated psyche of those who have happened to occupy coveted chairs. This predicament manifests itself in mutual jealousy among the officers, petty acts of snobbishness, their urge for exploitation of their subordinates, and their wives' desire to flaunt the status of their husbands. It all appears as if after the white sahibs departed for their homes the brown sahibs filled their places. Agastya's insights into the IAS find an echo in every Indian heart acquainted with this legacy of the Raj:

> District administration in India is largely a British creation, like the railways and the English language, another complex and unwieldy bequest of the Raj. But Indianization (of a method of administration, or of a language) is integral to the Indian story. Before 1947 the Collector was almost inaccessible to the people; now he keeps open house..., even though he still exhibits old accoutrements (but now Indianized) of importance—the flashing orange on the 'roof of the car, the passes for the first row at the sitar recital, which will not start until he arrives and for which he will not arrive until he has ensured by telephone that everyone else who has been invited has arrived first. In Madna, as in all of India,

> one's importance as an official could be gauged by how long one could keep a concert (to which one was invited) waiting. (10)

English, August: An Indian Story as an imaginative document maps in some starkly naturalistic detail the decline that occurred in the IAS with the passage of time. The Service expected to be selfless became a vehicle for self-aggrandizement on the part of those who happened to man it. The Collector of Madna, Srivastava, his predecessor, Mr. Antony, the Superintendent of Police, Kumar, and other officers, Bajaj and Menon—all together present, through their words and actions, an image of Indian 'steel frame' which has rotten to the roots. One charge made against this novel is that it 'seems to be competing with the Taluka office for tedium, documentary with relentless accuracy of every single syllable of the conversation of the self-satisfied and uninteresting bureaucrats who flock its pages' (Rao 79). This charge is valid, but only at the superficial level. It is through the lived lives of 'the self-satisfied and uninteresting bureaucrats' that the real core of the anti-heroic banality of modern Indian youth and life comes out in the novel.

Works Cited

Chatterjee, Upmanyu. *English, August: An Indian Story.* London: Faber and Faber, 1988. Print.

———. In Interview. *India Today*. (December 7, 2000). Print.

Kripal, Vinay. Introduction. *The New Indian Novel in English: A Study of the 1980s*. Delhi: Allied Publishers, 1990. Print.

Mukherjee, Meenakshi. "The Intellectual in a State of 'Anomy': Achebe's *No Longer at Ease* and Chatterjee's *English, August: An Indian Story*", *New Quest*. 92. (March-April, 1992). 109-11. Print.

Rao, Vimala Rama. Rev. of *English, August: An Indian Story*. *The Literary Criterion*. 27. 4 (1992). 78-79. Print.

Spiller, Robert E. "Literary History", James Thorpe (ed). *The Aims and Methods of Scholarship in Modern Languages and Literature*. New York: MAL, 1970. Print.

Thorslev, P.L. *The Byronic Hero: The Types and Prototypes*. Minneapolis: Univ. of Minnesota P, 1962. Print.

18

To Be Is To Connect: Harmony and Humanist Vision in Amitav Ghosh's *In An Antique Land*

K. Damodar Rao

In An Antique Land takes off from where *The Shadow Lines* has concluded. The veiled permeation of harmony carefully orchestrated in the form of distressing fragmentation, religious divide, communal riots and splintered souls in *The Shadow Lines* gives way to unbridled celebration of cross-cultural euphoria, intense internationalism in *In An Antique Land*. In *The Shadow Lines*, the narrator-protagonist, filled as he is with idealism and exuberant view of life juxtaposes people and lives from diverse places—Calcutta, Dhaka, London and weaves together an intricate, unified pattern. The connecting principle is the narrator's streak of humanism that binds the diverse backgrounds together. The same thrusting, pulsating humanist vision is in evidence in the novel, *In An Antique Land* in a singular, unique and assertive fashion; that is, without constrictions and boundaries. Ghosh's characters from *The Circle of Reason* days cross the boundary lines quite felicitously travelling across continents while the author jubilantly celebrates the connections in civilizations, similarities in beliefs and customs, castigates the oppressive interventions and colonial incursions. As Ramachandra Guha points out, there is a strong thematic unity to Ghosh's *oeuvre*. The polemic against the nation-state is one of the strains which carries forward the moral agenda of his novels. Guha says: "He (Ghosh) relentlessly questions the 'shadow lines' that divide human beings by nation, class, culture or religion; it is no accident that all his books move back and forth across time and across continents" (451). Here in this novel, he juxtaposes people, places, histories and values of two ancient civilizations, India and Egypt, and moves freely cutting across continents—Egypt, London, the United States, The Gulf, and Mangalore.

Ghosh's fiction erases artificial boundaries, man-made shadow lines as if in assertion of the famous Sanskrit saying, *Vasudhiaka kutumbam* (all the people on the earth are one family). His work bears testimony to intellectual de-compartmentalisation facilitating the disciplines of thought and different branches of human knowledge to coalesce in rendering a note of panegyric to humanity and freedom. Ghosh comments on his fiction: "My fiction has always been about places that are states in the process of coming unmade, or communities coming unmade or remaking themselves in many ways" (Ghosh 2002: 40). An important feature of Ghosh's *oeuvre* is his anti-colonial, anti-hegemonic stand. Claire Chambers, while pointing out the chief concerns of Ghosh observes: "At the heart of Ghosh's corpus is the contention that knowledge is produced by structures of dominance, particularly the military, economic, and epistemic strategies of colonialism. His main focus is the impact that Western paradigms of knowledge have had and continue to have on India" (Chambers 1).

In An Antique Land is an astonishingly crafted, marvelously exciting work. Anna Sujatha Mathai's elation when she observes, "Not since I read A.K. Ramanujan's *Speaking of Siva* some years ago have I read a book so intellectually thrilling, so compelling, so revealing as Ghosh's *In An Antique Land*" (Mathai 32) has been shared by many. The work is part-ethnography, part-anthropology, fictional invention, documentation, autobiography, a chronicle and a travelogue; 'genre-confounding' (Mukul Kesavan 2002: 1) is a term frequently used to describe the book. It is a subversion of history, master narratives, the form of narrative itself.

Subversion is at the core of Ghosh's fiction. Material from three of the essays, "The Imam and the Indian", "An Egyptian in Baghdad" and "The Slave of MS.H.6" included in *The Imam and the Indian*, as well as his doctoral thesis is incorporated in the book. Ghosh attests when he says the book is "pure history with no trace of fiction in it" (2002: 24). As the author assumes the role of an ethnographer and enthusiastically revels in gathering information about minute details of cultural manifestations across geographical distances while transforming it into fictional account, the authorial vision shuns distinctions between literary genres, academic disciplines and even the critical tools of appreciation. As a result, a multi-genric novel manifests that defies artificial frontiers unfolding an overarching humanism, harmony and wholeness. Ramachandra Guha observes: "*In An Antique Land* is a marvelous exemplification of the creative trespassing across scholarly boundaries and across the line between what is ostensibly 'fact' and what merely 'fiction'" (451). James Clifford perceives the work as a type of "new" cultural retrieval: "In weaving together his modern and medieval histories, Ghosh crosses the borders of ethnographic writing, particularly those shared with the novel and travel literature" (Clifford 27).

Ghosh as researcher occupies centre stage in the book and from his viewpoint the proceedings of the narrative are unfolded. In fact, there are three parallel narratives in the book. The core action of the novel revolves around Ghosh's own experiences as anthropologist working for a DPhil at Oxford. This narrative is interrupted by and intertwined with Ghosh's stay in Egypt studying the lives of the fellaheen of Latafia and Nashaway. These two narratives are further intercepted by the protagonist's attempts to establish the identity of an Indian slave catalogued as 'Number MS H. 6' in the University Library at Jerusalem. The retrieval of the identity of the slave reads like a gripping mystery drama, with the author finally succeeding in figuring out his identity through many historical evidences and connecting clues.

Although the author repeatedly said that he had no truck with the term 'postcolonial', "the content of his writing does irresistibly recall postcolonial literary productions" (Prasad 2007: 51). The retrieval of the name of a forgotten entity, of a marginalized slave in this instance, the many intersecting narratives crisscrossing past and present and geographical boundaries offer glimpses of the postcolonial and the postmodern in the subversive agenda of the author. In fact, the work is a subversion of postmodernity itself what with its superimposition on the medieval world he portrays. He attempts to re-create "a world of accommodations" which he believes "in some tiny measure, still retrievable" (Ghosh 1992: 237). He considers colonial intervention as a kind of rupture to humanist continuity: "Indeed, if one looks carefully at Ghosh's medieval construction one can see that his medieval pre-modern world has all the hallmarks of "*post*-modernity": syncretism, non-territoriality, multi-lingualism, hybridity, difference. Ghosh's restoration of this ruptured human continuity thus enacts a kind of historical detour which by-passes modernity completely, in effect wiping it out of history" (Mondal 31). Humanism and secularism might have been new to the west as the constructs of modernism at the turn of the twentieth century, but as a way of life the people of India and Egypt have experienced it for many centuries. Ghosh's vision scrupulously avoids the regimentation of Western concepts and offers a position that is all-inclusive which could be traced back to ancient Indian thought and South Asian cultural mores. His humanism and secularism do not proffer exclusions as in the Western context, but is all-embracing as is depicted in the medieval society of India and Egypt in this narrative. It is this superimposition of the pre-modern values over the postmodern and the postcolonial that makes his vision a diachronic, multicultural and pluralistic one.

Ghosh's humanism is the axis on which these disparate, multiple vantage points balance themselves. In this work, he presents two medieval societies which celebrated the ideals of oneness of harmony in practice. The very concepts sound eloquent in the modern context, more in theory than in practice. A telling juxtaposition in the novel sums up the chief concerns of the author. When his Egyptian friend, Zaghoul wonders whether he can reach Amitav's country by donkey, an image of visas, obstacles, and the war that stretched from Iraq to Afghanisthan flashes across his mind. But in twelfth century, the novel depicts, how a Jewish trader Abraham Ben Yiju started his journey from Tunisia, reached Mangalore coast, settled there for many years acquiring a Nair wife, Ashu, and a Tulu-speaking low caste slave, Bomma. The counterpointing of journey motif set in different time frames reveals that human relationships were cordial and harmonious in the twelfth century and the shadow lines have only grown murkier in the twentieth century. What is significant to note is the ease with which the narrator-protagonist moves between these time-frames "in splendid disregard for the conventions of academic history—where the time is, above all, continuous" (Guha 451).

The narrator-researcher-protagonist's journey itself is significant in many ways. With remarkable enthusiasm the researcher moves from the libraries of the Oxford to the Jewish Geniza; from the small dusty Egyptian villages where the narrator watches in wonderment the transformation that catapults innocent farmers, labourers into the twentieth century, to the American Libraries. In the process, the journey loses its physical contours, and becomes a spiritual discovery, a metaphor for connectedness. The moments of fulfillment are embedded in the small connections, "ironies of seemingly disparate cultures actually shaping and embodying the distant, rejected, unknown element" (Mathai 32).

The sense of fulfilment is complete with the reconstruction of the identity of the forgotten slave reaching its logical conclusion. The narrator draws illuminating links that bind those different religions, places, and cultures together. The concept of the slavery, in this part of the world, was also different from slavery as it came to be known "after the European colonial expansion of the sixteenth century" (Ghosh 259-60). Ghosh says:

> In the lifetime of Bomma and Ben Yiju, servitude was a part of a very flexible set of hierarchies and it often followed a logic completely contrary to that which modern expectations suggest. In the Middle East and northern India, for instance, slavery was the principal means of recruitment into some of the most privileged sectors of the army and the bureaucracy. For those who made their way up through that route, 'slavery' was thus

often a kind of career opening, a way of gaining entry into the highest levels of government. (260)

Among the Jewish merchants of medieval Cairo as well as with many tribes in Africa, slaves were sometimes gradually incorporated into their masters' households and came to be counted as members of their families. "Equally, in some vocations, the lines of demarcations between apprentice, disciple and bondsman were so thin as to be invisible" (Ghosh 260).

Ghosh goes on to find similar connections in medieval Indian mores. He discovers that the name of the slave, Bomma, is derived not from the Brahma of the Sanskritic pantheon, but from the much earlier Tulu deity, Berme or Bermeru, one of the Bhuta-spirits of Tuluva pantheon, absorbed by the all-inclusive Sanskritic incarnations of the later period. At the highest level this bond between master and servant assumes a spiritual dimension. In South India, "amongst the pietiest and fiercely egalitarian Vachanakara saint-poets of Bomma's own lifetime, for example, slavery was often used as an image to represent the devotees's quest for God" (Ghosh 260). In the poetry of the vachanakaras, poets became their Lord's servants and lovers. In their poetry slavery became the paradoxical embodiment of perfect freedom. The connections do not stop here. Ghosh goes on to find similarities in other cultures such as Sufism and Judaism.

The history-fiction interface in Ghosh's work calls into question the record of historical knowledge. As one critic points out, Ghosh, "while calling into question the 'truth' of historical knowledge, links the production of knowledge to the expansion of European colonialism; History, therefore, is revealed to be the history of appropriation" (Mondal 20). The book, in fact, begins with the Crusades and ends with the Gulf War. Once colonization started its frenzied march, it was no longer possible to speak "of things that were right, or good, or willed by God" but thrive on "the ascending ladder of Development..." and a language of "guns and tanks and bombs" (237). In addition, the vandalism of the Geniza by the Europeans betrays the insensitivity of the imperialists to the values and treasures of the East. The Geniza was the archive of the Synagogue which Ben Yiju attended in the early eleventh century and the letters referring to Bomma were lodged. The Geniza was used as a storehouse where writings containing the name of God were kept for fear of desecration. Ghosh's search for the identity of the subaltern brings him there and takes pride in the fact that it held the "greatest single collection of medieval documents ever discovered" (59). But inside there was only absence, as the documents have long since been moved. The dispersal of the Geniza material during the late nineteenth century under the impact of the European scholarship coincides with the age of high imperialism. By far the largest acquisition of the Geniza material was made by Soloman Schechter, a Reader in Cambridge University. It is no coincidence that of the many works mentioned in the 25-odd page notes appended at the end of the narrative there is not a single work by a European scholar that Ghosh acknowledges. The rupture of the postcolonial and the postmodern is in evidence in many such instances of Ghosh's *oeuvre*.

Ghosh's subversion of historical knowledge is also evident in his attempts at locating the tiny threads and positing them in a larger framework. The author marvels at the similarity of beliefs, myths and customs of the two ancient civilizations of Egypt and India. The Egyptian legend Sidi Abu Kanaka's grave is considered holy by their people. As it lay in the way of a canal being built, the authorities try to remove it; but it is in vain as all the modern machinery fails to dig it out. When the narrator is taken round a Bhuta temple he is told how bulldozers failed to break through the Bhuta shrine when engineers tried to build a road connecting Mangalore city to the port. The similarities are only striking.

The similarity of the past and present in long distances of old civilizations is a kind of revelation of the workings of cultures far removed from one another. The author goes to Egypt again and pays a visit to the tomb of Sidi Abu Hasira at Damanhour. When asked about his identity by an officer the narrator tells that he is neither Jewish, nor Muslim, nor Christian, he gets suspicious and takes him to the higher-ups. The papers are in order but what raises their suspicion was why he was there in the first place near the tomb of a Jewish saint in Egypt. The narrator thinks of telling him the story of Bomma and Ben Yiju but desists from it as he thinks there is nothing in his world that connects to his story—"the remains of those small, indistinguishable, intertwined histories, Indian and Egyptian, Muslim and Jewish, Hindu and Muslim, had been partitioned long ago" (339). A telling comment on the divisive nature of our times which the narrative strives to set right by many pointers in the directions of unity, connectedness, harmony, and cultural amity that humanity could still thrive upon.

Works Cited

Chambers, Claire. "Anthropology as Cultural Translation: Amitav Ghosh's *In An Antique Land.*" *Postcolonial Text.* 2. 3 (2006). 1-19. Print.

Clifford, James. "Looking for Bomma." *London Review of Books.* (24 March, 1994). Print.

Ghosh, Amitav. *In An Antique Land.* New Delhi: Ravi Dayal, 1992. Print.

———. "The System of Nation-state is under Strain." *Outlook* (August 19, 2002). 40-41. Print.

———. "At Home in the World International Festival of Indian Literature." *The Book Review.* 26. 4 (2002). 23-25. Print.

Guha, Ramachandra. "Where Fact Crosses Fiction." *Economic and Political Weekly.* (March 13, 1993). 451-52. Print.

Kesavan, Mukul. "The Written World." *The Hindu Literary Review.* Sunday (August 4, 2002). 1. Print.

Mathai, Anna Sujatha. "Exploring Humanist Vision." *The Book Review* (May 1993). 32. Print.

Mondal, Anshuman A. "Allegories of Identity: "Postmodern" Anxiety and "Postcolonial" Ambivalence in Amitav Ghosh's *In An Antique Land* and *The Shadow Lines.*" *Journal of Commonwealth Literature* 38. 3 (2003). 19-36. Print.

Prasad, Murari. "Transcending the Postcolonial: Amitav Ghosh's *In An Antique Land.*" *The Literary Criterion.* XLII. 2 (2007). 51-61. Print.

19

Plurality and Hybridity in Salman Rushdie's *The Moor's Last Sigh*

N. Ramesh Chandra Srikanth

Salman Rushdie's *Midnight's Children, Shame, Satanic Verses* and *The Moor's Last Sigh* address the issues of representative, contemporary political environment very effectively. Rushdie employs the technique of Magic Realism in comprehending the complex reality by his extraordinary use of language, story within the story and unconventional use of words, syntax and structure. In *The Moor's Last Sigh*, his second post-Fatwa novel, he adroitly represents his voice of uprootedness, belongingness, quest for identity through the incorporation of Magic Realism. In the novel the narrator questions the unitary history by 'peeling off' of the different layers of his own and of Indian history which have been superimposed on each other.

In *The Moor's Last Sigh*, Salman Rushdie describes the journey of Moraes Zogoiby (Moor), a half Christian, half Jewish narrator living in India. His struggle for identity takes him from Bombay to Spain due to religious clashes and cultural conflict that nearly tears Moor (and India) apart. Rushdie portrays his narrative with postmodern and postcolonial themes and techniques giving Moor's struggle a sense of epic proportions. Here Rushdie palimpsests Moor's struggle to establish his identity over the identity crises of historical icons and cultures. The value of pure multiculturalism as a remedy against social conflict is highly appreciable in this novel. While Rushdie suggests the danger of religious fundamentalism, he also suggests new-found doubts about pluralism and cultural hybridity through the experiences of Moor's family. The protagonist Moraes grows up in a pluralistic society of mixed heritage embedded in satire and sadness, history and humour.

Rushdie introduces major characters from across India's religious spectrum and other characters like Aurora, Moor's brilliant, Christian mother, a famous artist fighting to define herself between the east and the west. There is Abraham, Moor's Crooked Jewish father, and there is a Raman Fielding or Mainduck, a radical Hindu Nationalist with a British surname; between the story lines, Rushdie initially inserts famous characters from past, blurring the progression of time; references of Vasco de Gama, Martin Luther and Don Quixote meticulously glorify the cultural hybridity and plurality in cultural construction. Cantor says that for Rushdie, "All cultures, and especially Indian is Palimpsestic in nature" and he continues 'New Cultural Forces do not displace or erase prior ones, but simply write over them' (Cantor 137).

In the beginning of the novel itself, the protagonist, Moreas Zogoiby attempts to create his identity but the notion of the individual as a centered object is deconstructed and ends up instead with a decentered subject. The linear narrative is replaced by the concept of an open text. The story in *The Moor's Last Sigh* reveals how the protagonist Moraes Zogiaby thinks of the love between his parents, Aurora de Gama and Abraham Zogoiby. His parents' love crosses cultural boundaries since their families claim their respective descents from the Portuguese explorer Vasco de Gama and from the Jews expelled from early modern Spain.

He creates a direct lineage for Moor, related him to both Sultan and Spanish explorer, Vasco de Gama. Here Stephen Baker writes "The Mish-mash of influences, the juxtaposition of the European and the Indian can be said to represent a form of multiculturalism, absorbing the historical and cultural forces of west Europe on colonized societies" (Baker 233-46) and in post-colonial India, often, religion and politics could not be separated; Camoens (Moor's grandfather), for example, dreams of an independent India which could be "above religious because secular, above class because socialist, above caste because enlightened, above hatred because loving" (Rushdie 51). Here Moor describes, after Camoens' death "There was no room for a man who did not want to belong to a tribe, who dreamed... of peeling off his skin and revealing his 'secret' identity.... The secret, that is, of the identity of all men.... Of standing before the war-painted braves to unveil the flayed and naked unity of the flesh" (Rushdie 179).

Rushdie attacks Hindu fundamentalism through Raman Fielding, a Hindu who lives with one foot in politics and the other in the criminal world. He is the embodiment of use of power and religious intolerance. Rushdie also condemns the attitude of Abraham. Corrupted by his new found money and power in his search for an identity, Moor seeks to escape the binds of religion and desires to attach him to all other Indians. But India refuses to unchain itself from its religious shackles and Moor escapes to Spain. Moor flees India as Boabdil ran from Spain, as the story ends, the Moor/Boabdil parallel can be read as Rushdie's admonition against the dangers of fundamentalism and rigid definitions of self. It is very clear in the stand of the narrator and the writer in celebrating hybrid cultural association among Christian, Jewish, Muslim and Hindu traditions in twentieth century. Rushdie himself embodies this mélange:

> I was both, and nothing a jewholic anonymous, a cathjew nut, a stewpot, a mongrel cur. I was—what's the word these days?—atomized. Yessir: a real Bombay mix. (Rushdie 104)

In the text, Rushdie portrays and exposes a true version of the international, cross cultural, transnational individual in a negative image. The desire of expatriates to be recognized has led to an empty version of hybridity presenting an ugly life rather than enabling the prime characters. At this point, Rushdie makes a distinction between the hybridity of Bombay consciously.

> It may be hard for you to pity these lost souls in alligator shoes and sports—shirts with crocodiles over their

> nipples, but compassion is what is required here. Forgive them their sins, for these blood suckers are already in hell. (Rushdie 390)

Homi Bhabha states that the historical moment of political action must be thought of as part of the history of the form of its writing (Bhabha 23). According to Sara Suleri, in *The Moor's Last Sigh,* as in Rushdie's earlier novels, "there is an excessive novelty of the post-colonial condition juxtaposed with the excessive archaism of the idea of nationality" (Suleri 225).

These post-colonial traits of cultural identity and quest for 'Home' are adeptly deployed in the text through typical Rushdie technique of magical elements. Apart from the recent incidents, the novel appears striving for an ideal space that existed once in India, but is now vanishing due to contemporary communal politics. Eventually Rushdie tries to create a 'New' postmodern space in the novel at the end. Through the description of the fading Muslim Alhambrah at Granada, Rushdie evokes the value of 'The fabulous multiple culture of ancient history': "The Alhambrah, Europe's red fort, sister to Delhi's and Agra'.... Like a testament to...our need for flowing together, for putting an end to frontiers, for the dropping of boundaries of the self.... I watch it vanish in the twilight, and its fading, it brings tears to layers" (Rushdie 433).

Deepika Bahri writes, "Rushdie embarks...admitted by in a mood of trademark tolerance...on an examination of the hazards of indeterminancy and cultural pluralism under pressure from the need to articulate a modern determinate identity" (Bahri 197). Thus we can find Rushdie's Utopia of tolerance and multiculturalism forced upon the population by imperial power and Rushdie acknowledges the difficulties associated with implementing such ideals on society.

II

The protagonist Moraes' ambition to find his 'home' or place and the myth of hybridity is already witnessed as developed characters in Rushdie's previous novels *Midnight's Children, Shame, Satanic Verses.* These characters throw their didactic nature in this novel such as Aurora's art of paintings and her background. In the novel, there is a voice of singularity, such as Moraes's father, Alhambra and the boss of Bombay, Mainduck exploit to their advantage and end up in failure to achieve their home or identity. The phrase in the text '[t]he juggernaut is loose' (Rushdie 351) resembles postcolonial comedy and reveals the conflict of novel's central focus and the outcome of this confrontation. Through the use of typical phrases and syntax, he parodies the postcolonial hybridity making the contemporary Indian politics parallel to that of family history. In the novel the phrases, 'a sense of urgency', 'running out of time', 'living too fast' (Rushdie 2) explain the narrator's viewpoint as the 'truth' being concealed under the multilayered existence of life in the present-day world. *The Moor's Last Sigh* also records the emergence of a pervasive out of the struggle over cultural meaning in India and great parts of the Muslim world through the characters of Raman Fielding whose ideology is to follow the militant Hindu nationalists of Bharatiya Janata Party.

> Bombay blew apart...there had been nothing like it in the history of the city. Nothing so cold-blooded, so calculated, so cruel.... Bits of bodies were lying everywhere; human and animal blood, guts, and bones...who did it?... Hindu and Muslim areas were both attacked; men, women, children perished, and there was nobody to give the dignity of meaning to their deaths. (Rushdie 371-72)

The novel reflects and identifies the dream of cultural hybridity in twentieth century India. Moor's description of Aurora's Art, Uma, Moor's lover, A Fraud; Aurora's painting of her ancestors alongside St. Thomas The Apostle, Indian Jews alongside the Muslim League, The Hindus of Congress alongside Vasco de Gama provide strong examples of Rushdie's fear of unhindered pluralism and his ambiguity of multiculturalism. India being multilayered, pluralistic, hybrid and diversified, Rushdie here ridicules allegorically the corrupt politics in India. It cannot stop the events such as the riots of post Ayodhya, Bombay blasts and powerful control of centre by the underworld. The most obvious representative of the pluralist sensibility in this novel is the flamboyant, middle class, socialite painter Aurora Zogoiby, whose art work, like Rushdie's writing, is palimpsestic in style and hybrid in its source.

Rushdie's critique of rootless pluralism in the Moor seems more sustained and vituperative than elsewhere. The principal reason for this is that Rushdie's satire in the Moor is directed at liberal cosmopolitans in India who have sought their fanaticism as it is their fundamental right. Hence, the pluralist of the novel, whether they are represented affirmatively or critically by Rushdie are at one point or another, compromised by their association with the far right leaving the solidarity of India's pluralistic reality into question. Rushdie's critiques of the Shiva Sena in this novel drew cries of outrage in Bombay.

Rushdie cleverly places Aurora's hybridity in opposition to Abraham and Mainduck's singularity and represents a flipside of pluralism; the down side can be confusion, formlessness, chaos, a lack of vision or singleness of purpose. As the novel ends with Moraes' flight from India to Spain, there is last sigh of the Muslim Sultan Baobdil. The contemporary political events of India pervade everywhere in the novel. The family history of Aurora in the beginning of the novel is influenced by a mish-mash of ideas of individuals. Her grandfather, Franscisco da Gama, a modernist, follower of Betrand Russel and Annei Besant join the Home Rule Movement in 1916. His wife Epifania states 'masses and classes in same club! Shame and scandal! Sense is gone from the man,' and becomes silent. She vehemently says to her husband, 'it will blondify me with ugliness.' Then Franscisco retorts, 'old beauty is not enough' and Epifania bursts out stating,

> Old places, old behavior, old gods. These days the world is full of questions, and there are new ways to be beautiful. (Rushdie 16-19)

Both the characters in the novel do not agree on anything not even to be Eurocentric; her son Cameons follows his father and tells his wife Belle about the greatness of a new Post British world, a free country, a secular one.

> Dawning of a new world, Belle, a free country, Belle, above religion because secular, above class because socialist, above caste because enlightened, above hatred because loving...Belle, the freedom express of the train, soon we will stand that platform and cheer the coming of the train. (Rushdie 51)

Though Rushdie does not offer any hope in Moor, it is important to understand his autobiographical and personal emotions longing for his place through these characters in a subtle way. Rushdie packs his fiction with allusions to various Indian films, actors with metropolitan hybridity. In choosing references from films, the name 'Mogambo', Rushdie writes that his name is "carefully chosen to avoid offending any of the country's communities, it's neither Muslim nor Hindu, Parsi nor Christian, Jain nor Sikh" as this film highlights the artificiality of the modern form of multiculturalism. On the one hand, Rushdie is against the religious fundamentalism that threatens Indian society and suggests cultural hybridity as its remedy. But Rushdie also departs from an unqualified advocacy of such hybridity.

III

Aurora, a Catholic falls in love with Alhambra a Jew, and crosses all the borders of religion class and even mores and they are never married at the end of the novel. She is influenced by the Nehruvian National Movement, her paintings become popular on the walls and caricatured her in papers.

> Painted on walls, caricatured in the papers, the maker of images became an image herself. (Rushdie 116)

Aurora's nature of black sheep can be seen when she makes her servant Lambhajan's deformity of leg as natural and could witness the exploitation of the Margins by the central force representing then corrupt political agenda in the country.

While Vasco Miranda encourages her to have her own identity 'secret' to follow the true direction of her heart to the reality of dreams, Aurora moves away from Naturalism and creates a fantasy land called 'Mooristan' or Palimpsest and desires to represent the golden age of hybridity as it existed historically in the Arab period of Southern Spain, in Andalusia embedded with cultures of Christian, Jewish, Muslim living side by side over boundaries for years. This is an authentic appraisal of Rushdie's strong opinion for the literary search of his identity. The impact of these cultures resulted nothing on any one and the result was hybrid architecture, literature and culture. The novel is full of issues that identifies Rushdie's dream of cultural hybridity in twentieth century India. When disillusioned Zeeny Vakeel reappears in *The Moor's Last Sigh* lamenting on the deterioration of pluralistic diversity.

> Yet he knew, in his dreams, that this place was and would continue to be his home;...and the surrounding foreignness had become permeable, was beginning to dissolve. (Rushdie 94-95)
>
> Vasco Miranda had been urging upon her, the true direction of her heart; that is to say, inwards, to the reality of dreams. (Rushdie 179)

Thus *The Moor's Last Sigh* can be seen as a celebration of conjoining many different histories and cultures in Spain and to read India through Spain and cherish its hybridity and diversity. Rushdie adroitly promotes a parallel between the composite culture of India Hindu as majority and other cultures as Margins and they come together to form a mélange of Muslim Spain. Here at this point Rushdie and his alter ego Moraes view this newly emerging Hindu fundamentalism in India as a threat to the rich culture of hybridity. The images of self conscious narration, conspicuously arcane and technical language, long lists of objects used to create either a cramped and busy world or a barren and empty one and grammatically incorrect or "back—broke" sentences in *The Moor's Last Sigh* and in almost all his novels exemplify his inner revelation towards his quest for identity in this genre of hybrid multiplicity. Rushdie packs his fiction with allusions to various Indian films, actors, orienting towards metropolitan hybridity through his prime characters. He also creates another story of India's reality that is 'so plural and shifting' focusing on identity markers like caste, religion, language or place or community being deteriorated and calls for redefinition. Ultimately, Rushdie presents a difficult contradiction, a contradiction best summarized by Paul Cantor.

> Place where worlds collide, flow in and out of one another, and washofy away. Place where an air man can drown into water, or else grow gills.... One universe, one dimension, one country, one dream, bumpo'ing into one another, Call it Palimpsestine. And above it all, in the palace, you. (Rushdie 226)

But contrary to this threat, Spain and India enjoyed a fluidity that can be witnessed in Aurora's paintings by creating a 'place/ home' on canvas.

> And I was happy to be there, because the story unfolding on her canvases seemed more like my autobiography than the real story of my life. (Rushdie 227)

IV

In fact the entire novel itself is a nostalgic looking back at what once existed in Aurora's family, her art, her palimpsest painting of Madonna, without child. In other words, the important theme of the novel is secularism more than hybridity. All the main characters of the novel are unbelievers but seemed to be secular in their portrayal. On the other hand, Epifania, Flory, Mainduck are all marginalized in the text. With the impact of Fatwa on Rushdie, he attempts to create a staunch identity through this novel that anyone who represents a faith in god is violently marginalized. In *The Moor's Last Sigh*, Rushdie leaves the reader with this unanswered contradiction raising criticism in some minds on his value as a pluralist, postcolonial writer. Here we can ponder and find answer to his earlier position with this *genre* of multiculturalism and a more subtle understanding of India's complex cultural interaction, a grand design offered by Rushdie in his fiction ignoring the complexities of that culture. But in reality, the human condition is tense with contradictions and self-doubts. When Camoens is against occupation, hostile to many English families, Rushdie does not indict him, he praises him:

> To me the doubleness in grandfather Camoens reveal his beauty; his willingness to permit the co-existence within himself of conflicting impulses is the source of his fall, gentle humanness. (Rushdie 32)

Works Cited

Bahri, Deepika. "Before and After Midnight: Salman Rushdie and the Subaltern Standard." *Native Intelligence: Aesthetics, Politics, and Postcolonial Literature*. Minneapolis: University of Minnesota Press, 2003. 152-99. Print.

Baker, Stephen. "You Must Remember This. Salman Rushdie's *The Moor's Last Sigh*." *Bloom's Modern Critical Views: Salman Rushdie*. Comp. Harold Bloom. Philadelphia: Chelsea House, 2003. 233-46. Print.

Bhabha, Homi. *The Location of Culture* (London: Routledge, 1994), 20. Print.

Cantor, Paul A. "Tales of the Alhambra: Rushdie's Use of Spanish History in *The Moor's Last Sigh*." *Bloom's Modern Critical Views: Salman Rushdie*. Comp. Harold Bloom. Philadelphia: Chelsea House, 2003. 121-44. Print.

Cundy, Catherine. *Salman Rushdie*, Manchester: Manchester UP, 1997. Print.

Rushdie, Salman and Elizabeth West, eds., "Introduction." *Vintage Book of Indian Writing 1947-1997*. London: Vintage, 1997. Print.

Rushdie, Salman. *Midnight's Children*. London: Picador, 1981. Print.

———. *The Moor's Last Sigh*. New York: Vintage Books, 1995. Print.

———. *Imaginary Homelands: Essay and Criticism, 1981-1991*. London: Granta Books, 1991. Print.

Suleri, Sara. "Woman Skin Deep: Feminism and Postcolonial Condition". *Critical Inquiry* 18. 4 (1992): 756-69. Print.

Vinita, Damodaran et al. *Post Colonial India—History, Politics & Culture*. New Delhi: Manohar Publishers, 2000. Print.

20

Kerala Imagined in Arundhati Roy's *The God of Small Things,* Geeta Abraham Jose's *By the River Pampa I Stood* and Nirmala Aravind's *A Video, a Fridge and a Bride*

S. Devika

Fiction, which is rooted in a particular place or community and which affords an insight into the culture, customs, traditions, ethos, and social system of the place or the community, is popular with several women writers like Kaveri Nambisan, Manju Kapur, Dina Mehta and others who have depicted in their fiction the life of various regions of India such as Coorg or Punjab, or communities like the Sikhs or the Parsis. In 1997, Arundhati Roy's *The God of Small Things,* which portrays the life, social mores, caste politics, traditions, customs and beliefs of the Syrian Christian community in Kerala, put Kerala very firmly on the fictional map of Indian Writing in English, set as it is in the small town milieu of Ayemenem in Kottayam. Since then, there have appeared several novels by Malayali women writers in English which are set in the milieu of Kerala and which aesthetically capture a slice of the life of upper-caste communities like the Syrian Christians, the Nairs, or the Namboodiris.

In this paper I would like to examine the dynamics of life in Kerala as portrayed in Arundhati Roy's *God of Small Things*, Geeta Abraham Jose's *By the River Pampa I Stood* and Nirmala

Aravind's *A Video, a Fridge and a Bride*. A vivid sense of place and a palpable consciousness of community—the Syrian Christian community—unites Roy, Aravind and Jose. Nirmala Aravind's only novel *A Video, a Fridge and a Bride* (1995) is a domestic novel set in the 1980s in the city of Trivandrum and the faraway suburbs of rural Pallisery which pulsates with middle-class Syrian Christian life. Another semi-autobiographical saga of a Syrian Christian family in Kerala, *The God of Small Things* (1997) captures the intellectual, social, cultural, political, sexual and environmental landscapes of Kerala. Geeta Abraham Jose in her debut novel *By the River Pampa I Stood* (2007) paints, like Roy and Aravind, a vivid portrait of the Syrian Christians of Kerala—their historical background, the descriptions of people, the feudal set up and the social discrimination, all an integral part of the social fabric of the community. Here I shall examine the image of Kerala that emerges from a study of these three works, focusing primarily on the caste-class divide, the phenomena of religious conversion, communism and gulf migration in counteracting the divide, besides highlighting the gender issues in institutions like marriage and family and the shaping influence of the environment.

The breakup of the primitive communist social set up in Kerala with the beginning of Aryan influence around 500 AD saw the emergence of a society sharply divided along caste lines, giving rise to numerous communities on the basis of occupation, religion, caste and sub-caste. The occupational identity of the lower castes that were generally made to carry out manual labour and cultivation, brought into their lives the scourge of untouchability. The feudal structure of the agrarian society involving upper-caste landlords and labourers paved the way for slavery in the society of Kerala. Feudalism, untouchability and slavery, the natural fallouts of caste hierarchy, resulted in many inhuman practices that stripped the lower castes of human dignity and self-respect for centuries. The concerted efforts of British administrators and Christian missionaries led to a series of Proclamations in the 1850s by which slavery was legally abolished in Kerala.

The first dent on the system was made in the twentieth century by social reformers like Sree Narayana Guru who campaigned for the abolition of caste practices, and in post-Independence Kerala, communism and legislative reforms combined to ameliorate the condition of the oppressed. The caste prejudice of the upper caste Syrian Christian community is an important theme that shapes the narrative in Arundhati Roy's *The God of Small Things*, Geeta Abraham Jose's *By the River Pampa I Stood* and Nirmala Aravind's *A Video, a Fridge and a Bride*.

Roy's *The God of Small Things*, primarily a story of the forbidden love between an aristocratic Syrian Christian woman and an untouchable *paravan* and its horrendous consequences, exposes the bourgeois mentality and caste prejudices that lie entrenched in the minds of the dominant upper castes. Early in the narrative we are given a stark picture of the indignity to which untouchables were subjected in pre-Independence Kerala:

> Mammachi told Estha and Rahel that she could remember a time, in her childhood, when Paravans were expected to crawl backwards with a broom, sweeping away their footprints so that Brahmins or Syrian Christians would not defile themselves by accidentally stepping into a Paravan's footprint.... Paravans, like other Untouchables, were not allowed to walk on public roads, not allowed to cover their upper bodies, not allowed to carry umbrellas. (Roy 73-74)

In the democratic set up of post-Independence Kerala, social emancipation still remains a dream for the untouchables. Pappachi would not let paravans into the Ayemenem House because they cannot be allowed "to touch anything that Touchables touched" (Roy 73). The novel reflects the changes in social hierarchies brought about during the 1960s in Kerala by the Naxalite movement aiming at a reconstruction of society. The untouchable Velutha, an accomplished carpenter and mechanic is hired at Chacko's pickles and preserves factory and put in charge of general maintenance. When this generates a great deal of resentment among the other Touchable factory workers to whom Paravans are not meant to be carpenters, Mammachi placates them by paying Velutha less than she would a Touchable carpenter but more than she would a Paravan: "She said that it was a big step for a Paravan" (Roy 77). However, Vellya Paapen, an old world paravan who has seen the walking backwards days fears that his son's social advancement does not augur well for a paravan. True to his apprehensions, when the reckless Velutha steps over the line and ventures to love an upper-caste Syrian Christian woman, the iron hands of hegemony rush to deal a deathblow to him in an "attempt to instil order into a world gone wrong" (Roy 260). As Jain rightly avers, Velutha's expertise cannot absolve him of his untouchable status and he becomes a victim of inexorable social prejudices (130).

Geeta Abraham Jose's *By the River Pampa I Stood* also narrates the story of love between an upper caste Syrian Christian woman and an untouchable, set in pre-Independence Kerala. It depicts the complexities of feudal arrangement in an affluent, agrarian, aristocratic Syrian Christian family in Kuttanad and the dire consequences of disrupting that social order. In the feudal days, it was customary for landowning families to produce, store and eat their own rice as a matter of prestige. With its long line of illustrious forefathers and an unbroken Syrian Christian lineage the Ponnumpurackal family boasts of "nineteen hundred years old heritage and the Brahmin ancestry prior to it" (72). The Ponnumpurackal family engages a number of labourers who worked on the farm. While the men do the ploughing, sowing, transplanting, reaping, threshing, parboiling and sifting of grain, their women help the womenfolk of the household in the kitchen, though, for fear of contamination, the untouchables are "not allowed to do certain kinds of work like cooking or grinding chutney where direct contact with the food was required" (Jose 34). In return for their labour they are provided food, shelter and security. These dependants, through long tradition, owe allegiance to the master and live on the premises of the family estate in tidy little huts made of mud bricks, with thatched roofs and floors plastered with cow dung. Yoshua, the feudal lord Mathen's faithful Man Friday, even thanks his stars for belonging to a fine master who never beat him.

A forbidden love relationship between Annamma, the daughter of the Ponnumpurackal family, and Yoshua's son

Thoma, a strapping young untouchable farmhand threatens to upset the system that has been in place for centuries in the hegemonic social order. Mathen, the proud patriarch, not one to encourage any mixing of blood that diluted the aristocratic, ancient Syrian Christian tradition, even cut off his son Varghese for marrying an English woman. His daughter's affair with an untouchable calls for stringent action from him. Mathen, the wrathful father and benevolent lord offers Thoma the choice of losing his life or living in the high ranges as the master of his own piece of land, out of sight of his daughter and the Ponnumparackal family. Thoma, who had known a lifetime of deprivation and who resented being treated "*like Nandini, the cow. Or Chinnu, the sow. Or Kaiser, the dog. Or Meena, the cat*" (Jose 80), opted for the latter—to live like a human being. Unlike Velutha in *The God of Small Things* who pays with his life for his transgression, Thoma is given a second lease to erase his past, his love and his family, and start a new life in the far away hideout.

Nirmala Aravind's *A Video, a Fridge and a Bride* exposes the shameful fact that, even in the 1980s—age of enlightenment and equality, caste prejudices and antagonism lie ingrained in the minds of the upper castes of Kerala. The narrative traces the travails of Cheriachen, a member of that branch of a landowning Syrian Christian family in Pallisserry near Tiruvalla in Central Travancore. He tries to find a suitable match for their daughter Lissy, who has neither a fat purse nor a pretty face to offer. Sick of being paraded before a string of prospective grooms—"cynical bargain hunters" (Aravind 193). Lissy allows herself to be charmed by the persistent attentions of Jose, a union activist colleague at her bank. What hits the reader hard is the caste prejudice that surfaces when the low-caste Pulaya proposes to Lissy:

> He smells like one of the labourers your father employs.... Look at his face. He is as black as charcoal. And his hands, they are broad and squat with dirty fingernails; they should be tilling soil or breaking stones. (Aravind 225)

When her family gets wind of the affair, the adherents of orthodoxy and aristocratic tradition bewail the catastrophe: "He is a Pulaya, an untouchable.... Dear God, this foolish girl is the granddaughter of Padinjaramannil Korulla Eapen before whom an untouchable would not stand straight. Has she gone mad?" (Aravind 248).

There is a quick-freeze from the quixotic to the mundane for Lissy when Comrade Jose reveals to her the reason behind his insistence on a church wedding in Vellakada instead of a civil ceremony. It is to avenge the caste discrimination he faced as the first Pulaya boy to sing in the church choir, when Syrian Christian snobs like the organist never spoke to Jose and the lovely daughter of the priest refused to drink the water that Jose gave her. Lissy sees through his scheme when he tells her, "That glass of water is still standing there at St. John's Church. Do you know who is going to drink it?" (Aravind 262) and realizes that his love is only a mask, a dignified expression to hide the dark current of desire "to possess, to oppress, to have and to hold in thrall" (Aravind 263), the typical neo-colonial instinct to have what he never had and could never hope to have.

Roy's *The God of Small Things,* Aravind's *A Video, a Fridge and a Bride,* and Jose's *By the River Pampa I Stood* depict the three-fold phenomena of religious conversion, communism and gulf migration which have worked with varying degrees of success as antidotes to casteism in Kerala. Apart from drawing the picture of a Syrian Christian way of life, they also reflect the power structures in the traditional Christian community that work against the newly converted Christians to reinforce caste and class divisions. Hindus, Christians and Muslims have for centuries been the three major religious groups that made up the social fabric of Kerala. Each asserts itself as a distinct cultural marker with its own traditions, customs, practices, beliefs, superstitions, caste/class prejudices, etc. While the Hindu community, organized on a rigid social hierarchy, has always been caste-ridden, Christian and Muslim communities, in spite of internal divisions based on wealth, have remained largely casteless. The advent of British administration in Kerala in the nineteenth century brought the missionaries who put their heart and soul into mass religious conversions. The oppressed low-caste Hindus were encouraged to embrace Christianity in order to escape the scourge of untouchability. "Christianity, they were told, was a religion that believed in the equality of men. Had not Christ set a supreme example by befriending people from the lower strata of society in his time?" Jose writes in *River Pampa* (41). As added incentive they were given food and money, and they came to be known as "Rice Christians." Roy's satiric pen is quick to point out how their bid to equality misfired, and only created a cleft on the basis of caste in the hitherto homogenous aristocratic Christian community:

> It didn't take them long to realize that they had jumped from the frying pan into the fire. They were made to have separate churches, with separate services, and separate priests. As a special favour they were even given their own Pariah Bishop. After Independence they found they were not entitled to any Government benefits like job reservations or bank loans at low interest rates, because officially, on paper, they were Christians, and therefore casteless. (74)

In Jose's *River Pampa* pulaya farmhands of Ponnumpurackal like Yoshua and others who sought refuge in Christianity to wipe away the stigma of untouchability from their lives soon realized that they had made a terrible mistake, for the caste feelings remained as strong as ever: "So the poor folk were destined to their old fate—untouchability wrapped up in a colourful package called Christianity and handed back to them" (Jose 41).

Aravind too in *A Video, a Fridge and a Bride* shows how Syrian Christians who consider themselves a class apart marginalize the new Christians and discourage the merging of the two streams. Lissy, in a desperate attempt to persuade her folks to agree to her marriage with a non-Syrian Christian boy, argues:

> "Jose is a Christian, like any of us. He belongs to our church," said Lissy, gathering up all her courage.
>
> "The audacity of the girl! Christian, indeed!" Annamma's eyes were narrow slits.

> The Major snorted. "The fellow's a Pulaya, and he is not like any of us. Does a Pulaya have a soul to be saved?" (Aravind 248)

The three novelists project the view that the strategy of conversion to Christianity, an egalitarian religion, failed to work the miracle of removing caste differences and prejudices in the society of Kerala.

In a context where the Church took the side of the rich and the powerful, Marxism was touted as a "simple substitute for Christianity," replacing God with Marx, Satan with the bourgeoisie, Heaven with a classless society, and the Church with the Party, as Roy satirizes (Roy 66). The renaissance movement of Kerala initiated by anti-feudal struggles to reform the hierarchical Hindu society provided the leeway for Marxism and its ideologies like rationalism, socialism and communism to penetrate into the consciousness of Kerala. In the 1930s, Communism was touted as the remedy against the feudalistic forces that opposed social change. Soon Kerala became a bastion of Communism in India and saw the first democratically elected Communist Government come to power just months after the formation of the modern state of Kerala in 1957. The utopian ideal of a classless, casteless society captured the imagination of the intelligentsia represented by its leader E.M.S. Namboodiripad who, in Roy's words, is "the flamboyant Brahmin high priest of Marxism in Kerala" (Roy 67).

Communism receives the full blast of Roy's criticism in *The God of Small Things* for creeping into "Kerala insidiously. As a reform movement that never overtly questioned the traditional values of a caste-ridden, extremely traditional community" (Roy 66). Roy satirizes the Marxists of Kerala who always "worked from *within* the communal divides, never challenging them, never appearing not to", offering "a cocktail revolution," which was a "heady mix of eastern Marxism and orthodox Hinduism, spiked with a shot of democracy" (Roy 66-67). She paints the portraiture of the typical Communist in Comrade K.N.M. Pillai who "walked through the world like a chameleon. Never revealing himself, never appearing not to. Emerging through chaos unscathed" (Roy 14). She exposes and derides the hypocritical Comrade who, on the one hand, mouths Communist platitudes, and on the other declares that "these caste issues are very deep-rooted" (Roy 278). Roy insinuates that communism in Kerala only creates the illusion of a class war to stay afloat. And Nirmala Aravind couldn't agree more when she asserts:

> That's what these chaps who spout Marxism are all like beneath the bluster.... They're just mixed up. I'm talking about the white collar Marxists. It's a pose, nothing more, like our government's socialism. (Aravind 258)

Thus Roy and Aravind take their unflinching stand on communism as having no effect in ushering drastic social change in the casteist social hierarchy of Kerala.

We get yet another facet of Communism in Roy's novel in the capitalist Chacko. Though for the wealthy, estate-owning Syrian Christians of Kerala communism "represented a fate worse than death" (Roy 66), Chacko becomes "a self-proclaimed Marxist" (Roy 65) who invites pretty women from his factory to his room, and on the pretext of enlightening them on labour rights and trade union law, flirts with them outrageously. Ammu's cynical eye sees this as "a case of a spoiled prince-ling playing *Comrade! Comrade!*" An Oxford avatar of the old zamindar mentality—"a landlord forcing his attentions on women who depended on him for their livelihood" (Roy 65).

On a positive note, Roy concedes that the high literacy level in the state of Kerala is largely because of the communist movement. It is responsible for the labour class coming into their own and organizing themselves into trade unions to fight for their rights like higher wages, shorter working hours. "On their shoulders they carried a keg of ancient anger, lit with a recent fuse. There was an edge to this anger that was Naxalite and new" (69). Also, it emboldened the untouchables to slough off their demeaning caste names and demand "not to be addressed as Achoo Parayan, or Kelan Paravan, or Kuttan Pulayan, but just as Achoo, or Kelan, or Kuttan" (Roy 69).

Jose too in *River Pampa* alludes to the adoption of grander names among the newly awakened lower castes as a pointer to the democratization, social transition and, in short, the winds of change blowing over modern Kerala:

> Earlier the "*amma*" suffix to the name was used only by the high caste Hindus and the Syrian Christians of Kerala. The low castes were not allowed to use grand names. If they were Hindus, they could do with names like Thevi, Kali, Chirutha, Neeli, Chathan, Kittan or Chindan; if Christians, it could be Maria, Anna or Thara and the like without the "*amma*" suffix. As times changed, the low caste folk began to realize that they had the freedom to choose any name under the sun for their offspring. (110)

Jose attributes this visible change chiefly to the prosperity that the Gulf boom has brought to Kerala since the mid-1970s. The poor farm folk of Ponnumpurackal were no longer poor, because, as drivers, plumbers, fitters, office-boys, waiters they toiled in the sweltering heat of the desert and "back home, the thatched roofs and mud floors disappeared. Solid, concrete structures came up.... With fish bone structures on top through which glamour, culture and style came into their lives.... Life went on. But the rhythm had changed" (Jose 120). Aravind's novel too projects the elevation in the social status of the working and the lower middle classes due to migration to foreign countries. Aley, an old woman who swept the courtyard and washed the clothes at Cherichen's ancestral home at Pallissery only did so because of her loyalty to the family. "Aley had a daughter who was a nurse in West Germany, and she no longer needed to toil for a living. When the daughter came on leave, Aley would not come to work for a few days as it made the girl very angry" (Aravind 82).

Roy too alludes to the substantial rise in the standard of living of the Gulf migrants when she contrasts "the new, freshly baked, iced, Gulf-money houses built by nurses, masons, wire-benders and bank clerks who worked hard and unhappily in faraway places" with the "resentful older houses tinged green with envy, cowering in their private driveways among their private rubber trees. Each a tottering fiefdom with an epic of its own" (Roy 13). Aravind's Pallissery too bore the imprint of the Gulf boom: "a stretch of lush paddy would be marred by the florid two-storey monstrosity set by its side, the dream child of some expatriate Malayalee flush with new money" (Aravind 52). Jose caricatures the *nouveau riche* Gulf Malayalee who "invests all his hard earned money in buying a dilapidated, ancient house, renovating it to suit his newly acquired tastes, the old *nalukettu* portion of the house being preserved as a convenient camouflage to deceive others" (Jose 75), all in an attempt to buy "heritage" with the hard-earned money from the sand dunes of Arabia, "as easily as they could buy "careers" for their sons and "husbands" for their daughters" (Jose 9). As demonstrated in these novels, the most dynamic aspect of life in modern Kerala is the migration of the labour class especially to the Middle East, which contributed to the blurring of social divisions between the haves and have-nots and completely changed the socio-economic scenario in Kerala.

The God of Small Things, *By the River Pampa I Stood*, and *A Video, a Fridge and a Bride* offer a glimpse of the lot of another oppressed group in the society of Kerala—the women. The matrilineal system that prevailed in Kerala among the Nair and the Ezhava castes ensured that the woman was a powerful partner in marriage. However, the Aryanisation of Kerala contributed to a general decline in the status of women. While women have had the opportunity to be educated, this education has not translated into equality and emancipation for the woman in the patriarchal society. Roy, Jose and Aravind lay bare the issue of Syrian Christian women confronting patriarchal norms imposed on them in their various roles as wives, mothers, daughters, etc. We get several snippets of the dictates of patriarchy in Roy's novel: "single-mindedness...in a young girl in those days was considered as bad as a physical deformity" (Roy 24); "a college education was an unnecessary expense for a girl" (Roy 38); "choosing between her husband's name and her father's name didn't give a woman much choice" (Roy 37); "though Ammu did as much work at the factory as Chacko, he always referred to it as 'my' factory, my pineapples, my pickles. Legally this was the case because Ammu, as a daughter, had no claim to the property" (Roy 57). All this "thanks to our wonderful male chauvinist society" (Roy 57), as Ammu herself scorns.

Jose highlights the typical patriarchal image of the woman as "a burning candle" (Jose 5) and satirises the mentality that makes a sinner of any woman who broke rules or "reversed the Dos and Don'ts" (Jose 5) of a society highly sensitive to the slightest infringement of its conventions. Aravind too projects a male-dominated society where: "women shouldn't have opinions. There's no need for them, to add to the confusion" (Aravind 47); high educational qualifications make it difficult for a girl to get a suitable match (Aravind 63); parents are afraid to encourage a daughter to be ambitious (Aravind 175) and decide everything, "from the length of her sleeves to the number of movies she could see in a year" (Aravind 193); and weak-willed women allow their lives to be ordered by domineering men (Aravind 237).

These novels also take a look at the institution of marriage as it operates among the Syrian Christians of Kerala and analyze how it works hand in glove with patriarchy to discriminate against women. The central concern of Aravind's novel is the contemptible practice of dowry that is widespread among Syrian Christian community, that treats the woman as a commodity to be bargained for and which forces a middle-class father like Cheriachen to "save every paisa from the day a daughter is born" (Aravind 10). Jose too points a finger at the dowry system which deprives a Syrian Christian woman of the right or claim to anything in her father's house. Once the dowry is paid, and the knot tied, "her surname was changed; her identity merged with that of her husband" (Jose 28), which leaves an unemployed woman dependent on her husband and at his mercy. The narrator states that "Mathen had displayed great magnanimity by permitting Saramma, his wife, to go home on short visits to nurse her sick mother" (Jose 27). In *The God of Small Things* Pappachi is a male-chauvinist husband who, in an attempt to keep his wife subservient to him, ruthlessly clips her wings—first, in Vienna, he stops her music lessons when her talent is adjudged "potentially concert class" (Roy 50); and back in Ayemenem, when Mammachi's pickle business picks up, he does everything to demoralize her: "Every night he beat her with a brass flower vase" (Roy 47) to show Mammachi her place. However, marriage gives the Syrian Christian woman a respectability that is denied to a divorcee. The ignominy of divorce is captured accurately in Baby Kochamma's attitude towards Ammu:

> She subscribed wholeheartedly to the commonly held view that a married daughter had no position in her parents' home. As for a *divorced* daughter...she had no position anywhere at all. And as for a *divorced* daughter from a *love* marriage, well, words could not describe Baby Kochamma's outrage. As for a *divorced* daughter from an *intercommunity love* marriage—Baby Kochamma chose to remain quiveringly silent on the subject. (Roy 45-46)

One of the recurrent themes in these novels is the familial and societal attitudes towards marriages that cross the boundaries of caste, race and community. In *River Pampa*, the narrator's marriage in the 90s to a low caste non-Syrian Christian doctor raises a hullabaloo in the family. Varghese's marriage to Alice in the same novel or Chacko's to Margaret in *The God of Small Things*, both women of a superior race, is also frowned upon by their families in Kerala. There were unwritten laws "that lay down who could be loved and how. And how much" (Roy 31). Those who defy the traditions of the Syrian Christian community like Annamma in *River Pampa*, Ammu in *The God of Small Things* and Lissy in *Video* are forced to face stringent hostility and even ostracism both within the family and the society. They are punished for their sin of trying to marry an untouchable or taking an untouchable lover—Annamma is condemned to spinsterhood; Lissy is put under house arrest and forced to apply for a transfer to a distant place; and Ammu is asked to pack her bags and leave, to be refused even the dignity of a decent burial in the parish church four years later. Thus, caste feelings and patriarchal norms work hand in glove with marital laws in the conventional and orthodox Syrian Christian community of Kerala to keep the power structures in place.

Kerala, the land of lush greenery and shimmering waters, Kathakali and Mohiniyattam, and the magic of Ayurveda, may seem a veritable paradise to the outsider, a perception further reinforced by its sobriquet "God's Own Country." To the

Malayali this fertile land is an intrinsic part of his consciousness and identity, defining his habits, customs, rituals and way of life. The novels of Malayali-Anglian writers are intensely concerned with the regional landscape and the social structure of Kerala shaping individual lives. In Roy's *The God of Small Things* and Jose's *River Pampa*, the environment plays a vital part in the narrative, for the destiny of the characters is seen to be shaped by the rivers in both these novels. River Pampa with its mysterious ways changes the course of Annamma's life in *River Pampa*: "Had it been in her stars? That unmistakable link between the waters of the Pampa and Annamma's life? The river had been playing mean tricks on her right from her infancy" (Jose 64).

Though Estha and Rahel in *The God of Small Things* know that the Meenachal river is not "always what she pretends to be" (Roy 210), they see her as a friend, and use her as the transit to the utopian world of the History House. On the fateful night of Sophie Mol's drowning, the river is dark and quiet, "an absence rather than a presence, betraying no sign of how high and strong it really was" (291). It becomes the locale for transgression for the children and the pair of lovers Ammu and Velutha, the "worst transgressors" who "broke all rules...crossed into forbidden territory" (Roy 31) to be "where they weren't supposed to be" (Roy 55). The degeneration of the river—"once it had the power to evoke fear. To change lives. But now its teeth were drawn, its spirit spent" (Roy 124)—reflects not only the changing texture of life in Kerala but also the environmental concerns of the novelist.

Thus, Kerala serves as a fictional locale in the novels of Roy, Aravind and Jose. With a reformist's zeal, these writers wield the weapon of satire to expose caste and gender exploitations and inequalities in the society of Kerala. They stand for a social change that shall emancipate man from the fetters of conservatism and create a new world where, as the narrator of *River Pampa* (138) fervently hopes, "a person is not judged based on his pedigrees but on his personality…families no longer take interest in parading dynastic pedigrees or aristocratic connections," and "academic achievements and high-powered careers would overpower the old concepts."

Works Cited

Aravind, Nirmala. *A Video, a Fridge and a Bride*. New Delhi: Rupa, 1995. Print.

Balakrishnan, Dr. E. *The History of the Communist Movement in Kerala*. Ernakulam: Kurukshetra Prakasan Pvt. Ltd., 1998. Print.

Jain, Seema. "Gender and Caste Issues in Arundhati Roy's *The God of Small Things*." *The Commonwealth Review* 15. 2 (2004): 124-31. Print.

Jose, Geeta Abraham. *By the River Pampa I Stood*. New Delhi: Srishti, 2007. Print.

Nair, Adoor and K.K. Ramachandran. *Slavery in Kerala*. Delhi: Mittal Publications, 1986. Print.

Roy, Arundhati. *The God of Small Things*. New Delhi: India Ink, 1997. Print.

Visvanathan, Susan. *The Christians of Kerala*. New Delhi: Oxford UP, 1993. Print.

21

Khushwant Singh's *Death At My Doorstep*: A Multicultural Exploration

N. Anil Krishna

Khushwant Singh (1915-2014)—the maverick Indian writer—is a multifaceted personality whose genius is manifested in being a historian, candid political commentator, a keen observer of men and events, and a social critic. As a literary personality, Khushwant Singh proved his greatness in attempting many literary forms. Besides a rich corpus of fictional work, Khushwant Singh has written a classic two-volume history of the Sikhs, a number of translations and non-fiction books. His non-fictional works include: *The History of Sikhs* (1953), *The Sikhs Today* (1959), *Ghadar 1915: India's First Armed Revolution* (1966), *Tragedy of Punjab* (1984), *We Indians* (1993) *Truth, Love and Little Malice* (2002), *The End of India* (2003), *Agnostic Khushwant—There is no God* (2012). Irrespective of the genre, Khushwant Singh has made an indelible mark on the reader's mind.

Khushwant Singh's *Death At My Doorstep* deals with expressions of identity and self-respect while bringing in a touch of pathos. It affirms that multiculturalism as a principle to be celebrated and acted upon requires from us all, a receptivity to difference, an ability to recognize our familiar self in the strangeness of others. Thus, it transcends community, religion and nation for an establishment of identity and Khushwant Singh does it elegantly without any exaggerated ornamentation.

He views that multicultural ethic has replaced one nation, one culture idea and ventures out to explore this aspect in our context of multi-ethnicity, multi-linguism, multi-religious situations. In this pluralistic society, Khushwant Singh tries to evolve unifying centres around which our identities can revolve like concentric circles. This ultimately leads to integrated man—the primary objective of the multicultural existence.

Khushwant Singh's *Death At My Doorstep* is a collection of obituaries written over the years. He considers death as "essential fact of life which makes no exceptions." He writes:

> It comes to kings as well as beggars, to the rich and the poor, to saints as well as sinners, the aged and the young. You simply cannot turn a blind eye to it and fool yourself into believing that death comes to other people but will spare you. It will not. It is best to prepare yourself for it and when it comes, welcome it with a smile on your lips. (xi)

He claims to have written obituaries, the first being entitled "Posthumous" which was written when he was still in his twenties. Khushwant Singh was so enamored by mortality that he penned his own epitaph well in advance:

> Here lies one who spared neither man nor God
> Waste not your tears on him, he was a sod
> Writing nasty things he regarded as great fun
> Thank the Lord he is dead, this son of a gun. (167)

Death At My Doorstep chronicles the author's dialogue with celebrities—Dalai Lama, Z.A. Bhutto, Sanjay Gandhi, M.O. Mathai, Mountbatten, Nargis Dutt, R.K. Narayan, Faiz Ahmed Faiz, Protima Bedi, Bhisham Sahni and a host of others on the topic of mortality. The author, in the course of his narration, hints at their cosmopolitan philosophy of life underlying multicultural way of subsistence. Khushwant Singh, however, does not narrate the life of these personalities *per se* but as it weaves through fantasy, sarcasm, and humour, obliquely hinting at the ensuing events. In 1948, Krishna Menon was the High Commissioner in London and Khushwant Singh was the Press Officer in charge of Public Relations. Mr. Khushwant Singh comes to know that Her Highness, The Rani of Mandi passed away. A gentleman by name Mr. Kenyon visits Khushwant Singh and introduces himself as the representative of the biggest firm of undertakers in England and puts a parcel on the table and says:

> 'Sir,' 'you must have read of the death of Her Highness, the Rani of Mandi?'
>
> 'Very sad,' replied Khushwant Singh.

Mr. Kenyon proceeded to open the parcel he had brought and continued, 'Her Highness left a will to the effect that on her cremation, her body was to be draped in her favourite sari that she had worn for her wedding. Despite our vast experience, we have no idea how Indian ladies drape their sari. I took the liberty of coming to ask for your help in the matter (xxi). Without a pause Khushwant Singh answers with his 'damn' wit:

> 'I am sorry Mr. Kenyon, though I have some experience of taking saris off, I have none of putting them on.' (xxi)

Mr. Kenyon marched out angrily and this incident betrays the variations of cultural expressions.

Khushwant Singh "demystifies death" in this collection of obituaries and engages in a veritable discussion on the issue of multicultural interest. In his interaction with "The Dalai Lama on Death," the author asks:

> "Your Holiness, I know Buddhists regard the existence of God as an open question. I go along with that. But I cannot accept your belief in reincarnation. There is no scientific evidence to support it." (5)

The Dalai Lama roars with laughter and replies:

> 'You have a point there! But if I did not believe in reincarnation, I would be out of business!' (5)

A morbid discussion on the "undiscovered country from whose bourn no traveler returns" will be of no interest and does not sustain as a work of art. Knowing this, the author ingeniously intersperses his narration with incidents of multicultural interest armed with wittiness thus imparting readability.

In the Chapter entitled "Fear of Dying," the author ventures to broach the issue of mortality to prove that "Death is not a fiction; it is a profound reality, more real than anything in life." He differs with Acharya's views on death and adds:

> Having allowed himself to become a Bhagwan, he has forfeited the right to say, 'I do not know.' Nobody, not even Bhagwan Rajneesh, knows what happens to us when we die. And as long as we do not know we will continue to dread it. (6)

Khushwant Singh's description of the spiritual leaders is replete with derision and disdain and serves as warning bells to the "believers." Khushwant Singh's love for his country is brought to the fore in the chapter "Nearing Death: Old Age." He worked as the editor of *The Hindustan Times* for quite a reasonable period of time. In the third year of his tenure as editor, when his contract was due for renewal, K.K. Birla, the owner of the news paper asked:

> "Sardar Sahib, aren't you thinking of retiring?" (18) The Editor replied: "I will retire when I am taken to the cremation ground." (18)

He further writes:

> Actually, I plan to be buried so that my rotten guts can enrich the soil of my motherland after I have gone. (18)

The author discusses the profundity of death with the former Prime Minister V.P. Singh, in the chapter "Death as a Houseguest." V.P. Singh suffered from blood cancer of the bone marrow for the past nine years; his kidneys were impaired. He had to undergo blood transfusion every seven days. V.P. Singh tells Khushwant Singh with a wistful smile:

> I have had death staying with me for nine years.... Every week I ask death: 'is it time for you (death) to take me along?' and she replies: 'no, not yet.' (19)

The author counters with his favourite quotation from Allama Iqbal:

> I have a lot of work that remains unfulfilled; now you better wait for me....

> ...When I feel my end is near, I tell the Badey Mian up in the clouds,
> "Mian Sahib, I will come to you when I have fursat (spare time)." (20)

V.P. Singh responded 'Wah! Wah!' in approval and praise.

Though known for salacious gossip, Khushwant Singh here mulls over seriously on the theme of mortality. The chapter "Nargis Dutt: Mother India," narrates the author's proximity with the celebrity and the vacuum ensued after her death. He writes:

> Beautiful she was in all senses of the word. Shaped in classic mould enshrining a heart of gold which went out to the poor, the blind and the paraplegic. Her smile was bewitching, her laughter contagious. She had the gift of eternal youth and died looking as young in her fifties as she had in her teens.... My chief claim to fame as a Member of the Rajya Sabha was that I sat next to Nargis and was the envy of my brother parliamentarians. That seat has remained unoccupied since last August. But the void she leaves in the hearts of millions of her countrymen will never be filled. (120)

The Chapter "Gurucharan Singh Tohra: Be Taaj Badshah" delineates the domination of Tohra in Sikh politics for over half a century. Khushwant Singh writes about the historical details pertaining to SGPC and Khalistan movement. He comments on Tohra:

> He did not have the qualities of a visionary statesman who could have led a vibrant and progressive community to greater heights of prosperity and find an honourable place in the annals of history...my handsome friend has gone to sleep amongst the dead. My eyes filled with tears. What great things this man could have accomplished if he had the vision and the will to do so. (63)

Death At My Doorstep is Khushwant Singh's meditation on the possibility of death in a multicultural Indian set up. He has touched upon several personalities—M.O. Mathai, Sanjay

Gandhi, Z.A. Bhutto, Mountbatten, Balwant Gargi, Ali Sardar Jafri, Faiz Ahmed Faiz, Protima Bedi—who left an indelible mark on Indian social and political scene. However, Death as an imperious guiding force permeates his narration.

Work Cited

Singh, Khushwant. *Death At My Doorstep*. New Delhi: Roli Books, 2013. Print.

22

Rohinton Mistry's *Such a Long Journey*: Perspectives of Multiculturalism and Double Displacement

Baishali Bhaumik Mitra and *B. Gopal Rao*

Multiculturalism as a new paradigm recognizes the effects of globalization by accounting for the migrant's cultural differences. No matter which view on multiculturalism as a policy one takes, it seems beyond dispute that a truly multicultural perspective cannot but acknowledge that migration is a move with far-reaching consequences for the host societies but also, often more drastically, for the individual migrant. Arguably one of the most pressing problems for those forsaking their homes for a new country is the construction of a new identity. In more accessible terms, the central concerns for many who feel themselves uprooted are how to make life in the diaspora 'liveable.' The phrasing here is deliberately vague. 'Liveable' can refer to an attempt to reproduce the old country in the new, however it might also imply in some cases that the country of origin is happily discarded in favour of the country of adoption. The implications of what 'liveable' entails are negotiated along a spectrum of possibilities ranging from assimilation to a new culture to the retention of the old, or, put differently, along a continuum from sameness to difference.

Multicultural fiction does not have to accept a cultural tradition to adopt it uncritically. It may well encompass stories in which protagonists feel uneasy with their cultural tradition and modify or even discard it. Rohinton Mistry's works are a case in point as he reflects complex implications of multicultural differences. The fiction of Mistry is typical for immigrant experience and it is concerned with both multicultural as well as postcolonial issues respectively.

The paper examines how Mistry views Canadian and Indian societies' treatment of cultural diversities. At the centre of interest will be questions of race and ethnicity, difference and assimilation. To understand multiculturalism it is pertinent to discuss how the 'Other', as represented in Mistry's fiction fares in the face of institutionalized tolerance. Is multiculturalism experienced as liberation or does it provoke racism in a more subtle form (because it may in itself be informed by a racial bias)? One has to figure out how the paradigm of difference underlying multicultural modes of society is experienced as a prerequisite for a dignified existence in the diaspora, or whether it is an assumption that prevents the immigrant from opting for other models of integration, such as, for example, assimilation or acculturation. Particularly interesting in this context is the role that other categories of difference play. For example, is home as well as host culture experienced differently by the protagonists of Mistry's fiction?

Once other categories of difference, such as age, social class, etc., are introduced, do second generation immigrants experience Canadian multiculturalism as liberation from a colonialism which they themselves have not had to suffer? How do members of former colonial elites such as Mistry's Parsis experience the racism of lower-class ghettoes?

At the centre of Mistry's narratives from 'there' are likewise issues of culture and identity. Operating with the vocabulary of post-colonialism, the question at the centre of interest will be the relevance of difference and to what extent Mistry subscribes to it. He reflects a certain awareness of cultural difference but offers vistas beyond post-coloniality by taking recourse to cultural exchange but also to humanist positions.

Rohinton Mistry is a writer of Indian Diaspora and his works reflect his status as a member of a twice-displaced people.

He explores the relationship with Parsi community in India's troubled historical context by a process of self-preservation and through an act of transformation. The element of compassion which runs through his novels is "informed by an experience of double displacement" and is instilled with the author's sense of "identification with and alienation from their new and old homelands" (Bharucha 57). As an Indian Parsi and then an immigrant in Canada, Mistry is a symbol of double displacement as well as multiculturalism. This sense of dislocation is a recurrent reality in the lives of the protagonists of all his works. There is always the prominence of the human will to disengage from the fetters of subaltern existence throughout his works. He observes that multiculturalism brings together a set of issues that relate to the need for minority community, a sense of belonging to it, the importance of a secure sense of identity, of importance and recognition, particularly and the need to recognize and maintain difference with others.

As a socio-political novelist, Rohinton Mistry has emerged as a significant literary figure during the recent years. Mistry's *Tales from Firozsha Baag*, describes the daily lives of the inhabitants of a Bombay apartment complex. The stories are remarkable for the representation of the Parsi dilemma. Hope prevails in these stories, as Mistry's carefully and compassionately drawn characters survive and work through difficult circumstances toward a brighter future. The stories can be divided as Indian stories and stories of migration, yet the two categories are often blurred within the stories themselves. Mistry's *Such a Long Journey* brilliantly portrays Indian culture and Parsi family life, set against the backdrop of India's volatile postcolonial politics. The novel is Mistry's attempt to repossess the past and is definitely a Diasporic discourse as the title itself signifies as essence of journey.

In 1995 he published *A Fine Balance* which was nominated for the prestigious Booker Prize. Set in India in mid-1970, the time when the Government declared a state of emergency. *A Fine Balance* focuses on the lives of four unlikely people who find themselves living in the same humble flat in the city as they desperately fight the ominous course of destiny, but find out that the more they try the more they are caught in it. His novel *Family Matters*, describes the members of a blended family who are trying to cope with the failing health of their father. Meantime, the father relives his past, a past beset by thwarted love and crushing social strictures.

According to Bharucha, Mistry's writings are—"a time-warp, common to most Diasporic writers, and occasional lapse into nostalgia." However, Mistry is also a Parsi Zoroastrian whose ancestors were forced in to exile by the Islamic conquest of Iran. He was a Diaspora even in India and his writings are influenced by this sense of double displacement. Although he lived in Canada since 1975 and took citizenship, he continues to write about India. Even when he does focus on Canada, he represents his adopted country as the sight of Parsi Diaspora, a place where the immigrant Parsis renegotiate their identity. While exploring in his stories, the relationships at the heart of this community, their cultural identity, Mistry seeks to shed light and embrace the Diasporic Parsi experience whether that be in North America or in India. Being a member of the Parsi Diaspora writer Mistry is able to present issues related to the plight of the Parsis in a way that provides insight and compels empathy. He reflects back on the country he left and portrays a society on the path to extinction, knowing that he is part of the process. Depending on this perspective, the trajectory of his life and his art either reflect or counter the Parsi experience. "Almost all the Parsi writers exhibit consciousness of their community in such a way that the community emerges as a protagonist from their works though on the surface these works deal with their human protagonists" (Singh 66).

Subsequently Mistry's works can naturally be read on many levels—as Parsi history, testimony of Indian postcolonial reality as well as Diasporic experience. From both these perspectives there is always a Diasporic trait of nostalgia and loss in his writings, which can be directed towards a geographical as well as psychological Diaspora. Identical to Bharati Mukherjee, Mistry's multi-layered works can be linked to his personal status as a migrant, with his odyssey of journey, physically from Bombay to Canada—and racially, as a Zoroastrian, from Iran to India, where they settled down in the coastal areas in the west. Mistry grew up in a Parsi Baag in Bombay, a distinctive feature of the cityscape. In emigrating he followed a demographic trend that has been blamed for the decline of the Parsi culture; however, it also led to his remarkable success as a writer.

Consequently, Mistry's literature reflects his position as a member of the twice-displaced people, and explores the difficulty an immigrant faces in a society that recognizes their cultural difference, and yet fails to embrace that difference. It also investigates the relationship of the Parsi community in India's troubled historical context. The conscious autobiography of the race, in his portrayal becomes the unconscious autobiography of the race, especially in his comprehension of life. He is able to capture "the authenticity of Parsi life as he has distanced himself by immigrating to Canada and successfully produced the effect of an insider/outsider" (Luhman viii). Therefore, his grievances are mostly the exuberance of the Parsi psyche. Even though westernized, he had painful experiences that led him to an identity crisis, as his natural hold of the indigenous culture unconsciously hinders with the logical grasp of foreign culture. Also, he shows an Indian's knowledge about corruption being an ingrained part of life at all levels in India. He reiterates how an ordinary citizen can get nothing done without bribes. Dr Paymaster, the family physician of Gustad Noble, points out: "that municipal corruption was only a microcosmic manifestation of the greed, dishonesty, and moral turpitude that flourished at the country's centre" (312).

As a Parsi, Mistry finds him at the margins of Indian society and therefore his writings confront and oppose that absorption by the dominating culture. Nevertheless being in the west despite the nostalgia and loneliness, his stance does change from what it used to while he was in India. The perpetual identity crisis moves towards a continuous strive to maintain a fine balance. He objected to the Canadian multiculturalism as this liberal framework claims to accord recognition to non-mainstream writers, even though it functions to further consolidate their minority position. He further insists that non-white authors should be regarded as Canadian writers, not as representatives of racial or ethnic groups. He is aware of the assimilationist pressures encoded in state constructions of multiculturalism. In rejecting current constructions of Canadian multiculturalism, he proposes as alternative idea that is not based on an opposition between assimilation and exclusion. The stance of the writer obviously represents his dissatisfaction as an expatriate in the west.

Nonetheless, Mistry's works, in a way, are the discourse of hybridity, the very artefact of migration. This perhaps explains the characteristic melancholy that pervades his works. It also reflects his negative criticism of the so-called expression 'home town.' Even then Mistry comes one step forward to conclude that the acceptance of hybridity may be the only hope for survival.

In an interview Mistry confesses, "I've been asked why I keep writing about India, and specifically Bombay even though I left 26 years ago. It remains my focus and makes it all worthwhile because of the people...their capacity for laughter, their capacity to endure" (interview by Ali Lakhani at Vancouver International Writers' Festival). He often embodies his accepted country as the location of a Parsi Diaspora, a place, where immigrant Parsis renegotiate their identities and their relationships with one of India's most endangered communities.

In all the migration stories in *Tales from Firozsha Baag*, thus Mistry indicates the necessity of moving beyond the nationalist methodology—where "the desire to come to terms with oneself in place and time and in relation to others, is a national instinct" (Tarras 10). The stories of Firozsha Baag reveal the expatriate sensibility and immigrant Canadian identity of Rohinton Mistry. Hence the reason for a typical Indian local colour that pervades through all the stories could be assigned to the writer's sense of nostalgia and homesickness. In "Swimming Lessons," we find the mother of the narrator says:

> she said he must be unhappy there, all his stories are about Bombay, he remembers every little thing about his childhood, he is thinking about it all the time even though he is ten thousand miles away.... I think he misses home and us and everything he left behind. (243)

This could well justify Mistry's obsession with Bombay life, even though often it is an angular vision. The generous spread of native words throughout renders the local colour to his tales. In "Auspicious Occasion" the Firozsha Baag is recreated by Mistry with the use of—Behramroje, dugli, pheytoe, navjote, dhandar-paato, Sali-boti, loban, ailchee, chasni, AsemVahoo, etc. The story, "Of White Hairs and Cricket" is a sort of reminiscences from boyhood. The narrator, a fourteen year old boy, remembers his father, mother and grandmother—mamaiji. A Sunday is re-enacted in bits and pieces, while the boy's nimble fingers are wielding tweezers, pulling out the white hairs from his daddy's scalp. All these successfully emphasize the home colour. The narrative technique of "The Ghost of Firozsha Baag" is extremely interesting in an individualistic dialect if a Catholic ayah from Goa,—"After reaching first floor I stooped to rest. My breath was coming fast-fast. Fast-fast, like it does nowadays when I grind curry masala on the stone" (44). "Swimming Lessons" also possesses a unique narrative style, as it is printed in two styles, ordinary and italics. The difference in printing style signifies the juxtaposition of Firozsha Baag-Bombay-India with Canada.

Mistry's *Such a Long Journey* is a novel which is in line with the realist tradition in which narrative is pushed forward in arithmetical progression and is chronological rather than spatial in the development of the plot. There is a strange mingling of comedy, tragedy, humour, and satire as well as with an affluent framework of beliefs, superstition, and failure of ideologies, frustration, humanism, radicalism and optimism. The opulence of the novel is attained in the creation of the protagonist Gustad Noble, the pattern of whose life and sufferings are rhythmic with the migration pattern and the resulting agony and despair of the Parsi race as well as with the pattern of universal human misery. Like Oedipus, Gustad achieves his human dignity through compassion and endurance to withstand against all chances. However, the novel can be studied as the exuberance of a migrant writer's Parsi psyche.

Justifying Rushdie's summing up the peculiar penchant of immigrant writers in "Imaginary Homelands" as an "endeavour to repossess their own history...whose fragments have been lost" (10-11), a technique reminiscent of M.H. Abram's lamp/mirror theory, Rohinton Mistry's debut novel *Such a Long Journey* becomes the reflection of the outside reality as well as the expression of the inner soul. *Such a Long Journey* both creates a vivid picture of Indian family life and culture and tells a story rich in subject matter, characterization and symbolism. It is set in 1971 Bombay, when India went to war over what was later to become Bangladesh. This is the political context for the unfortunate events that disrupt the personal lives of the kind-hearted Parsi man, Gustad Noble, and his family and friends. He skilfully parallels public events involving Indira Gandhi with the misfortunes of the novel's principal characters. The story's private dimensions are not merely weighed against political circumstance; they are revealed as the personal manifestations of the same reality, as the lives of his characters become entangled in the vituperative dishonesty and incompetence of the government.

The Parsis were particularly disturbed by the increasing radicalism of the national movement strongly influenced by the neo-Hindu renaissance. As a minority community, Parsis feel a sense of inequality and injustice. Discussing the apprehensions of minorities in *Multiculturalism, Liberalism and Democracy,* Rajeev Bhargava observes:

> they should not be discriminated on account of particular features of their religion and culture nor be compelled to set aside their cultural particularity. Somehow, a space has to be found to accommodate cultural particularity within the political sphere shaped by Indian liberal individualism and publicanism, for neither on their own is able to deal with extremely important issues raised by multiculturalism. (16)

They felt they had very limited access to the socio-religious nationalism of the Congress movement under Tilak and Gandhi. These fears encouraged the Parsis to oppose even the concept of the Home Rule on India. Parsis "who became especially active in the national movement, were opposed by the majority of the community as traitors to the British and, consequently, to their own community" (Kilke 213). *Such a Long Journey* manages brilliantly to portray Indian culture and Parsi family life setting it against the backdrop of India's unstable postcolonial politics. The action takes place in 1971 in Bombay at the moment war breaks out between India and Pakistan. In this depiction of the political backdrop the troubled life of Gustad Noble is played out.

Such a Long Journey, in Mistry's attempt to recuperate the past, is definitely a Diasporic discourse. It not only depicts the long journey of Gustad Noble who seems to be pitted against fate, yet, desperately tries to sail through against the odds of life, but also symbolizes the long journey of the Parsis from Iran to India and then to the west. The thick cover of Parsi ethnicity, the essence of Parsi spirit and the angles and angularities of Parsi way of life in *Such a Long Journey* is Mistry's obsession with his own origin and is definitely the sign of his perception of the Iranian as well as Indian Diaspora in which the Parsis are caught. He proves, "no mosaic, no multiculturalism can cut man off the roots he sprouts and sucks sustenance from" (Sharma 37). His involvement with the past is the result of himself falling into the Indian Diaspora, enhancing a sense of double Diaspora in his writing. He keeps returning to the shred and traces of the lived and hoary past. There is always a feel of being fallen in the lake of fire with an irrevocable Heaven lost behind.

The destruction of Gustad's wall and his pulling out of the black out papers is turned into a positive occurrence and letting in the light as well as proximity with the outside is indicative of may be letting in the Indian reality into the isolation of the Parsi world where "new melodies break forth from the heart; and where the old tracks are lost, new country is revealed with its wonders" (11)—this could be Mistry's postmodern attitude towards assimilation, which could only be understood by coming out of the narrow boundaries and realizing a certain broadmindedness, which is achieved only by living in the west. As the novel progresses, Gustad turns the offensively stinking wall into "the wall of all religions" (183). And this open mindedness can be the consequence of Mistry's Western broadmindedness and a sense of liberation in the outlook.

Such is Mistry's power that he makes, to imitate John Donne, "one little room, an everywhere." Without apparent effort, manipulation or contrivance, Mistry creates characters that are liked instantly and is followed gladly as long as the novel leads. Mistry's works possess an "international dimension" where in the writer's "national consciousness" evokes a humanist vision (Fanon 199). Arising out of these dimensions of the novel are the forces of conscience and consciousness.

For Gustad it was a long journey through this cold, hostile world, whereas Dinshawji, Bilimoria and Tehmul have undertaken a long journey. At the same time it is for all, a journey from hopelessness to hope, from despondency to optimism. Here the journey of man towards his destination also remains his spiritual quest to gain the fine balance.

In order to subvert the privilege of colonial hegemony in language and to do away with the dominance of the master narratives of the west, Mistry, like most other Diasporic writers, followed the post-colonial mode of resistance against the use of the colonizer's language. As a result, his texts are splendid celebration of the Parsi idioms. He faithfully captures the Parsi tone and rhythm in his writing. He does not use it to create a mere effect of exoticism but carries it on steadily and consistently so as to convey its position as natural as any other Indian language and render it a status with its distinctive phonetic features in the scenario of global English. He "emerges as a true Indian writer, for the scenes, the situation, the characters and even the language reflects the typical Indian culture vividly" (Myles 91). In *Such a Long Journey* we come across phrases like "it is like a taveej, a protection" (150) and words like 'jaadumantar', 'bhaia', 'yaar', 'humkokuchnehimaloom', 'masala', 'gaswalla', 'paanwalla', 'morcha', 'besharam', 'parinam', etc. which justify Mistry's postcolonial attitude of rebel against the west even though it is his homeland now.

He seems to be aware of his international audience. He describes in detail in his writings, the Parsi religious customs, prayers, and costume and funeral rites at the fire temples and the Towers of Silence. In his use of Parsi customs and untranslated words like dugli, Behramroje, dustoor, navjote, etc. there is a distinctive assertion of his cultural identity and a peculiar resistance of the Parsi to conform or identify with the logocentrism of either the British or the Indians. The hybridity of Mistry's use of two disconnected discursive policies can be read as a supporting act—to claim and safeguard cultural terrain for the Parsi. At the same time the use of purposely Parsi words and culture has a nostalgic task of resituating the writer in his early days in Bombay.

In the migration stories of *Tales from Firozsha Baag* and in the novel *Such a Long Journey*, thus, Mistry, through a series of intertwining discursive creation, articulates the ambivalent space between the 'old' and the 'new' as well as 'here' and 'there'. Caught between two cultures, his characters are always busy defining their own hybridity. Like them, Mistry himself is a South Asian Canadian Parsi who negotiates between diverse cultural traditions and explores cross cultural hybridity, both within and beyond the national border.

Therefore, in conclusion, an advocacy of multiculturalism is not exactly free of problems. It tends to essentialize and harden identities that generate radical exclusions of people. Its encouragement of cultural particularity appears to deepen division and undermine the common foundation necessary for a viable society. Mistry's fiction unequivocally states that multiculturalism supports aggregative community power over individual freedom by according unequal right to oppressive cultures it corrodes values of liberal democracy.

Multiculturalism requires recognition or respect for culture which in turn is possible only after a degree of interaction, familiarity and mutual understanding among minority communities. This clearly brings up a crucial epistemological issue central to the debate on multiculturalism in Mistry's works. It is interesting to note that moral, religious and cultural diversity has not always appeared puzzling to us. Without the dissolution of religious and rationalist certainties, issues such as the possibility of genuine multicultural understanding or sound intercultural judgements would have never been foregrounded and Mistry's works amply testify to this argument.

Works Cited

Bhargava, Rajeev, Amiya Kumar and R. Sudarshan Bagchi, *Multiculturalism, Liberalism and Democracy.* USA: Oxford University Press, 2007. Print.

Bharucha, Nilufer. *Rohinton Mistry: Ethnic Enclosures and Transcultural Spaces*. Jaipur: Rawat, 2003. Print.

Fanon, F. *The Wretched of the Earth*. Harmondsworth: Penguin, 1967. Print.

Kilke, Eckegard. *The Parsees in India: A Minority as Agent of Social Change*. New Delhi: Vikas Publishing House, 1995. Print.

Lakhani, Ali. Personal Interview, off camera, conversation with Rohinton Mistry. Vancouver, July 1995. Radio.

Luhman, T.M. *The Good Parsi: The Fate of Colonial Elite in a Post-Colonial Society*. VIII. New Delhi: Oxford UP, 1996. Print.

Mistry, Rohinton. *Tales from Firozsha Baag*, New Delhi: Rupa Books, 1987. Print.

———. *Such a Long Journey*. London: Faber and Faber, 1992. Print.

Myles, Anita. "Thematic Concerns in *Such a Long Journey*". *The Fiction of Rohinton Mistry*. Ed., Jaydipsinh Dodiya. New Delhi: Prestige Books, 1998. Print.

Rushdie, Salman, *Imaginary Homelands: Essays and Criticism: 1981-1991*. New York: Penguin Books, 1992. Print.

Sharma, N.P. "Parsi Culture and Vision in Rohinton Mistry's *Such a Long Journey* and Firdauskanga's *Trying to Grow*". *The Fiction of Rohinton Mistry*. Ed., Jaydipsinh Dodiya. Delhi: Prestige Books, 1998. Print.

Singh, Avadesh Kumar. "Community with Parsi novels in English." Rpt Novy Kapadia and A.G. Khan. *Preface to the Parsis*. ed., Madyan Sanjan. New Delhi: Creative Publishers, 1997. Print.

Tarras, David. "Introduction." *A Passion for Identity*: *An Introduction to Canadian Studies*. Ed., David Tarras and Eli Mandel. Toronto: Methuen, 1987. 10. Print.

Viswanath, Geeta. "Modes of Resistance in the South Asian Novel." Rpt *The Fiction of Rohinton Mistry*. Ed. Jaydipsinh Dodiya. New Delhi: Prestige Books, 1998. Print.

23

Multiculturalism in Chitra Banerjee Divakaruni's *The Mistress of Spices*

Soumyajyoti Banerjee and *Amrita Basu*

Chitra Banerjee Divakaruni is a contemporary Indo-American poet and fiction writer whose writing tackles the intricate and multi-faceted identity issues faced by immigrants, with an emphasis on those experienced by women. In 1976, Chitra Banerjee Divakaruni left Kolkata (then Calcutta), India as a young adult and moved to the United States. Her experience of immigrating "caused Divakaruni to re-evaluate her homeland's culture, and specifically its treatment of women" (Sofky). A characteristic feature of Divakaruni's novels like *The Mistress of Spices* (1997), *Sister of My Heart* (2000), *Vine of Desire* (2002) and *Queen of Dreams* (2004) is that she combines the elements of Indian American experience and magical realism, drawing parallels between the realistic and the cosmic. Her stories mainly deal with the search for identity—both individual and communal and a sense of emotional completion achieved by fusing the two. In order to express experiences as well as internal struggles, in her novels, women are always in the forefront of action. Another characteristic feature of Divakaruni's novels is that she often weaves a divine order and mysticism into the gritty reality of the lives of her women characters. As a result, women protagonists in her fiction often enter a state of liminality, "a space between ruptured pasts and unpredictable futures, residing in an ever changing present and giving rise to discourses which enable new narratives to be formulated" (Brah). A case in point is the female protagonist in 'The Mistress of Spices' who has been Nayantara, the pirate queen, Sarpa-kanya, the old-one's apprentice and now Tilottama in a journey which leaves her at the end as Maya. We never know what was or is the original nature of her spirit. She is ever sailing into uncharted and amazing areas of experiences where the transformations require more than time and distance, even desire. Women like Tilo, making diasporic journeys in Divakaruni's novels, often identify fault-lines and fissures in their search for self-definition. Thus her novels are an adventurous foray into the complex mind of women.

The present paper attempts a reading of the politics of multiculturalism in Chitra Banerjee Divakaruni's novel *The Mistress of Spices*. As stated, the protagonist of the novel, Tiolottama (popularly called Tilo), owns a spice shop in California. She supplies ingredients for various Indian recipes, simultaneously possessing an uncanny ability to penetrate deep into the personal life of each of her customers and prescribing different spices as remedies for their different problems. Tilottama prescribes range of spices to evoke desired emotional reactions from people and it may be looked at from the standpoint of evocation and practice of "Indianness." She suggests spices as remedies for various problems, in the process playing a typical Indian agony-aunt for the expatriate community and much of an alternative-medicine professional who can read the problems of others' bodies and others' minds, and knows the value of Indian spices. In the process, suggesting remedial spices also becomes a soul searching inner journey for Tilottama as the novel ventures into the magical and wonderful world of the woman in whose hands "the spices come to life." Espin has commented that although the contradictions involved in immigrant experiences (specifically for women) can lead to emotional or other problems, most immigrant women "manage to survive and emerge from the emotional struggle" (Espin 10). How this is achieved in the novel makes interesting study when one analyses the opening lines of the concerned novel, *The Mistress of Spices*:

> I am a Mistress of Spices. I can work the others too. Mineral, metal, earth and sand and stone.... But the spices are my love. (3)

The opening lines are very poignant. Tilo is "a" mistress of spices. So, it is assumed that there may be other mistresses. Second, she uses the word "spices" that is the plural form, so she considers the spices as a unified category and at the same time she belongs to each and every member of the spice family. The juxtaposition of mistress and love is equally important here as she says that she loves the spices but she is their mistress. Later she goes on to reveal: "If you stand in the centre of this room and turn slowly around, you will be looking at every Indian spice that ever was—even the lost ones—gathered here upon the shelves of my store" (3). The word store is another important word because it is a metaphor of commodity-exchange. It is not a place associated with love, but it is certainly more in line with the association with mistress. In a society that generally sees adult women as sexual rivals, especially wives and mistresses, and in one that is inclined to see a mistress's function as disruptive rather than constructive, these lines appears rather odd. Here mistress may be said to be modeled on the ancient concept of the courtesan. Courtesans were artistically gifted women, who in the past were pictured as consorting with kings and other members of the royal dynasty and enjoyed a fabulously rich lifestyle, being the custodians of culture and fashion. They also enjoyed a lot of respect in society. Courtesans were under the patronage of the King or the nobility and would provide favours only to them. It is interesting to see that before giving out her name Tilo opens her lines with her status as mistress of spices. She defines her identity, though finds it difficult to stress her individuality. It reflects her unequal power relations and partial social exclusion in the novel. The concept of a stable identity is derived from rootedness in a locality, owning land, having a neighbourhood. She has forged a complex relationship with the self by owning a store, and becoming a mistress of spices.

The next phase of the novel unfolds different people in front of us. Tilo through her magical artistic vision sees what they want or lack in their life and sets out to correct it through customized dosage of spices in each individual's life without the subject realizing it. Most problems seem to emerge from the family. Indians suffer from a dependency complex (Kakar

1983, 89) with sometimes the familial bond being so strong that even the loosening of the family bond, not to mention an actual break, may be a source of psychic stress and heightened inner conflict (Kakar 1983, 91) as is evident in the characters in the novel. Surprisingly, this makes the narrative even more "Indian" though located in a foreign land. Thus for Ahuja's wife Tilo feels:

> Child-longing, deepest desire, deeper than for wealth or lover or even death. It weighs down the air of the store, purple like before a storm. It gives off the smell of thunder. Scorches...A handful of turmeric wrapped in old newspaper with the words of healing whispered into it, slipped into your grocery sack when you are not looking. The string tied into a triple flower knot, and inside, satin-soft turmeric the same color as the bruise seeping onto your cheek from under the dark edge of your glasses. (16)

Tilo's heart also cries out for Ratna, another migrant lady who suffers regular, routinised torture at her husband's place. She feels: "Fenugreek, I asked your help when Ratna came to me burning from the poison in her womb, legacy of her husband's roving. And when Ramaswamy turned from his wife of twenty years to a newer pleasure" (47).

At a personal level, Tilo's selection of spices as a tool to create emotions in people reflects gender-oriented underpinnings in her choosing to work within the domestic aesthetic praxis. At a socio-political level, the spice-shop emerges as a diasporic space where identities are repeatedly destabilized by the mutability of the diasporic's situation in the land of domicile (hostland) and the corresponding re-adjustment of his relations with the place he/she calls home by habit (homeland). The call for repeated re-negotiation of identity makes the shop and by extension, diaspora a volatile space. The store transforms a part of terrestrial space into a place of historical life for people (Bhabha 143) to quote Bhabha in another context. Supriya Chaudhuri and Rimi B. Chatterjee in their work *The Writer's Feast: Food and The Cultures of Representation* state that: "The physical realities of migration and resettlement produce two types of psychic accommodation. One, which may be labelled as nostalgia, where the land left behind is equated with the food that can never be recovered. In the other—which may be labelled as cosmopolitanism—a dazzling array of global cuisines greets the gourmet traveller in the great cities of the world" (xiv).

For traumatised people displaced by history who have lost much of the material inheritance of a prosperous, cultured and happy past, remembering food is a form of preserving their roots. In the process, feasting and plenitude became part of a cumulative narrative of a golden past, a story which compensates to a small extent for the loss of ancestral roots, property, and social and economic security (Chakravarty 126). Bunny Crumpacker opines: Food memories, most of them forgotten or blurred, are a mystical heritage, long since digested and gone, but still lingering in our souls. Personal food, ethnic food, family food, the food of the culture in which we grew up, the food our mothers gave us—this is the eating that determines who we are, what we love, what disgusts us, and makes us feel better (xii). Thus Tilo, through spices sets upon an endeavour to play an agony aunt for the people in the community.

Bhikhu Parekh posits that tendencies to equate multiculturalism with racial minorities and seeing it as promoting a thinly veiled racism is not what multiculturalism is about. It is a far more encompassing concept. He argues that multiculturalism is in fact "not about minorities" but "is about the proper terms of relationship between different cultural communities," which means that the standards by which the communities resolve their differences, e.g., "the principles of justice" must not come from only one of the cultures but must come "through an open and equal dialogue between them" (13). This is exactly what is achieved through the use of spices in the novel which is our area of exploration.

Complex Problems, Combination of Spices

While Ahuja's wife and Ratna face problems from their respective husbands, Geeta has to confront the ire of her own family members for choosing a life of American Independence where a girl can choose her own marriage partner and stay with him before marriage. Slowly, the problems start getting more and more complex, and Tilo has to take recourse to combination of spices to heal others rather than her earlier relying on individual spices for individual cases. Thus, when she comes face to face with Jagjit's case; Jagjit is a young Sikh boy continuously threatened by white racist boys, Tilo feels: "And here is cinnamon, hollow dark bone that I tuck unseen in your turban just before you go. Cinnamon friend-maker, cinnamon *dalchini* warm-brown as skin, to find you someone who will take you by the hand, who will run with you and laugh with you and say "See this is America, it's not so bad…." And for the others with the pebble-hard eyes, cinnamon destroyer of enemies to give you strength, strength which grows in your legs and arms and mostly mouth till one day you shout *no* loud enough to make them, shocked, stop" (39). Thus cinnamon is considered the spice which will increase tolerance and assertiveness; it will help a boy like Jagjit to learn to say no. However, the chapter cinnamon has an elaborate reference to Lanka or the red chilli which hints at the nature of events to come. Thus, in this same chapter dedicated to cinnamon, Tilo weaves a paean to Lanka. The solution to the racist problem through the use of spices reveals to be binary in nature, one developing tolerance (through cinnamon) and another, fighting back (through the red chilli). In which direction the narrative will move is indicated by the choice of spices:

> Let me tell you about chillies. The dry chilli, lanka, is the most potent of spices. In its blister-red skin, the most beautiful. Its other name is danger.... *I Lanka was born of Agni, god of fire. I dripped from his fingertips to bring taste to this bland earth….* Chilli, spice of red Thursday, which is the day of reckoning. Day which invites us to pick up the sack of our existence and shake it inside out. Day of suicide, day of murder. *Lanka, lanka.* Sometimes I roll your name over my tongue. Taste the enticing sting of it. So many times the Old One has warned us against your powers.
>
> 'Daughters, use it only as the last remedy. It is easy to start a flame. But to put it out?' That is why I hold on, *lanka*, whose name the ten-headed Ravana took for his enchanted kingdom. City of a million jewels

> turned at the last to ash. Though more than once I have been tempted.... In the inner room of the store, on the topmost shelf, sits a sealed jar filled with red fingers of light. One day I will open it and the chillies will flicker to the ground. And blaze. *Lanka*, fire-child, cleanser of evil. For when there is no other way. (37)

While elaborating the level of competency needed to handle each spice, Tilo remarks that the chilli grows in the very centre of the magical spice island, in the core of a sleeping volcano. Until the third level of apprenticeship is reached, no one is allowed to approach working with the chilli. Tilo also remarks that the presence of Lanka is like an ever looming threat as any day it may provoke one to take it out of the jar and use it. Lanka becomes symbolic of the dormant, inner violence present in all of us. It can come out any day. To ward off the looming tension, Tilo moves into the history of the spice Lanka.

To borrow from Rogobete, tracing and interpreting a food's story is also about mapping a cultural geography; a food is both a product of particular times and places, and part of the process of globalisation. Like "any good biography or travelogue," a food's story reveals a "much bigger story" (Rogobete 2007). Tilo talks of the rich ancient heritage of chilli, its illustrious past. At the same time she also tries to explain the contemporary use of the spice and how it may be used in the future to help the community. Tilo thus also acts as an art historian seeking to accommodate novelty while retaining some continuity with the aesthetic as understood in the past (Dickie). It is understood traditions often have to be reclaimed and revitalized as part of modernity to establish their continuity. At the same time, the legitimacy of modernity depends on how it conforms to tradition (Ramakrishnan 6). Tilo's mention of the grand history of chilli and its ever important presence in today's scenario also supports the argument.

Soon after the paean to the red chilli in Jagjit's case for whom Tilo has already prescribed the tolerance enhancing cinnamon, comes up Haroun's case. Haroun is a Kashmiri Muslim who has migrated to Oakland, California and is working as a cab driver there. Haroun gets into argument with the local whites of the region and therefore, he is mercilessly beaten up. This is the location in the narrative where to quote Homi Bhabha, "the very place of identification, caught in the tension of demand and desire, is a space of splitting" (44). Tilo initially prescribes cinnamon for Jagjit, then moves on to prescribe Kalo Jire for Haroun and all other Indian brothers in trouble, but everything moves towards failure. As Mendoza and Shankar point out, "assimilation remains an option; even a recommendation" as many contemporary immigrant and ethnic American texts present a suspicious, if not oppositional, attitude towards Americanization. They often challenge the myth of the American Dream, exposing the racism that immigrants face and the challenges that even the hardest working face in their quest to "make it." Such challenges may not always be resolved through tolerance.

Tilo casts a spell for the benefit of all Indians in America: "I will split once again tonight kalo jire seeds for all who have suffered from America. For all of them and especially Haroun, who is a hurting inside me, whose name each time I say it pulls my chest in two. I will lock the door and stay up all night to do it, through dimness the knife rising and falling steady and silver as holy breath. So that when he comes tomorrow evening (for tomorrow is Tuesday) I can hand him the packet and say, "Allah ho Akbar, may you be safe, in this life and always...I will whisper into air purifying prayers for the maimed, for each lost limb, each crushed tongue. Each silenced heart" (173).

But Tilo soon realizes that kalo jire is not so potent a spice to stall violence when America rushes by. "Kalo jire wasted once again, what apology can I offer you? I can say only what you know already. It is too late for you to work your power. One spice alone is left that can help Haroun now" (231).

Incidentally Tilo associates kalo jire with Ketu (itself considered a shadowy planet) in the system of *navagrahas* (since spices are also associated with grahas in the novel). Rahu and Ketu are actually not considered planets proper but as the nodes of the moon and hence important. It is interesting to see that the spice associated with Haroun which is kalo jire is the spice of the planet ketu. In the system of Indian astrology, there are two shadowy planets. A traditional healer should have a sound knowledge of astrological discourses; the workings of the *grahas* or the planets in our lives. Tilo, as the mistress of spices, somehow manages to choose a marginal spice ruled by a marginal planet for the Kashmiri Muslim immigrant Haroun. There are two things important here, first, ketu though a navagraha, is a marginal planet as it is the last one in the schema of planets, the scheme being Surya, Chandra, Mangal, Budh, Brihaspati, Shukra, Shani, Rahu and Ketu. Second, ketu is often associated with violence, fears, unknown enemies, etc.; all of which find reflection in Haroun's case.

With the help for Haroun repeatedly failing, Tilo starts suffering from a lack of self-confidence. This spreads to the lack of her self-confidence in her own looks and body. The socio-political gets intertwined with the personal here at this juncture of the novel. In steps a devastatingly handsome American man and Tilo soon experiences the throes of loosing out her heart to him. One cannot say that Tilo is not aware of her precarious situation. She even mentions at a point of time: "A Mistress must carve her own wanting out of her chest, must fill the hollow left behind with the needs of those she serves" (69).

It is interesting to see that while she still relies on Indian herbs and spices to accentuate her beauty, the outfit she chooses is American. This is where Tilo arrives at a critical juncture where she has to choose between her identity as the mistress of spices or she has to set out into a foray into an unknown world. But her very identity of a mistress also hints at the idea that one cannot abdicate power one has not held. She is not a wife, she is a mistress of spices, however creative a power the spices may confer on her. "O spices.... Can I not love you and him both. Why must I choose" (190), she asks in a moment of desperation. She is not afraid to enter conflagration and consuming in Shampati's fire (261), a sure punishment for aberrant mistresses because she has already entered this conflagaration in love.

Dick Hebdige in addressing the subculture of punks in the United Kingdom posits that a dominant culture incorporates any alien culture through two forms: the commodity form and the ideology form (90-99). If, for the purpose of this paper, we extend Hebdige's definition of incorporation through commodity and ideology and apply it to the immigrant condition within the space of California in the novel, we find, as Hebdige argues, the first form-commodity turns difference into something to be embraced and purchased, that is Indian spices and herbs are affordable commodities and may be easily purchased, including its people are affordable; and no matter how they treat Indians, they are going to escape from the clutches of the law. This creates tensions in some who extend it to a perverted idea that everything Indian is affordable because an Indian marker of culture like valuable herbs and spices is reduced to the category of material goods. The second form discussed by Hebdige is ideology, that is presenting people belonging to the alien culture in such a way that they do not appear as "the other" but rather as a part of the dominant culture. The combined role of home and host cultures in conditioning the diaspora's sense of belonging to a definitive and stable space cannot be overstated. The diasporic's identity in this space is thus generated by the collective imagination of a community that has evolved from the migrant's contact with the new host-land cultures and the distancing from a familiar homeland culture and its established systems of knowledge production. This ironically finds expression in a very twisted way in the novel where routinised violence emerges as an established system of action against migrants and they in turn resort to violence as the only solution to violence. Slowly the cases Tilottama faces also become tougher day by day, for example, Jagjit getting involved in a drug racket or like Haroun, even Mohan being mercilessly beaten up in a violent racist attack. Kalo jire, the spice she selects for helping Haroun, has already been wasted multiple times.

Descriptions of irritation triggered by such external incidents could also be interpreted as masking deeper feelings of hurt and frustration. Once again in her life Tilo has to reject the mantle of the caring, sacrificing woman, the fantasy of idealized femininity, which is internalised from childhood and cast a spell with the spice of violence, with a constant looming threat of losing her own identity. Chitra Banerjee Divakaruni, through Tilo, puts into print women creator's deepest fears: the fear of being trapped and imprisoned in her store which confines her life, at the same time a fear of male sexuality, male power and male duplicity, and not least a fear of losing her own identity. This echoes Haroun's deepest fears, of being trapped and imprisoned in a no-solution situation, at the same time a fear of what may come if one does not rise to the occasion and take action against the racist attacks. C. James Trotman argues that multiculturalism is valuable because it "uses several disciplines to highlight neglected aspects of our social history, particularly the histories of women and minorities and promotes respect for the dignity of the lives and voices of the forgotten" (113). By closing gaps, by raising consciousness about the past, multiculturalism tries to restore a sense of wholeness in a postmodern era that fragments human life and thought" (Trotman).

The spice Lanka helps Tilo to close the gap between the past and the present so that she can move boldly into the future without anything holding her back. Lanka achieves the same for Haroun too who is resolved to start life anew. Thus, Lanka emerges as a final salvation for Haroun. Emboldened, Tilo tries it out for herself too, the fire of Lanka to combat Shampati's fire. Lanka emerges as a spice to break away, fight back and rebel rather than assimilate. While Haroun gathers courage to face the situation with resilience, Tilo sees a vision of the First Mother in the mysterious spice island, the one who had warned her about Shampati's fire in case she dares to use the spices for her own benefit. The exchange of words is important:

> "Tilo you should not have broken open the red jar—"
>
> "Mother it was time."
>
> "—should not have released its power into this city that has too much anger in it already."
>
> "But Mother, the anger of the chili is pure, impersonal. Its destruction is cleansing, like the dance of Shiva. Did you not tell us this yourself?"

> She only says, "There are better ways to help those who come to you."
>
> "There was no other way," I say in exasperation. "Believe me. This land, these people, what they have become, what they have done to—. Ah, rocked in the safe cradle of your island, how can you understand?" (235)

It is interesting to see that the imagery of being burnt Shampati's fire is almost like the Hindu *sathi* of burning oneself at one's husband's funeral pyre. It also hints at purity through fire, because Tilo does not burn away into ashes after this ordeal. Rather, imbibed with new courage and newer priorities in life, Tilo starts off into another new journey with her dream man, this time with another cosmic name for herself—Maya.

Conclusion

The novel *The Mistress of Spices*, examines with clinical precision, the process by which people get alienated from the host-nation. It probes the sources of violence that have been internalized by the host-nation. Deeper subliminal layers of ideological perspectives present in the novel point to the similarities in the manner in which Divakaruni presents alternative ideas of self, community and nation for a woman and a man, intertwining socio-political with personal destiny. When seen against the essentialising socio-political discourse of the nation, the personal and random aspects of everyday life also acquire the halo of the heroic and the homogenous. Thus, both destinies influence, and in turn are influenced by each other. Issues of power and desire, contest and consent, aggression and accommodation revolve around the multicultural praxis in the novel. Full of people negotiating the immigrant experience, in *The Mistress of Spices* Divakaruni skillfully "builds an enchanted story upon the fault line in American identity that lies between the self and the community" (Merlin 207). Diverse people problems are solved through the use of diverse spices. According to Bhattacharya, "immigrants to do not simply accept the 'melting pot' roles expected of assimilated Americans"—instead they continually redefine their sense of identity (66) and "such identities are continually constituted within the crucible of the materiality of everyday life; in the everyday stories we tell ourselves individually and collectively" (Brah 8). Chitra Banerjee Divakaruni's novel offers a crucial site to explore how characters maneuver their lives and identity struggles. As has been famously remarked "as migrants cross borders, they also cross emotional and behavioral boundaries.... One's life and roles change...with them, identities change as well" (Espin 241). "Although such experiences are stressful, they also provide opportunities for creating a 'new' identity" (Ramakrishnan 2011) and this new identity is achieved through the help of spices in *The Mistress of Spices*.

Works Cited

Bhabha, Homi. *The Location of Culture*. London: Routledge, 1994. Print.

Brah, Avtar. 1996. *Cartographies of Diaspora: Contesting Identities*. Routledge: London and New York, *1996*. Print.

Chakravarty, Suchandra. "Lost Land, Remembered Flavours." Supriya Chaudhuri and Rimi B. Chatterjee, Ed. *The Writer's Feast: Food and The Cultures of Representation*. New Delhi: Orient Blackswan, 2011. 125-35. Print.

Chaudhuri, Supriya and Rimi B. Chatterjee. *The Writer's Feast: Food and The Cultures of Representation*. New Delhi: Orient Blackswan, 2011. Print.

Courtesan culture. http://www.wikigender.org/index.php/Courtesan_Culture: Complexities and Negotiations Accessed on 10 April 2012. Web.

Dickie, George. "All Aesthetic Attitude Theories Fail: The Myth Of The Aesthetic Attitude." *American Philosophical Quarterly* 1.1 (1964): 56-66. Print.

Divakaruni, Chitra Banerjee. *The Mistress of Spices*. London: Blackswan, 1997. Print.

Espin, Olivia. *Women Crossing Boundaries: A Psychology of Immigration and Transformations*. New York: Routledge, 1991. Print.

Hebdige, Dick. *Subculture: Meaning of Style*. London: Routledge, 1979. Print.

Kakar, Sudhir. qtd in Ajay Gehlawat. *Reframing Bollywood: Theories of Popular Hindi Cinema*. New Delhi: Sage, 2010): 8. Print.

Mendoza, Louis and S. Shankar. Introduction. *Crossing into America: The New Literature of Immigration*. New York: The New Press, 2003. xiii-xxvi. Print.

Merlin, Lara. 1998. "Review of *The Mistress of Spices*". *World Literature Today*. 72 (1) 207. Print.

Parekh, Bhikhu C. *Rethinking Multiculturalism: Cultural Diversity and Political Theory*. London: Macmillan, 2002. Print.

Ramakrishnan, E.V. *Locating Indian Literature: Texts, Traditions, Translations*. New Delhi: Orient Blackswan, 2011.

Rogobete, Daniela. "Sweet Taste of India: Food Metaphors in Contemporary Indian Fiction in English." in Edward W. Said *Reflections on Exile' and Other Literary Cultural Essays*. London: Penguin Books Ltd., 2001. Print.

Sofky, Elizabeth. "Cross-Cultural Understanding Spiced with the Indian Diaspora." *Black Issues in Higher Education*. (18 September 1997). Print.

Trotman, James C. *Multiculturalism: Roots and Realities*. Bloomington: Indiana UP, 2002. Print.

Author Index

Subject Index